NARRATIVE OF THE LIFE OF FREDERICK DOUGLASS, AN AMERICAN SLAVE

broadview editions
series editor: Martin R. Boyne

Anon., Frederick Douglass, 1843. Onondaga Historical Association
Research Collection, Syracuse, NY.

NARRATIVE OF THE LIFE OF FREDERICK DOUGLASS, AN AMERICAN SLAVE

Frederick Douglass

edited by Celeste-Marie Bernier

broadview editions

BROADVIEW PRESS – www.broadviewpress.com
Peterborough, Ontario, Canada

Founded in 1985, Broadview Press remains a wholly independent publishing house. Broadview's focus is on academic publishing; our titles are accessible to university and college students as well as scholars and general readers. With over 600 titles in print, Broadview has become a leading international publisher in the humanities, with world-wide distribution. Broadview is committed to environmentally responsible publishing and fair business practices.

Library and Archives Canada Cataloguing in Publication

Douglass, Frederick, 1818-1895, author
    Narrative of the life of Frederick Douglass, an American slave / Frederick Douglass ; edited by Celeste-Marie Bernier.

Includes bibliographical references.
ISBN 978-1-55481-342-1 (softcover)

    1. Douglass, Frederick, 1818-1895. 2. African American abolitionists—Biography. 3. Abolitionists—United States—Biography. 4. Slaves—United States—Biography. 5. Autobiographies. I. Bernier, Celeste-Marie, editor II. Title.

E449.D68 2018   973.8092   C2018-900337-5

Broadview Editions
The Broadview Editions series is an effort to represent the ever-evolving canon of texts in the disciplines of literary studies, history, philosophy, and political theory. A distinguishing feature of the series is the inclusion of primary source documents contemporaneous with the work.

Advisory editor for this volume: Martin R. Boyne

Broadview Press handles its own distribution in North America:
PO Box 1243, Peterborough, Ontario K9J 7H5, Canada
555 Riverwalk Parkway, Tonawanda, NY 14150, USA
Tel: (705) 743-8990; Fax: (705) 743-8353
email: customerservice@broadviewpress.com

Distribution is handled by Eurospan Group in the UK, Europe, Central Asia, Middle East, Africa, India, Southeast Asia, Central America, South America, and the Caribbean. Distribution is handled by Footprint Books in Australia and New Zealand.

Broadview Press acknowledges the financial support of the Government of Canada through the Canada Book Fund for our publishing activities.   Canada

Typesetting and assembly: True to Type Inc., Claremont, Canada
Cover Design: Aldo Fierro

PRINTED IN CANADA

Contents

List of Illustrations

List of Illustrations

A narrative of the life of Frederick Douglass

Acknowledgements

In preparing this edition for publication I would like to acknowledge my heartfelt gratitude to the following trailblazing Douglass scholars: William L. Andrews, Houston A. Baker, John W. Blassingame, David Blight, Angela Davis, Ira Dworkin, Leigh Fought, Henry Louis Gates Jr., Peter P. Hinks, Earnestine Jenkins, Lee Jenkins, Heather L. Kaufman, Gregory Lampe, Bill E. Lawson, Deborah McDowell, William McFeely, John R. McKivigan, Sarah Meer, Benjamin Quarles, John David Smith, John Stauffer, Robert B. Stepto, Jeffrey Stewart, and Zoe Trodd. For sharing generously from their research specifically for this edition, I would like to signal my sincere gratitude to the following internationally renowned Douglass historians and literary theorists: Robert S. Levine, Hannah-Rose Murray, Alasdair Pettinger, Alan Rice, and Fionnghuala Sweeney. I would like to express my profound gratitude to Walter O. and Linda Evans for their exceptional generosity in granting me access to their unpublished Frederick Douglass collections. A lifelong friend, Claire Freeman, provided invaluable foreign-language expertise without which I would have been unable to examine Douglass's European editions. I would like to extend my heartfelt gratitude to the National Humanities Center for the Senior John Hope Franklin Fellowship that made the research and writing of this edition possible. The inspirational expertise of the National Humanities Center's Brooke Andrade, Sarah Harris, and Joe Millelo in finding and sourcing rare materials played a key role in the completion of this volume. Richard Newman and Lois Whittington provided invaluable support and kind assistance during my time there. I am deeply indebted to the following colleagues at the University of Edinburgh for giving their wholehearted support for this project: Janet Black, Michelle Houston, Charlie Jeffries, Dorothy Miell, Jeremy Robbins, and Andrew Taylor. This edition is dedicated to Richard Anderson.

This edition is published to coincide with a major exhibition, *Strike for Freedom: Slavery, Civil War, and the Frederick Douglass Family in the Walter O. Evans Collection* which will be on view at the National Library of Scotland, Edinburgh, and with additional exhibits at the Frederick Douglass National Historic Site, Washington, DC and the Banneker Douglass Museum and Maryland State Archives, and with the publication of the book (co-authored with Andrew Taylor), *If I Survive: Frederick Douglass and Family in the Walter O. Evans Collection* (Edinburgh University Press, forthcoming).

Introduction

Originally published in 1845, *Narrative of the Life of Frederick Douglass, an American Slave*, the first autobiography of Frederick Douglass (1818–95), a renowned freedom-fighter, statesman, activist, and author, is uncontested as the definitive text within his writings and as *the* canonical autobiographical work in nineteenth-century African American literary production. Yet his biography—not to mention his memory—remains a swirling quicksand of shifting perceptions and changing interpretations. Against a backdrop of Civil Rights, Black Power, and Black Lives Matter eras, and on the two-hundredth anniversary of his birth, there is a Douglass for every political cause, revolutionary platform, literary tradition, cultural agenda, and vision for social change.

While John Blassingame's emphasis that the *"Narrative* far outstripped any of its predecessors" ("Introduction," in Blassingame et al. xxxii) is indisputable regarding the record-breaking publication sales for Douglass's first autobiography, I would urge readers not to read his work in isolation. The only way in which to do justice to Douglass's lifelong re-creation of his many-sided public and private sense of selfhood is to read the *Narrative* not as a canonical, definitive, or representative work but as one among many stand-alone narratives authored by hundreds of formerly enslaved and self-emancipated writers living across the Atlantic world.

Among Douglass's contemporaries, countless self-emancipated authors-turned-activists were responsible for publishing autobiographies of equally extraordinary political, social, historical, and artistic power. Among them can be found the following individuals: Sojourner Truth (c. 1797–1883), William Wells Brown (c. 1814–84), Harriet Jacobs (1813–97), Henry Bibb (1815–54), William Grimes (1784–1865), Solomon Northup (1807/08–c. 1863), Harriet Tubman (c. 1820–1913), Elizabeth Keckley (1818–1907), Moses Roper (c. 1815–91), William (1824–1900) and Ellen (1826–91) Craft, and Henry Highland Garnet (1815–82).

Nothing is to be gained and everything is to be lost by reading Douglass as the representative enslaved liberator and his *Narrative* as the representative autobiography. At our peril do we reimagine Douglass's "story of the slave" to the exclusion of all others. It is only by examining Douglass's *Narrative* in comparative perspective that a full picture of the "grim horrors of slavery" (p. 239) emerges as encompassing a full gamut of physical, psychological, emotional, imaginative, social, political, and cultural realities. Readers are also urged not to examine Douglass's *Narrative* in isolation from his own vast array of published and unpublished writings. He was a prolific writer no less than a reformer, and his works not only include multiple autobiographies and written accounts of his speeches but also a novella, poetry, historical and philosophical essays, political tracts, travel diaries, and correspondence. For Douglass, his *Narrative* was in no way definitive regarding his credentials as an author and activist.

Equally, and of heightened urgency during a Black Lives Matter era, it is our social and political responsibility to confront the stark fact that the autobiographies written by Douglass and by the many other formerly enslaved individuals that have been handed down to us are the stories of the survivors who made it to freedom. It is only when we recognize the atypicality and the exceptionalism of their lives that we can begin to come to grips with the traumatizing reality that the vast majority of women, children, and men who were bought and sold lived and died in slavery. While I urge readers to undertake further research into the written testimonies produced by enslaved peoples living across the African diaspora, I also recommend that they turn to their music and art-making traditions. When words failed and access to the written record was denied, the stories of the dead women, children, and men who told no tales live on "hidden in plain sight" in their songs, oral stories, musical instruments, paintings, burial markers, architecture, gardens, culinary practices, hairstyling traditions, quilting patterns, basket weaving, silversmith work, and earthenware production, among much more. Just as the women, men, and children whose names we will never know used every means necessary to survive by finding a way out of no way, so too is Douglass's *Narrative* as much a monument to loss and to the lives that can never be remembered as it is a testament to the facts and fictions of his own life.

During his anniversary year of 2018 and in a current Black Lives Matter era, while there have been many Douglasses—Douglass the activist, Douglass the statesman, Douglass the autobiographer, Douglass the essayist, Douglass the orator, and Douglass the politician—the Frederick Douglass we need now is no representative, iconic, mythic or legendary "self-made man" but a fallible, mortal, and human individual: a husband, father, brother, and son. Writing toward the end of his life, Douglass admitted in his final autobiography, *Life and Times*, that "I have lived several lives in one: first, the life of slavery; secondly, the life of a fugitive from slavery; thirdly, the life of comparative freedom; fourthly, the life of conflict and battle; and, fifthly, the life of victory, if not complete, at least assured" (581–82). This offers a blueprint for contemporary Black liberation struggles. If we dispense with the final stage, the "life of victory"—a state of existence that, even for Douglass, was more imagined than real—and instead turn to his penultimate belief in a "life of conflict and battle," his rallying cry lives on to inspire today's activism: "Agitate! Agitate! Agitate!" (qtd. in Foner, *Life*, vol. IV, p. 314).

Frederick Douglass as Author, Editor, Publisher

"My part has been to tell the story of the slave," Frederick Douglass confides in *Life and Times*, his final autobiography, which he published in 1892, just a few years before he died. Over the decades, he remained immovable in his conviction: "The story of the master never wanted for narrators" (372). Born into US plantation slavery as Frederick Augustus Washington Bailey in Maryland in February 1818, this formerly enslaved field laborer turned ship caulker was reborn into freedom as Frederick Douglass following his escape to the north 20 years later on 3 September 1838. Living at the height of the internal slave trade, he was just one among thousands of African American women, men, and children who made it out of the "prison-house of bondage" (p. 81) against all odds and on pain of death. A self-emancipated author no less than an activist, he was also one among thousands who took it upon themselves to use their autobiographical experiences not solely to do justice to personal abuses but to "tell the story of the slave." Formerly enslaved women and men including Douglass were early pioneers of the slave narrative genre, a US literary form in which Black writers retold their life stories in order to convert white mainstream audiences to the abolitionist cause.

Living in the decades before the Civil War, radical reformers such as Moses Roper, Henry Box Brown (c. 1816–97), William Wells Brown, William and Ellen Craft, Solomon Northup, Henry Bibb, Harriet Jacobs, Elizabeth Keckley, and Douglass wielded the pen as a powerful weapon in their antislavery arsenal. On the antislavery podium as well as on the written page, they bore witness to their personal histories not as an end in themselves but as catalysts to their no-holds-barred examination of the "story of the slave." In the service of the cause, both female and male narrators such as Douglass repackaged their lives and sacrificed private details to lend maximum weight to their representation of Black women, children, and men who had been bought and sold into slavery. Black subjects typically come to life within the pages of "written by her- or himself" and "as told to" slave narratives as bodies of evidence and objects of proof rather than as personal, fallible, and individualized human beings.

"Speaking of marks, traces, possibles and improbabilities we come before our readers" (176), Douglass candidly writes in his sole work of fiction, *The Heroic Slave*, which he published in 1853. He readily confides the burden he faced in beginning to tell the "story" not of any enslaved individual but of the "heroic slave" Madison Washington. As a self-emancipated freedom-fighter, Washington was an enslaved man, born in Virginia, who was subsequently lionized for liberating the women, men, and children shackled on board the *Creole* slave ship on its way to the markets of New Orleans over a decade earlier in November 1841. Douglass readily admitted to his failure in trying to recount Washington's story despite his fame and notoriety in the international press. He was beset on every side by the near impossibility of putting flesh on the bones of a man who may well have assumed renown as a Black liberator but whose life had been entirely obliterated from official US history. Douglass was bitter in his denunciation of the injustice that "*one* of the truest, manliest, and bravest of her children, one who, in after years, will, I think, command the pen of genius to set his merits forth, holds now no higher place in the records of that grand old Commonwealth than is held by a horse or an ox" (175; emphasis in original). He deplored the stark reality "that a man who loved liberty as well as did Patrick Henry [1736–99], who deserved it as much as Thomas Jefferson [1743–1826], and who fought for it with a valor as high, an arm as strong, and against odds as great, as he who led all the armies of the American colonies through the great war for freedom and independence, lives now only in the chattel records of his native State" (175).

Ever mindful of the insurmountable difficulties facing any attempt to penetrate beneath the "chattel records" in order to memorialize Black lives, Douglass was forced to turn away from the slave narrative genre to reimagine the life of this "heroic slave" in fictional form. As he realized only too well, if the quest to do justice to a lionized self-emancipated leader was all but impossible, how much harder was it to come to grips with the biographies of his own family members, many of whom had been unable to escape but had lived and died in slavery. As he admits in his second autobiography, *My Bondage and My Freedom*, published in 1855, "[g]enealogical trees do not flourish among slaves" (p. 34). During his lifetime, Douglass was denied access to accurate information concerning the birth and death dates of his mother, Harriet Bailey, while the very identity, let alone the biographical information, belonging to his father remains an ongoing area of controversy. To the day he died, Douglass had no idea regarding the year or month in which he was born despite his repeated attempts to glean this information from the descendants of his white slaveholding family. "I have no accurate knowledge of my age, never having seen any authentic record containing it," he was forced to concede (p. 93).

In 2018, we are now free to consult the "authentic record" that was withheld from Douglass, due to the decision made by Mary A. Dodge (1833–96), one of his slave-owners' descendants, to donate the relevant plantation ledgers to the Maryland State Archives in the early twentieth century. "Frederick Augustus son of Harriott" can now be immediately identified in a ledger tabulating "Negros ages" and kept by Aaron Anthony (1767–1826), Douglass's white master, while his date of birth is recorded as "Feby ... 1818" (see Figure 1). US legal officials took stock of the "Personal Estate of Capt. Aaron Anthony of Talbot Co.—19 Dec. 1826" in a document titled "Account of Sales and Inventories 1827" (see Figure 2). The "Ages of Negroes and their appraised value" dominates this sales account as inadmissible proof of the fact that Anthony's ownership of human property lay at the heart of his wealth. A nine-year-old enslaved child identified solely by the name of "Frederick" and valued at "110" US dollars appears as number 17 in the list of 25 individuals that Anthony owned. "Hester," a 17-year-old woman valued with her child to a total market value of $220, is also included in this list. While she and her baby circulate here only as a "chattel record," she would assume dramatic center stage in Douglass's first autobiography, *Narrative of the Life of Frederick Douglass, an American Slave*, published nearly 20 years later in 1845.

According to the "Talbot Co. Distributions 1825–1845, folio 58—27 Sept 1827" legal brief compiled in the same year, "James Chambers and Wm. A. Leonard were appointed to divide the negroes of late Captain Aaron Anthony of Talbot County" (see Figure 3). Chambers and Leonard fulfilled their obligations by bequeathing the following enslaved people to white slaveholder Thomas Auld: "1 Negro Milly and infant / 2 Tom / 3 Nancy / 4

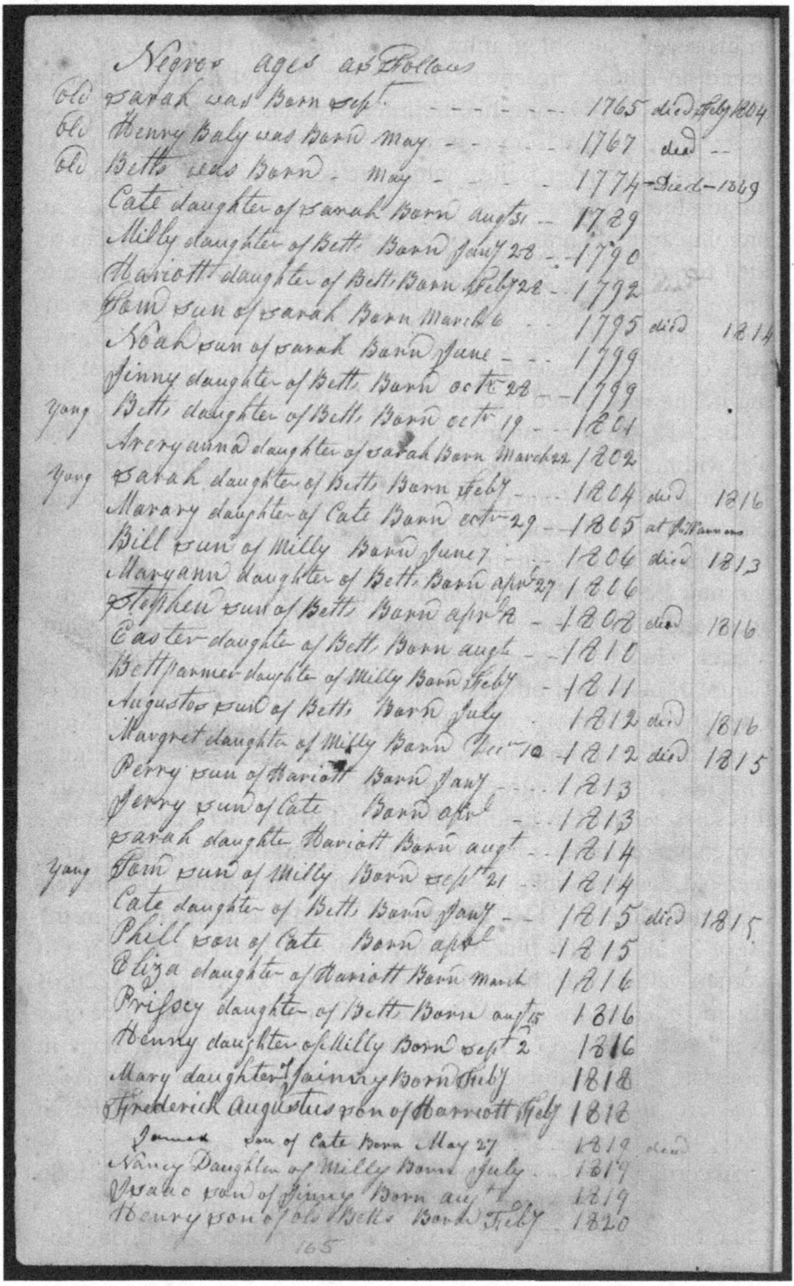

Figure 1: Aaron Anthony, "Negroes Ages as Follows," Special Collections, Maryland State Archives, Annapolis, MD.

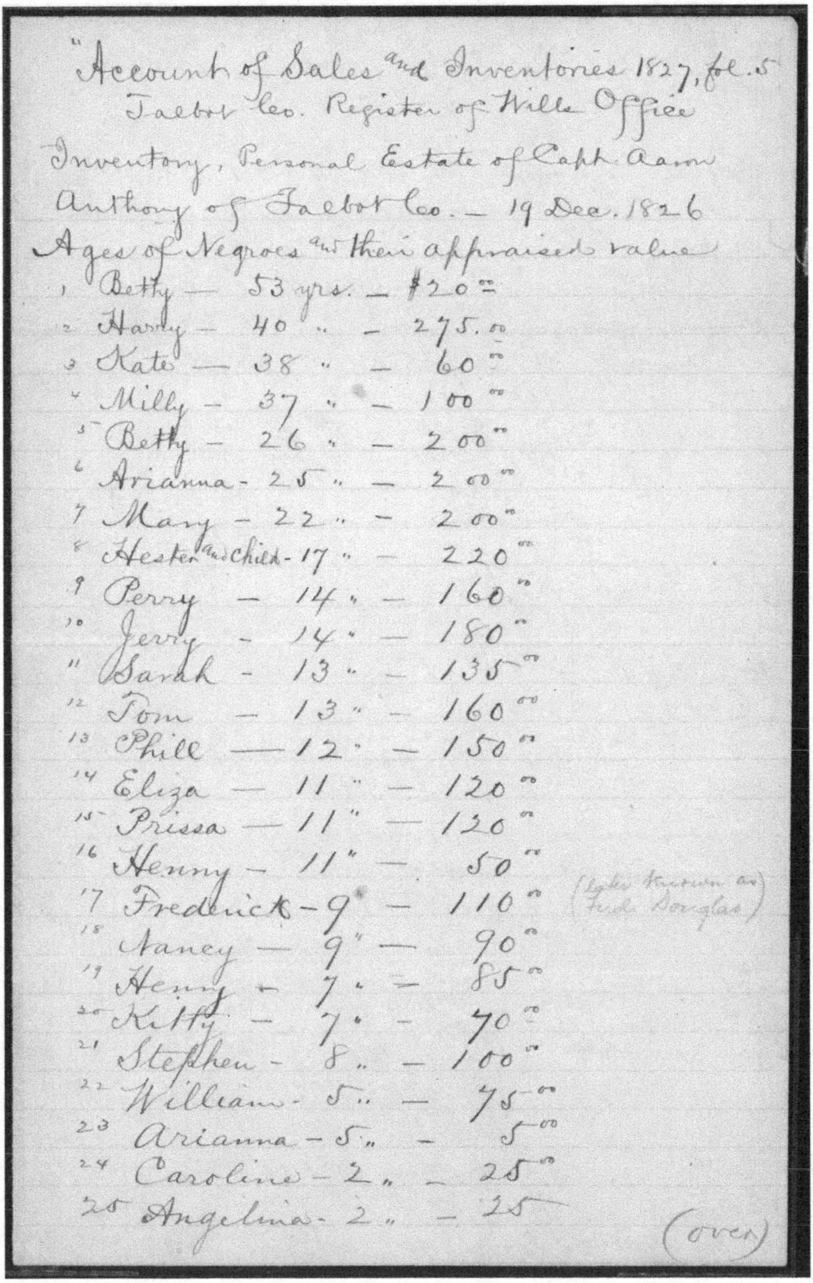

"Account of Sales and Inventories 1827, fol. 5
Talbot Co. Register of Wills Office
Inventory, Personal Estate of Capt. Aaron
Anthony of Talbot Co. — 19 Dec. 1826
Ages of Negroes with their appraised value

1	Betty —	53 yrs. —	$20 =
2	Harry —	40 " —	275.00
3	Kate —	38 " —	60 "
4	Milly —	37 " —	100 "
5	Betty —	26 " —	200 "
6	Arianna —	25 " —	200 "
7	Mary —	22 " —	200 "
8	Hester and child —	17 " —	220 "
9	Perry —	14 " —	160 "
10	Jerry —	14 " —	180 "
11	Sarah —	13 " —	135 "
12	Tom —	13 " —	160 "
13	Phill —	12 " —	150 "
14	Eliza —	11 " —	120 "
15	Prissa —	11 " —	120 "
16	Henny —	11 " —	50 "
17	Frederick —	9 " —	110 " (later known as Fred. Douglas)
18	Nancy —	9 " —	90 "
19	Henry —	7 " —	85 "
20	Kitty —	7 " —	70 "
21	Stephen —	8 " —	100 "
22	William —	5 " —	75 "
23	Arianna —	5 " —	5 "
24	Caroline —	2 " —	25 "
25	Angelina —	2 " —	25

(over)

Figure 2: "Account of Sales and Inventories 1827," Special
Collections, Maryland State Archives, Annapolis, MD.

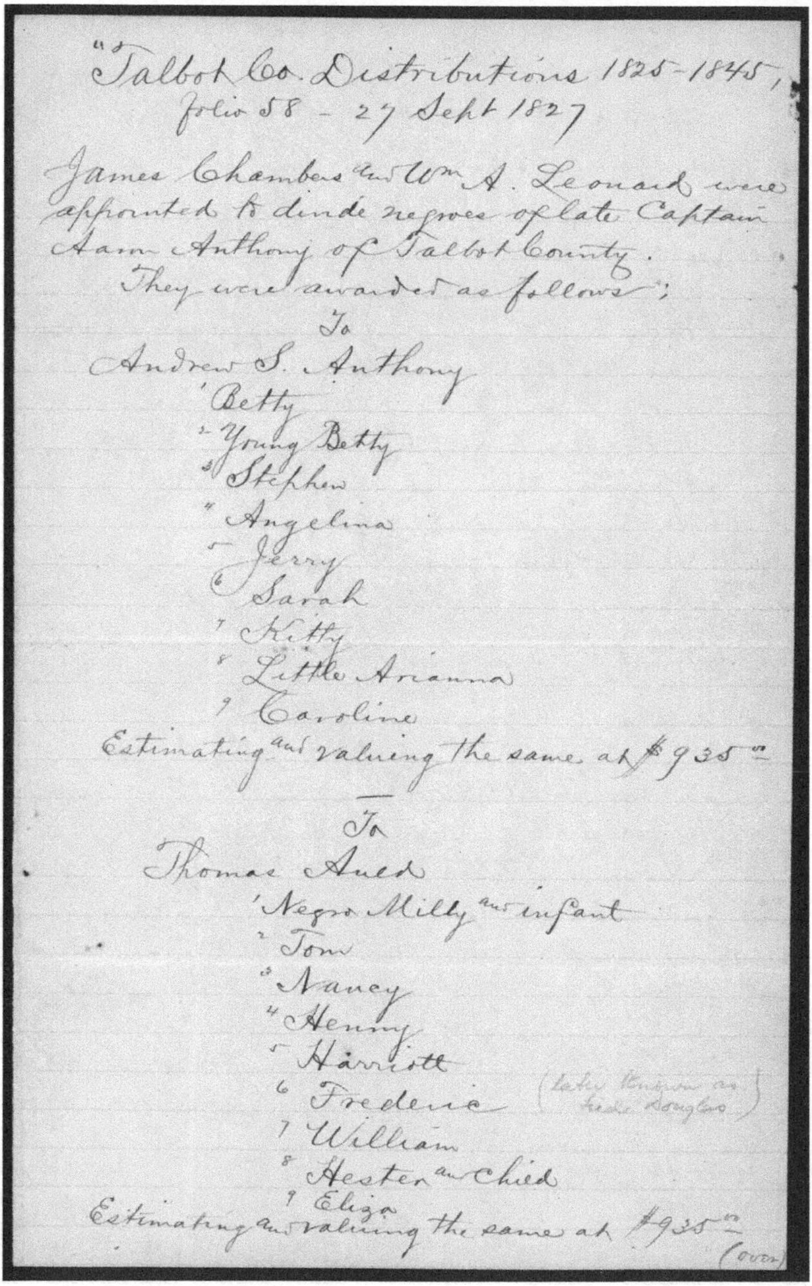

"Talbot Co. Distributions 1825-1845,
folio 58 - 27 Sept 1827

James Chambers and Wm A. Leonard were
appointed to divide negroes of late Captain
Aaron Anthony of Talbot County.
They were awarded as follows:
To
Andrew S. Anthony
    1 Betty
    2 Young Betty
    3 Stephen
    4 Angelina
    5 Jerry
    6 Sarah
    7 Kitty
    8 Little Arianna
    9 Caroline
Estimating and valuing the same at $935 —

To
Thomas Auld
    1 Negro Milly and infant
    2 Tom
    3 Nancy
    4 Henny
    5 Harriott
    6 Frederic (later known as Fred Douglas)
    7 William
    8 Hester and child
    9 Eliza
Estimating and valuing the same at $935 —
(over)

Figure 3: "Talbot County Distributions," Special Collections,
Maryland State Archives, Annapolis, MD.

Henny / 5 Harriott / 6 Frederic / 7 William / 8 Hester and child / 9 Eliza." A final tally "Estimating and valuing the same at $935.00" is categorical evidence of US chattel slavery's equation of Black humanity solely with dollars and cents and according to which all rights—physical, emotional, spiritual, sexual, and intellectual—were not only denied but also entirely eradicated in legal documentation. While all these enslaved women's and men's names are listed in ink and accompanied by no handwritten textual emendation, next to "Frederic" an unknown hand has written in pencil, "(later known as Fred Douglas [sic])."

Decades later, Douglass memorialized this terrible rite of passage in his *Narrative* by declaring, "[w]e were all ranked together at the valuation. Men and women, old and young, married and single, were ranked with horses, sheep, and swine. There were horses and men, cattle and women, pigs and children, all holding the same rank in the scale of being, and were all subjected to the same narrow examination" (p. 120). While these legal documents readily confirm that Anthony's enslaved people were "ranked together," Douglass's poignant examination of the emotional toll they all experienced is of course entirely missing from this official archive. As he writes in the *Narrative*, "I have no language to express the high excitement and deep anxiety which were felt among us poor slaves during this time" (p. 121). Nowhere is there more hard-hitting confirmation of Douglass's despair regarding Black women, children, and men consigned to the lifeless death that is the "chattel record" than the gaps within the historical archives concerning his own genealogy. At the same time, his confession that he had "no language" with which to bear witness to the suffering endured by enslaved people is a terrible indictment of slavery's unrepresentable realities.

For Douglass, the answer to beginning to reimagine lives that survived only as "marks, traces, possibles and improbabilities" undoubtedly lay in his cultivation of an experimental literary prowess and an unequivocal oratorical power. From the 1840s onwards, he came to national prominence by delivering speeches that soon became the blueprint for his first *Narrative*. Over the decades, he harnessed his voice and authorial skill to tell and retell the story not only of Frederick Augustus Washington Bailey "the slave" but of Frederick Douglass "the freeman." At the same time, however, he never lost sight of the limitations of either the written or the spoken word when it came to doing full justice to slavery as a site of unspeakable—and unwritable—atrocity.

Douglass's war against the eradication of the legendary icon Madison Washington from the history books was on a continuum with his protest against the "invisibilization" of the erstwhile anonymous Frederick Augustus Washington Bailey in the "chattel records."[1] As he recognized, the fight for visibilizing Black lives was not confined to the battleground of history but extended to the dominant US records and national archives from which African American women, children, and men, enslaved and free, were repeatedly excluded. He insistently called for "literature not ledgers" as an antidote to the incarceration of Black peoples, enslaved and free, within "chattel records."

A few years prior to writing *The Heroic Slave*, Douglass was jubilant regarding a new tradition not only of slave narrative writing but also of Black-authored dramas, histories, essays, speeches, and poetry. As he wrote to white radical abolitionist Gerrit Smith (1797–1874) in 1851, "[t]he fact that Negroes are turning Book makers may possibly serve to remove the popular impression that they are fit only for Boot blackers & although they may not *shine* in the former profession as they have long done in the latter, I am not with out [sic] hope that they will do themselves good by making the effort."[2] A prolific author and indefatigable activist on the abolitionist circuit, Douglass sought not only to do himself "good" but to "shine" by writing three autobiographies alongside hundreds of speeches, essays, tracts, letters, and poems on a multitude of historical and cultural topics. No genre, form, or topic was off-limits. At the same time that he rejected the white racist prescriptions surrounding Black lives endorsed by a proslavery ideology, he maintained an unceasing fight against white abolitionist paternalism and deeply entrenched systems of romantic racialism.[3] Fully aware that he and hundreds more formerly enslaved narrators were addressing their narratives primarily to pro- as well as anti-slavery audiences, Douglass was not alone in developing self-aware literary practices. Working to end slavery by any means necessary, Douglass relied on the satirical techniques of the subversive trickster at the same time that

---

1   In the current era, "invisibilization" has emerged as a core term assisting scholars in doing justice to the ways in which Black lives, enslaved and free, have been not only eradicated and erased but also distorted and denied in the dominant official records.

2   Frederick Douglass to Gerrit Smith, 21 January 1851, in Foner, *Frederick Douglass: Selected Speeches and Writings* 172; emphasis in original.

3   For an examination of the nineteenth-century concept of "romantic racialism" see Fredrickson.

he embraced revolutionary rhetoric. For Douglass, language was a powerful tool by which he not only defended the equal rights of all Black women, children, and men but signaled his own refusal to be categorized, stereotyped, or pigeonholed within a white US imaginary.

"I was generally introduced as a 'chattel'—a 'thing'—a piece of southern 'property'—the chairman assuring the audience that it could speak," Douglass writes in *My Bondage and My Freedom*, his second autobiography, published in 1855 and over a decade after the publication of his *Narrative* (360). He pulls no punches regarding his suffering at the hands of not only white slaveholders but also of white abolitionists. Douglass remained constantly vigilant against any attempts by white patrons, sponsors, political radicals, and general audiences to script, censor, or edit either his life or his testimony. While he recognized that he was no longer for sale on the auction block following his self-emancipation in 1838, he realized only too well that he was being bought and sold in abolitionist campaigns that traded in shamelessly sensationalist, dehumanizing, and derogatory language when it came to Black women and men. He was especially appalled to note the advice he was given: "It was said to me, 'Better have a little of the plantation manner of speech than not; 'tis not best that you seem too learned.'" Douglass remained respectful of white abolitionist sensibilities by observing, "[t]hese excellent friends were actuated by the best of motives, and were not altogether wrong in their advice." And yet he steadfastly refused to defer to their authority: "still I must speak just the word that seemed to me the word to be spoken by me" (*My Bondage* 362). For Douglass, this quest renders his life's work as a reformer indivisible from his life's work as a writer. Notably, on Douglass's sudden death on 20 February 1895, Helen Pitts Douglass (1838–1903), his second wife, honored her husband's life not by celebrating his political activism but by designating his profession as "Literary (Author, Editor, Publisher)."[1] As a man for whom the right to literacy was secured only on pain of persecution and very real personal threat, the right to recognition as not only an "Author, Editor, Publisher" but also a "*Literary*" one was to remain as important as his political activism.

This new edition of Douglass's first autobiography is published in 2018, the two-hundredth anniversary of his birth, to celebrate his lifelong declaration of authorial independence. As the sheer volume of his published and unpublished writings demon-

---

1 Frederick Douglass's death certificate is available online:
https://www.loc.gov/resource/mfd.45004/?sp=2.

strates, Douglass's bestselling autobiography, which circulated in the United States and Europe from 1845 onwards was no isolated event. Even a cursory examination of the Frederick Douglass Papers held in the Library of Congress and the Frederick Douglass Collection owned by the Moorland Spingarn Research Center at Howard University establishes that he was a self-reflexive and experimental autobiographer, powerful orator, incisive essayist, radical historian, intimate diarist, contemplative philosopher, lyrical poet, brilliant political commentator, thoughtful correspondent, and canny photographic subject. In view of his designation as an "Editor, Publisher" as well as an "Author," he was also a pioneering newspaper and magazine editor responsible for founding and maintaining the following radical and revolutionary publications: *The North Star, Frederick Douglass's Paper, Douglass' Monthly*, and *The New National Era.*

A testing ground for Douglass's experimental aesthetic strategies, his *Narrative* is at the center of his productivity and remains key to unlocking his groundbreaking use of language and oratorically inspired literary forms. In this work, he sheds light on the survival strategies endorsed by Black people, enslaved and free, which ran a gamut of physical, psychological, imaginative, sexual, cultural, spiritual, and political resistance. Just as no one size fits all regarding the types of slavery or guises of white supremacy, nor does one literary form fit all. Douglass developed ever more experimental practices in recognition of the fact that he had "no language" in which to do full justice either to the experience of enslavement or to the condition of emancipation.

This edition of Douglass's *Narrative* begins by examining his complex relationship to the slave narrative genre and literary language. He repeatedly admits to his failures of literary expression throughout this first autobiography. Here and elsewhere he recognizes the impossibility of reimagining the atrocities of slavery in either spoken or written form. Working to do justice to Douglass's seismic importance not only as an American but also as a transatlantic author and activist, I then trace the reception of his *Narrative* following the work's publication in editions that appeared not only in Boston but also in Dublin, Ireland, and London and Leeds in England. I examine his first autobiography as a bestselling European publication by coming to grips with the additional materials he included in these editions. At the heart of these works is his ongoing war regarding the representation of his own likeness across his frontispiece portraits. I also provide readers with access to the pioneering oratory and essays he published contemporaneously with the *Narrative*, including the letter he wrote to Thomas Auld following his emancipation. The challenges Douglass faced in liberating himself from white abolitionist control were only to be matched by the conflicts he experienced in gaining his emotional and psychological—not to mention his physical—freedoms from his former slave master.

I conclude this anniversary edition of the *Narrative* by introducing readers to Douglass's own family—Anna Murray Douglass, his first wife of over 40 years, and his daughters and sons, Rosetta Douglass Sprague, Lewis Henry Douglass, Frederick Douglass Jr., Charles Remond Douglass, and Annie Douglass. For reasons Douglass never explained, his family members are themselves relegated to "chattel records" in his *Narrative*. They remain a non-presence despite the invaluable social, political, economic, cultural, intellectual, and historical roles they had to play in his own "struggle for the cause of liberty" (see Appendix D7, p. 270). It is no exaggeration to state that without each of his family members' fulfillment of their various indispensable roles as household managers, domestic carers, food preparation specialists, laundry workers, Underground Railroad operators, grassroots campaigners, proofreaders, typesetters, and delivery agents, and even as his amanuensis, there would be no Frederick Douglass.[1] As we see in Rosetta Douglass Sprague's biography of the invisibilized life of her mother, had Anna Murray, herself a free woman, decided not to use her financial resources to aid this particular fugitive slave, Frederick Augustus Washington Bailey would have very likely remained in slavery.

"The Blood-Stained Gate": Douglass's *Narrative* and the "Story of the Slave"

"'Let us have the facts,' said the people. So also said Friend George Foster, who always wished to pin me down to my simple narrative. 'Give us the facts,' said Collins, 'we will take care of the philosophy.'" So Douglass reminisces in his second autobiogra-

---

1 As a case in point, Douglass's eldest daughter, Rosetta, repeatedly acted as her father's amanuensis by not only copying out his speeches but also editing them and producing the final typescripts prior to their publication. She was not alone. Douglass's second wife, Helen Pitts Douglass, also performed this role, as did Fredericka Douglass Sprague Perry, Rosetta's daughter.

phy, *My Bondage and My Freedom*, regarding the pressures he faced from white abolitionists in his early years as an antislavery campaigner (361). "'Tell your story, Frederick,' would whisper my then revered friend, William Lloyd Garrison,'" he confides. Tellingly, any stipulations by white reformers George Foster, John Collins, and William Lloyd Garrison (1805–79) that he confine himself solely to the "facts," that he write only a "simple narrative," or even that he tell only his own "story" proved unacceptable to Douglass. He admitted, "I could not always obey, for I was now reading and thinking." He was fully equipped to "take care of the philosophy" by assuming the roles not only of the autobiographer, orator, historian, and political commentator but also of the dramatist, intellectual, and thinker. He insisted on his right to freedom of expression and freedom of thought by confirming, "[i]t was impossible for me to repeat the same old story month after month, and to keep up my interest in it.... It was new to the people, it is true, but it was an old story to me; and to go through with it night after night, was a task altogether too mechanical for my nature" (361). He refused to confine himself to the "same old story" by insisting on his right to exercise his formidable cerebral as well as creative power: "It did not entirely satisfy me to narrate wrongs; I felt like denouncing them" (361–62). According to the predictions of his white male sponsors, his behavior promised to be nothing less than catastrophic for the antislavery cause: "'People won't believe you ever was a slave, Frederick, if you keep on this way,' said Friend Foster" (362).

In May 1845, at the age of 27, Douglass refuted the claims made by non-believers that he never "was a slave" by publishing his first autobiography, *Narrative of the Life of Frederick Douglass, an American Slave*, at the antislavery office in Boston. Douglass's *Narrative* was an instant bestseller. Writing in the Preface to the first edition published in Dublin, Ireland, he confirmed, "when I sailed for England in September, about 4,500 copies had been sold" (see Appendix A2, p. 176). As Douglass continued to face white-abolitionist attempts to influence his story on the antislavery lecture circuit, his *Narrative* showed equal signs of strain. While he authored his "Appendix" by indicting the hypocrisy of a slaveholding religion, he had no choice but to include prefatory materials written by white abolitionists Garrison and Wendell Phillips (1811–84). No "black message in a white envelope," as theorized by John Sekora, however, Douglass's *Narrative* supplies a black message in a *black* envelope. He chose to frame his white-

NARRATIVE

OF THE

LIFE

OF

FREDERICK DOUGLASS,

AN

AMERICAN SLAVE.

WRITTEN BY HIMSELF.

BOSTON:

PUBLISHED AT THE ANTI-SLAVERY OFFICE,

No. 25 CORNHILL.

1845.

Figure 4: Title Page, *Narrative of the Life of Frederick Douglass* (Boston: Anti-Slavery Office, 1845).

Figure 5: Frontispiece, *Narrative of the Life of Frederick Douglass* (Boston: Anti-Slavery Office, 1845).

authored apparatus which was typically included in all slave narratives as a means of authentication, by including a title page that is distinctive not only for including the title of his work but also for registering his declaration of authorial independence: "Written by himself" (see Figure 4).

Douglass traded on his widespread celebrity by inserting a delicately etched engraving of his own portrait as a frontispiece on the page immediately facing his title page (see Figure 5). In so doing, he guaranteed that his readers' initial encounter with his

Figure 6: Josiah Wedgwood, "Am I Not a Man and a Brother?" (1837). Prints and Photographs Division, Library of Congress.

Narrative remained defined by their exposure to an accurate likeness of Douglass himself as the author. No grotesque caricature of white racist imagining and no bent-over abolitionist icon purporting to represent enslaved humanity, he relies on his emotionally charged expression to confront the viewer as a psychologically complex protagonist in the portrait. On the one hand, his dignified likeness is the visual antithesis of villainous stereotypes that traded in barbaric fictions of a murderous Black masculinity. On the other hand, the detailed engraving of his physiognomy rejects the white abolitionist trade in a spectacle of Black martyrdom. Nothing could be further from white British ceramicist and abolitionist campaigner Josiah Wedgwood's (1730–95) "Am I Not a Man and a Brother?" medallion, in which a Black man with generic and caricatured facial features begs for white philanthropic uplift (see Figure 6), than Douglass's empowered portrait.

Douglass's likeness also survives as an unequivocal endorsement of his public letter addressed to A.C.C. Thompson, a white proslavery apologist. Writing in a vituperative vein, Thompson insisted, "'I knew this recreant slave by the name of Frederick Bailey,' (instead of Douglass.)." He was convinced that Douglass "was an unlearned, and rather an ordinary negro" and was "confident he was not capable of writing the Narrative alluded to."[1] Douglass silenced Thompson by publishing his response to these injurious charges in the second Irish edition of his *Narrative*. Writing from Dublin in 1846, Douglass was candid regarding the miraculous change wrought upon his character by freedom. "Frederick the Freeman is a very different person from Frederick the Slave," he argued, insisting, "[t]o judge me now by what I was then, is to do me great injustice" (cxxvi). As he informed Thompson, "You know when I used to meet you near Covey's wood-gate, I hardly dared to look up at you. If I should meet you where I now am, amid the free hills of Old Scotland, where the ancient 'Black Douglass' once met his foes, I presume I might summon sufficient fortitude to look you full in the face" (cxxvi). For Douglass, his meticulously rendered physiognomy and meditative gaze on offer within his likeness function as a visual fulfillment of his prophecy that he was now equipped to look not only Thompson but also his audience "full in the face." As a survivor turned witness to a life lived in bondage, he was burdened with remembering both his own traumas and those of the millions more who live and died in slavery. His decision to insert his signature beneath his portrait by using "Frederick Douglass," the name he adopted in his life as a freeman and for which he earned international renown, was yet another way in which he dispelled any doubts surrounding his literacy and his authorship.

Douglass's use of portraiture works in combination with his textual declarations of independence to ensure that he has the first word—and control over the first image—within his *Narrative*. He celebrated his role as the author of his own story to wrest control away from Garrison's "Preface" and Phillips's letter of introduction. As the array of experimental narrative techniques on offer in his text confirms, he rejected Garrison's patronizing claim that "Mr. DOUGLASS has very properly chosen to write his own Narrative, in his own style, and according to the best of

---

1 See the second Dublin edition, p. cxxiv.

his ability, rather than to employ some one else" (p. 85). For Douglass, the "best" of his "abilities" involved experimental strategies of self-representation that further complicated Garrison's insistence on his veracity: "I am confident that it is essentially true in all its statements; that nothing has been set down in malice, nothing exaggerated, nothing drawn from the imagination; that it comes short of the reality, rather than overstates a single fact in regard to SLAVERY AS IT IS'" (p. 85). Douglass gave the lie to Garrison's conviction by working with every tool at his disposal—factual or otherwise—to dramatize "SLAVERY AS IT IS." He saw no tactic as off-limits in his determination to delve deep beneath the surface. As an experimental writer, he transgressed the boundaries of literal truth and rejected the over-reliance on factual accuracy maintained by his white sponsors by "drawing" heavily from his "imagination" throughout his text. He deliberately worked with fictional devices as the sole means by which to cut to the heart of the lived realities of enslaved peoples that defied all dominant forms of representation.

Douglass's *Narrative* comes to life in uneasy relation to Garrison's conclusion that "[t]he experience of FREDERICK DOUGLASS, as a slave, was not a peculiar one; his lot was not especially a hard one; his case may be regarded as a very fair specimen of the treatment of slaves in Maryland" (p. 85). Across his autobiography, Douglass deliberately constructed individualized Black protagonists in a rejection of any reduction of African Americans, enslaved and free, solely to their use and reuse as "fair specimens" in the cause. Warring against Garrison's tendency to collapse the specificities of his life into the generic difficulties endured by "slaves in Maryland," Douglass sought not only to tell the "story of the slave" but also to tell the story of Frederick Augustus Washington Bailey turned Frederick Douglass. For Phillips, Douglass benefitted from yet further political currency in his symbolism not as a "fair specimen" of slavery but as an icon of white US revolutionary heroism. In his letter immediately following Garrison's preface, Phillips proclaims, "[t]hey say the fathers, in 1776, signed the Declaration of Independence with the halter about their necks," as he advised his friend that "[y]ou, too, publish your declaration of freedom with danger compassing you around." Phillips was candid regarding his realization of Douglass's exemplary courage by admitting, "I am free to say that, in your place, I should throw the MS. into the fire" (p. 91).

Douglass's decision to write a work of literature signals his declaration of independence from the consignment of his own and his family's lives solely to the plantation ledger. He begins his "story as a slave" in his *Narrative* by awarding center stage to his maternal ancestry: "My mother was named Harriet Bailey. She was the daughter of Isaac and Betsey Bailey, both colored, and quite dark. My mother was of a darker complexion than either my grandmother or grandfather" (p. 93). A victim of the "chattel records," Douglass's mother was listed solely as "Hariott daughter of Bett, Born Feb 22 1792" in Anthony's misspelt list of "Negroes Ages" (see Figure 1). Next to the entry of her name, a handwritten note starkly reads, "dead." Douglass's mother was denied not only a gravestone and burial but also a date of death according to this "chattel record."

While he had no access to this dehumanizing archive, Douglass anticipated its existence by assuming the role of his mother's biographer, despite the challenges he faced concerning his own lack of knowledge. As a formerly enslaved individual of mixed-race heritage, his insistence regarding his mother's "darker complexion" successfully overturned all racist assumptions that he owed his intellectual power to his supposed white ancestry. A decade later in *My Bondage and My Freedom*, he confirmed his dissatisfaction with the account he gave of his mother's life in his *Narrative* by deciding to include additional biographical information. "My knowledge of my mother is very scanty, but very distinct," he writes. "Her personal appearance and bearing are ineffaceably stamped upon my memory. She was tall, and finely proportioned; of deep black, glossy complexion; had regular features, and, among the other slaves, was remarkably sedate in her manners" (xxx). He admits to a "scanty" understanding regarding Harriet Bailey's personal history only to do painstaking justice to her exemplary beauty and heroic stature: "I learned, after my mother's death, that she could read, and that she was the only one of all the slaves and colored people in Tuckahoe who enjoyed that advantage," he observed. Douglass pulled no punches regarding his disbelief: "How she acquired this knowledge, I know not, for Tuckahoe is the last place in the world where she would be apt to find facilities for learning. I can, therefore, fondly and proudly ascribe to her an earnest love of knowledge" (58).

He carried within himself a living testament to his mother's scholarly prowess, and Douglass's middle names "Augustus Washington" variously speak to his mother's immersion in classical antiquity—through Augustus, the founder of the Roman empire—and US history—through George Washington, the first president. The fact that one of Douglass's middle names was

Washington may well account for his lifelong fascination with Madison Washington, their shared nomenclature very likely suggesting their shared heroism in Douglass's eyes. If Douglass's *Narrative* is considered in conjunction with the evidence provided by the surviving plantation ledger, Harriet Bailey may very likely also have sought to honor the life of her brother, Augustus Bailey (see Figure 1). As the record shows, Augustus was a child born into slavery in 1812 only to die four years later, less than two years before Frederick was born. If this is the case, Harriet Bailey adopted the widespread practice of preserving the memory of Black genealogical trees through a deliberate use of naming.

If the biographical uncertainties surrounding Douglass's mother's life present difficulties for researchers, then his father's identity—not to mention his father's history—remains impossible to resolve and is the source of ongoing intense debate. In his *Narrative*, Douglass gives only the scantiest information by stating, "My father was a white man" (p. 93). By comparison, he speculated in *My Bondage and My Freedom* that "[i]t was sometimes whispered that my master was my father" (52). Decades later, he refused to give any opinion in *Life and Times* by insisting on his ignorance: "Of my father I know nothing" (27). While Douglass may have felt he was unable to provide any categorical information regarding his father's identity, the generally held consensus among his nineteenth-, twentieth-, and twenty-first-century biographers is that his first master, Aaron Anthony, was almost certainly his father. However, my recent research into the Frederick Douglass Papers held in the Library of Congress introduces another possibility.

Ottilie Assing, a German-born philosopher, journalist, activist, and Douglass's long-term collaborator and friend, presents a very different candidate for his father. She writes in an unsigned, undated, and unpublished manuscript, "it is to be supposed that a favourite white slave of Lloyd—probably his own son, whom he afterwards made free, was F.D.'s father; at least a striking resemblance with the Lloyd family was said to be found in him." According to her declaration, written during Douglass's lifetime—she died in 1884—and of which he was very likely aware and yet chose not to publicly contradict, his father was almost certainly not Aaron Anthony but an as yet unidentified son of Colonel Edward Lloyd V (1779–1834). Adding fuel to the flames, much later in his life Douglass chose to describe himself in an interview with a journalist as the "son of a senator." The fact that the eldest of Edward Lloyd

V's sons, Edward Lloyd VI, became a Maryland state senator would suggest the likely candidacy for his paternity.[1] Douglass's refusal to resolve the issue, either because he would not or because he could not, leaves researchers with more questions than answers. Now 200 years following Douglass's birth, still further research is required to resolve this controversy.

Working to do justice to his lifelong conviction that "words are weapons," Douglass interrogated the expressive possibilities of language within the pages of his *Narrative* and across his speeches through his repeated attempts to memorialize one particularly traumatizing rite of passage that he experienced during his childhood. He writes of the unspeakable atrocities committed by Aaron Anthony against his "Aunt Hester," a woman who, as we have seen, was recorded with her unnamed child solely by her monetary value within the "chattel records." Douglass relies on an incendiary prose style to inform his readers that "I have often been awakened at the dawn of the day by the most heart-rending shrieks of an own aunt of mine, who he [Anthony] used to tie up to a joist, and whip upon her naked back till she was literally covered with blood" (p. 96). Douglass deliberately relies on graphic language and gory imagery to provide neither himself nor his audience any safe space from which to remain immune to a sense of shock and horror. He confides, "I remember the first time I ever witnessed this horrible exhibition. I was quite a child, but I well remember it. I shall never forget it whilst I remember any thing" (p. 96). No isolated event, he urges, "[i]t was the first of a long series of such outrages, of which I was doomed to be a witness and a participant" (p. 96). Douglass testifies to this incident's enduring emotional power by admitting, "[i]t struck me with awful force. It was the blood-stained gate, the entrance to the hell of slavery, through which I was about to pass. It was a most terrible spectacle. I wish I could commit to paper the feelings with which I beheld it" (p. 96). His repeated use of "remember" lays claim to the authority of his testimony, as he brooks no contradiction regarding the accuracy of his representation of white slaveholding barbarity. As an "outrage" that is hidden in plain sight, he is both unequivocal and opaque regarding his description of Hester's physical and emotional suffering. Witnessing this "horrible exhibition" as a child, he

---

1 A lifelong democrat, Edward Lloyd VI (1798–1861) "served as a delegate to the Maryland constitutional convention of 1850 as a state senator (1851–52)" (Blassingame et al. 124).

most likely had no way of comprehending Anthony's sexual as well as physical violation of his aunt's body during this "terrible spectacle."

In a self-consciously anti-heroic move in this scene, Douglass denies himself—and by extension his audience—any safe ground by describing himself as "a witness and participant." While he, no less than his reader, objectifies Hester's body by acting as a voyeur to her violation, he takes full responsibility—and invites his audience to do the same—for his, and their, complicity. Here and across his *Narrative*, Douglass seeks to reinforce the horror of slavery as a dehumanizing system in which no one was left innocent. The resounding power of his blistering language, in which he memorializes this experience as a "blood-stained gate" to the "hell of slavery," succeeds in devastating his audience when they learn of his sense of failure. Douglass underscores his authorial control by freely admitting that his inability to "commit to paper" his feelings arises not because of his own literary limitations but due to the enormity of Hester's suffering, which defies all textual forms. As shown here, while the Black woman's body and soul are all but destroyed by white slaveholding villainy, she remains no less vulnerable to Black male editorial control. On these grounds, there can be little doubt concerning the failures of the written word to do justice to Hester's story.

Douglass himself is fully aware of his own limitations. He does not hold back on his realization that, however unequivocal, spare, or evocative his use of textual language, neither his literary style nor his oratorical prowess can ever approximate the realities of the lived atrocities that were endured by enslaved women such as Hester. Ultimately, he refuses to consign Hester solely to the status of a victim by celebrating her exceptionalism on terms very similar to those of his mother: "She was a woman of noble form, and of graceful proportions, having very few equals, and fewer superiors, in personal appearance, among the colored or white women of our neighborhood" (p. 96). However much Douglass had "no language," Hester's life story as narrated by an enslaved author assumes multidimensional form in comparison with her non-appearance as an absent-presence in the ledgers authorized by slaveholders.

Since 2016, a major archaeological investigation has been undertaken into the environs of the Wye plantation where Douglass and Hester Bailey lived. As the report compiled by James M. Harmon, Anna Hill, Kristofer Beadenkopf, Jessica Neuwirth, Mark P. Leone, and Jean Russo confirms, material culture offers another route into enslaved histories that cannot be accessed via

Figure 7: Anon., Captain Aaron Anthony's House, Wye Plantation, Maryland, c. 1933. Prints and Photographs Division, Library of Congress.

written records.[1] At the same time, a sole photograph has survived showing Aaron Anthony's house, in which Douglass bore witness to Anthony's tragic acts against Hester (see Figure 7).

At the heart of Douglass's *Narrative* is his preoccupation with Black strategies of resistance that have otherwise been invisibilized within a white racist imaginary. Writing of the "wild songs" sung by enslaved women and men early in his life story, he declares that, "revealing at once the highest joy and the deepest sadness[, t]hey would compose and sing as they went along .... They would sometimes sing the most pathetic sentiment in the most rapturous tone, and the most rapturous sentiment in the most pathetic tone." They would sing "words which to many would seem unmeaning jargon, but which, nevertheless, were full of meaning to themselves" (p. 101). Across his autobiography, Douglass works not with a "simple narrative" but with a deliberately experimental literary style in which he comes to grips with enslaved people's "unmeaning jargon" that is "full of meaning." The distinction he makes between "words" that appear incomprehensible to white listeners but for which the interpretative possibilities could not be clearer for Black audiences offers a

---

1   Their report can be accessed online at the following link:
    drum.lib.umd.edu/bitstream/1903/14975/1/WyeHallPlantation.pdf.

useful roadmap for his readers in interpreting the storytelling layers of his *Narrative*.

Douglass exerts the utmost authorial control in his first autobiography by instructing his white audiences not on what they know but on what they will never know regarding Black oral histories and literary practices. He even admits to his own lack of understanding, not as a betrayal of his own deficiencies but as a catalyst to inspire white readers to a realization regarding their own ignorance. As he observes, "I did not, when a slave, understand the deep meaning of those rude and apparently incoherent songs. I was myself within the circle; so that I neither saw nor heard as those without might see and hear. They told a tale of woe which was then altogether beyond my feeble comprehension" (p. 101). According to Douglass's reckoning, if these songs defy his "comprehension," how much further beyond the pale were they for white mainstream readers with no experience of slavery? He deliberately rejects the role of an omniscient narrator by encouraging his readers to see the gaps and omissions within his own testimony. He works to ensure that his autobiography assumes heightened emotive power by trading in uncertainties in order to encourage his audiences to engage in self-questioning and personal critique. At the same time, Douglass repeatedly indicts white misreadings of both Black music and oral cultures in order to shore up his own authority: "I have often been utterly astonished, since I came to the north, to find persons who could speak of the singing, among slaves, as evidence of their contentment and happiness. It is impossible to conceive of a greater mistake. Slaves sing most when they are most unhappy" (p. 101). Audiences are consigned to the status of outsiders, as they have no choice but to bow to Douglass's insider knowledge. They are encouraged to heed the warning of one who has been "within the circle" regarding the impossibility of even beginning to understand the imaginative inner lives of enslaved peoples.

While Douglass deliberately conceals the full "meaning" of Black oral cultures for audiences of his *Narrative*, he goes to great lengths to detail his acquisition of literacy in order to silence his white racist disbelievers. For Douglass, the denial of an enslaved person's right to read lies at the heart of white slaveholding power. He is candid regarding the opposition of his second slaveowner, Hugh Auld, to the decision of his wife, Lucretia Auld, "to teach me the A, B, C. After I had learned this, she assisted me in learning to spell words of three or four letters. Just at this point of my progress, Mr. Auld found out what was going on, and at once forbade Mrs. Auld to instruct me further, telling her, among other things, that it was unlawful, as well as unsafe, to teach a slave to read" (p. 113). Auld's opposition to Douglass's education had the opposite effect, hardening Douglass's resolve to dedicate himself to the life of an author as well as an activist: "These words sank deep into my heart, stirred up sentiments within that lay slumbering, and called into existence an entirely new train of thought.... I now understood what had been to me a most perplexing difficulty—to wit, the white man's power to enslave the black man" (p. 113). Douglass instantly realized that the "white man's power" was successful only insofar as he was able not only to brutalize Black bodies but also to incarcerate their minds. "From that moment, I understood the pathway from slavery to freedom," he confides, observing, "I succeeded in learning to read and write" by being "compelled to resort to various stratagems" (p. 115).

In the process of "learning to read and write," for which Douglass relied on "various stratagems," he not only engaged in artful deceptions with white children but also relied on a seminal educational primer. He confirms, "I got hold of a book called 'The Columbian Orator.' Every opportunity I got, I used to read this book. Among much of other interesting matter, I found in it a dialogue between a master and his slave" (p. 115). For Douglass, Caleb Bingham's instructional tract—one of the few volumes he took with him when he escaped from slavery, first published in 1810 and endlessly reprinted during his childhood—set a powerful precedent by teaching him the power of language to effect real social and political change. Here was a lesson in moral suasion in words as they translated to revolutionary reform. He writes, "The slave was made to say some very smart as well as impressive things in reply to his master—things which had the desired though unexpected effect; for the conversation resulted in the voluntary emancipation of the slave on the part of the master" (p. 117).

A powerful paradox arises from the fact that while Douglass spent a lifetime insisting on the failures of language, his voluminous writings and oratory testify to his enduring belief in the power of words to effect the social, political, and moral transformation of a white master class. "I used to spend the time in writing in the spaces left in Master Thomas's copy-book, copying what he had written," he admits (p. 120). The image of the Black man's text as written in the margins of white official records offers a powerful lens through which to interpret Douglass's *Narrative*. Across his autobiography, he sets himself up not only as an editor but also as an interlocutor and interpreter of white master narratives.

In the *Narrative*, Douglass holds white southern slaveholding classes accountable both for the brutalization of enslaved bodies and for the annihilation of their imaginative inner lives. While hired out to "negro breaker" Edward Covey (1805–75), Douglass writes of his exposure to life-threatening physical assault. As he remembers, "I had been at my new home but one week before Mr. Covey gave me a very severe whipping, cutting my back, causing the blood to run, and raising ridges on my flesh as large as my little finger" (p. 129). And yet it was not the terrible violence endured by his body but his own "mourning over my wretched condition" that led to a psychological turmoil that nearly caused his premature death. "I was sometimes prompted to take my life, and that of Covey, but was prevented by a combination of hope and fear," he confirms. Writing over a decade later, Douglass the freeman comments on the life of Bailey the slave by insisting that his "sufferings on this plantation seem now like a dream rather than a stern reality" (p. 132).

For Douglass living a life in freedom, the overwhelming trauma of his enslavement subsequently lost its basis in "stern reality," due to his psyche's determination to relegate it to a dreamlike status and thereby take the edge off his exposure to unimaginable pain. According to his admission, he was able to live with the memory of slavery only if it was consigned beyond the pale of actual experience. A moment of intensified drama in his autobiography, Douglass's incarceration with Covey inspired a defining dramatic monologue in which he addresses the ships on the Chesapeake Bay. He marshals his oratorical power to decry his own suffering: "You are loosed from your moorings, and are free; I am fast in my chains, and am a slave! You move merrily before the gentle gale, and I sadly before the bloody whip!" (p. 132). Nowhere is Douglass's rejection of Garrison's insistence that there is no straining toward dramatic language in his text more evident than in this epiphanic moment in which he relies on theatrical devices and declamatory rhetoric to meditate on his fate.

Douglass's decision to stage a physical rebellion against Covey's authoritarian rule ultimately resulted in extreme corporeal suffering and led him not only to seek out the sympathy of his slave master—to no avail—but also to take comfort in the support of a fellow enslaved man, Sandy Jenkins. As he declares, "I found Sandy an old adviser. He told me, with great solemnity, I must go back to Covey; but that before I went, I must go with him into another part of the woods, where there is a certain root, which, if I would take some of it with me, carrying it always on my right side, would render it impossible for Mr. Covey, or any other white man, to whip me" (p. 136). While the "root" ultimately failed to protect Douglass in any real way, Black fraternal solidarity and African diasporic belief systems that lie beyond the ken of white authoritarian rule very likely provided him with the courage to resist white male oppression. As he confirms on his return to his white persecutor, "from whence came the spirit I don't know—I resolved to fight; and, suiting my action to the resolution, I seized Covey hard by the throat; and as I did so, I rose" (p. 137). Douglass writes of this reversal of his fate, a definitive moment in his biography, "[y]ou have seen how a man was made a slave; you shall see how a slave was made a man" (p. 133). According to Douglass's hard-hitting narration of his life story, violent acts of self-defense and spiritual belief systems work in conjunction with his belief in the power of language and philosophical reasoning, not only in his *Narrative* but also across his oratory and writings more generally.

An "Excellent Piece of Writing": Early Reviews of Douglass's *Narrative*

A transatlantic publishing phenomenon, Douglass's *Narrative* was reviewed in the national and international press to profound critical acclaim. As an anonymous reviewer writing in the *Liberator* on 23 May 1845 declared, "[t]his long-desired Narrative is now presented to the public, in a neat volume occupying 125 pages. It was written entirely by Mr. Douglass, and reveals all the facts in regard to his birth-place,—the names of his mother, master, overseer, &c.&c." The author jubilantly predicts that as a work written by a "fugitive slave" and one who is ideally placed to provide an eyewitness account of slavery's atrocities, "[i]t cannot fail to produce a great sensation wherever it may happen to circulate, especially among the slaveocracy.... The edition is going off rapidly.... It is for sale at 25 Cornhill. Price 50 cents." One week later, another unknown author commented in the same newspaper, "[a]ll who know the wonderful gifts of friend Douglass know that his narrative must, in the nature of things, be written with great power. It is so indeed. It is the most thrilling work which the American press every issued—*and the most important*" (emphasis in original). The writer attests to the autobiography's status not as a "simple narrative" but as a work of literature of unequivocal power: "There are passages in it which would brighten the reputation of any living author,—while the book, as a whole judged as a mere work of art, would widen the fame of Bunyan or De Foe."[1] This writer equates Douglass's *Narrative* with a "work of art" in order to situate it not within the history of the slave narrative but rather within a transatlantic literary tradition.

Yet more American and British reviews applauded Douglass's literary skill. "It is an exceedingly interesting as well as ably written work," one reporter wrote in the *Philadelphia Elevator* in a review that Douglass himself included within later editions of his *Narrative*.[2] His autobiography was not only highly commended by anonymous reviewers but also received resounding praise from renowned authors, editors, and activists such as Margaret Fuller (1810–50). Writing in the *New York Tribune* on 10 June 1845, Fuller observed, "In the book before us he has put into the story of his life, the thoughts, the feelings, and the adventures that have been so affecting through the living voice; nor are they less so from the printed page." She was convinced that "[i]t is an excellent piece of writing, and on that score to be prized as a specimen of the powers of the black race, which prejudice persists in disputing.... We prize highly all evidence of this kind, and it is becoming more abundant.... The Cross of the Legion of Honor has just been conferred in France on Dumas and Soulie, both celebrated in the paths of light literature. Dumas, whose father was a General in the French Army, is a Mulatto; Soulie, a Quadroon."[3] Fuller unwittingly honors Douglass's own jubilance

---

1 John Bunyan (1628–88) was an English writer most famous for *The Pilgrim's Progress* (1678–84); Daniel Defoe (1660–1731) was the author of *Robinson Crusoe* (1719) and *Moll Flanders* (1722).
2 See, for example, "Critical Notices" in the first Dublin edition of the *Narrative*.
3 Fuller is referring to Alexandre Dumas (1802–70), author of best-selling novels such as *The Three Musketeers* (1844) and *The Count of Monte Cristo* (1845), and Frédéric Soulié (1800–47), who was most famous for his novel *Les deux cadavres* (1832).

at the newly emerging tradition of Black "bookmakers not boot-blackers" by insisting that his *Narrative* was best situated within not a white but a Black literary tradition. Toward the end of the first year of the *Narrative*'s circulation, a reporter writing in the *Liberator* on 28 November 1845 urged that, "even as a literary production, this book possesses no ordinary claims.... The author, though uneducated, or rather self-educated, displays great natural powers; he utters his thoughts always lucidly, and often with a polished and vigorous eloquence." For this reviewer, as for so many others, Douglass's command over language was evidence that the "slaves' natural inferiority, has no foundation as regards such men as the writer, and therefore totally fails in its general application." Writing from Belfast in 1846, a religious minister, Isaac Nelson, was no less emphatic: "I regard the narrative of Frederick Douglass as a literary wonder."[1]

In the early days of its publication, the circulation of Douglass's *Narrative* often led to punitive consequences for those who tried to get it into the hands of southern audiences. In an article in the *Liberator* of 18 May 1849 titled "Arrest of an Abolition Missionary in Virginia," an unidentified reporter confirms, "We learn from the Alexandria Gazette, that on the 3d ult.. [i.e., 3 April], the Grand Jury of Grayson Co., Va., made a presentment against 'Jarvis C. Bacon.'" An individual on whom very little has been written, Bacon not only was charged with disseminating an unidentified work that was intended to incite slave rebellion, but was also under suspicion for "feloniously circulating a printed book, of the same tendency, entitled, 'A Narrative of the Life of Frederick Douglass, an American Slave.'" The repercussions were instantaneous: "On the same day, Judge Brown issued his bench warrant for the arrest of Bacon. On Wednesday morning he was arrested, and was examined before three magistrates of Grayson, by whom he was committed for further trial, and gave bail for his appearance before the County Court of Grayson, at its April term, to be further examined on the charge." Bacon's persecution at the hands of white slaveholding authorities offers a searing indictment of Douglass's conviction that language, when harnessed to the slave's cause, had revolutionary social, political, and moral power.

---

1 See "Critical Notices" in the first Dublin edition.

"Dragged Back into Bondage": Douglass's *Narrative* in Europe and His Bill of Sale

"I have repeatedly given as one of the reasons for leaving the United States, a fear, that in consequence of publishing a narrative of my experience in slavery, and exposing the conduct of my owner, he might, to gratify his revengeful disposition, attempt to reduce me to slavery." So wrote Frederick Douglass from Belfast, Northern Ireland, on 23 July 1846, in a letter he addressed to white abolitionist James Wilson (1787–1850). "My object was to be out of the way during the excitement and exasperation which I had good reason to apprehend would follow the publication of my narrative," he declared (McKivigan 145). Just two months earlier, on 15 May, the *Liberator* reprinted a report from the *Western Citizen* confirming that his fears were far from groundless. According to the testimony provided by Jeremiah B. Sanderson (1821–75), an African American abolitionist and one of Douglass's close friends, "A gentleman told me that, while coming from New York recently, he overheard several persons in the car, conversing about Douglass." As he recalled, "One of them said that a combination had been entered into by a number of slaveholders, the object of which was, to watch vessels leaving Great Britain, to note where Douglass left; and if he arrived into any other American port except Boston, to be prepared, and seize him immediately upon landing.... And what do they want? To kill him, and glut their revenge. Kill him by inches! Oh, it is horrible to think of!"

Justifiably fearing for his life, in August 1845 Douglass left his family—then consisting of his wife, Anna; daughter Rosetta; and three sons, Lewis Henry, Frederick Jr., and Charles Remond, as Annie was not born until 1849—to spend over 18 months touring Ireland, Scotland, Wales, and England. During this time, he earned undisputed fame as the quintessential "fugitive slave" and ultimate spokesperson for the antislavery cause on a European as well as a British and American abolitionist stage. A household name, he delivered speeches to standing-room-only audiences, wrote letters to celebrated critical acclaim, and published multiple Irish, English, French, and Dutch editions of his *Narrative*, which were all instant bestsellers. As he emphasizes in the Preface to the first Irish edition of the *Narrative*, published in Dublin in late 1845, "I have had public meetings in Dublin, Wexford, Waterford, Cork, Youghal, Limerick, Belfast, Glasgow, Aberdeen, Perth, and Dundee" with tremendous results: "An edition of 2000 copies of my Narrative has been exhausted."

Douglass begins that preface by repeating his conviction that he "wished to be out of the way during the excitement consequent on the publication of my book; lest the information I had there given as to my identity and place of abode, should induce my owner to take measures for restoration to his 'patriarchal care.'" Not content with admitting to his desire for self-preservation, he seeks to awaken his transatlantic audiences to a full awareness of US slaveholding villainy by confirming, "it may not be generally known in Europe, that a slave who escapes from his master is liable, by the Constitution of the United States, to be dragged back into bondage, no matter in what part of the vast extent of the United States and their territories he may have taken refuge." As he confides, fear for his own safety was not the sole motivation for his visit to Britain and Ireland, however. He foregrounds his biracial heritage by admitting to "a desire to increase my stock of information, and my opportunities of self-improvement, by a visit to the land of my paternal ancestors." While betraying his commitment to a program of "self-improvement," he also insists on his determination to whip up such moral outrage regarding "the contaminating and degrading influence of Slavery upon the slaveholder and his abettors, as well as the slave" on British and Irish soil as "to excite such an intelligent interest on the subject of American Slavery, as may react upon my own country, and may tend to shame her out of her adhesion to a system as abhorrent to Christianity and to her republican institution."

As a result of his transatlantic abolitionist campaign, Douglass joined the ranks of nineteenth-century African American abolitionists, enslaved and free, who visited Europe to garner support for the antislavery cause. Cannily flattering a British and Irish sense of their moral superiority, Douglass was one among many Black activists who were working to inspire an "intelligent interest on the subject of American Slavery" on the European stage in order to "shame" the US into antislavery action. His reform efforts can be situated alongside the careers of the following pioneering figures: Nathaniel Paul (c. 1793–1839), Zilpha Elaw (c. 1790–1873), Charles Lenox Remond (1810–73), Sarah Parker Remond (1815–94), J. Irving Glasgow (1837–60), William (1824–1900) and Ellen Craft (1826–91), William Wells Brown (1814–84), Moses Roper (1815–91), Henry Box Brown (1816–97), and John Anderson, to name but a few. And yet the overwhelming focus on Douglass's life and works within the surviving archives testifies to his uncontested status as the most celebrated Black activist bar none in the eyes of British and Irish audiences.

Scarcely a month into his European sojourn, Douglass wrote Garrison from Dublin on 29 September 1845, confirming, "[m]y Narrative is just published, and I have sold one hundred copies in this city" (McKivigan 58). In comparison to his US volume, Douglass printed the first Irish edition of his *Narrative* with a newly written preface as well as an appeal "To the Friends of the Slave." He also provided his transatlantic audiences with detailed information regarding the American Antislavery Society while soliciting contributions for their forthcoming Antislavery Bazaar in Boston. No reluctant self-publicist, he lent further authority to his autobiography by excerpting "Critical Notices" of his *Narrative* that he had handpicked from reviews in the British and American press. Douglass's second Dublin edition appeared only months later in 1846 in order to meet popular demand and included these same materials alongside his additional insertion of A.C.C. Thompson's "attempted Refutation of [his] Narrative" and his response. For Douglass, Thompson was to be applauded for doing "a piece of anti-slavery work, which no anti-slavery man could do" by irrefutably authenticating his fugitive slave status. As Douglass concedes, Thompson "agrees with me at least in the important fact, that I am what I proclaim myself to be, an ungrateful fugitive from the 'patriarchal institutions' of the Slave States" (cxxvi).

A publishing phenomenon, Douglass's *Narrative* was an instant bestseller. On 2 October 1845, as printed in the *Liberator* of that day, Richard Webb informed William Lloyd Garrison that he had "printed an edition of 2000 copies of his Narrative, and 100 are already sold in a few days in Dublin alone." Just under two months later, in the *Liberator* of 30 November, Webb wrote Garrison again to confirm that "[u]pwards of 600 copies of his book have been already disposed of, and this is a very large sale when it is considered that the book is little more than two months published, and that the whole of this sale has been private, and with hardly any assistance from the booksellers." The fact that there has been "hardly any assistance" from booksellers offers categorical proof of Douglass's celebrated renown: he was able to sell his *Narrative* solely on the basis of his own personal fame. On 6 December, Douglass contentedly wrote Webb from Belfast saying, "Well well my Books went last night at one blow. I want more I want more, I have many things to hope and— nothing to fear" (see Appendix B1, p. 187). Less than three weeks later, he again wrote Webb from Belfast to celebrate the fact that "the Books go off grandly" (Appendix B2, p. 188).

Unintimidated by Webb's power as the publisher of his *Narrative*, Douglass refused to take a back seat in the process. Across their correspondence, he not only gave vent to his dislike of the frontispiece portrait but also had no qualms in advising Webb about his preferred physical dimensions for the *Narrative*. Writing Webb from Perth in Scotland on 20 January 1846 (see Appendix B3), Douglass's imperious tone brooked no dissent: "If it be possible to make the alteration which you suggested about the length of the book—and to get it out in the time I mention in the last note—you will do so by al[l] means, I think it will look much better a little shorter" (p. 192). Douglass was also quick to reprimand Webb for his tardiness in getting books to him, which ran the risk of damaging his sales figures: "I am sor[r]y you could not send me the three hundred copies for which I sent last week. When the next edition is published, I wish you to have it bound up at once, so that I may not have to wait, as I have had to do for the last edition" (p. 192). The source of Douglass's anxiety is immediately explained by the fact that the sale of his *Narrative* was his sole source of financial support in the UK. As he concedes, "It is a great loss to me to be without my narrative as I am dependent on it for all my support in this Country" (p. 192).

In a later letter Douglass wrote Webb, most likely on 16 April (see Appendix B6), he endorsed a seemingly more capitulatory position by conceding, "I have addopted [sic] your advice as to how I might correct and amend the narrative" (p. 196). However, he instantly countered any such deference by again denouncing the portrait: "I don[']t like it" (p. 196). He also issued further instructions regarding his preferred size for the second edition by instructing Webb to make his *Narrative* "shorter and thicker agreeable to your suggestion" (p. 197). Douglass also demanded that Webb "[g]et as good, and if you can get better paper than that used in the first edition" (p. 197). Just two weeks later, on 25 April, Douglass admitted to Webb the challenges he faced in selling his books while fighting for the cause: "The <u>fighting</u> armour is by no means the most favorable one for a Book Seller" (Appendix B8, p. 199). Only months previously, he had written Webb of his struggles to sustain his role as an antislavery campaigner-turned-bookseller: "This battling is rather unfavorable to the sale of my book—but the cause first every thing else afterwards" (Appendix B4, p. 193). Douglass's priorities were set squarely on a life dedicated to abolition. Ever the antislavery campaigner, he refused to sacrifice the "cause" to anything, even the sale of his *Narrative*.

Under the close eye of his white American paternalist sponsors, Douglass's commitment to the "cause" was repeatedly called into question during his transatlantic campaign. White abolitionists such as Maria Weston Chapman (1806–85), secretary of the American Anti-Slavery Society, were unwilling or unable to recognize his exemplary contributions. As a result, his fight for freedom from white abolitionist constraints became yet more pressing. Without Douglass's knowledge, Chapman had written Webb on 29 June 1845, a few months prior to Douglass's arrival in the UK, to warn the Irish activist regarding the moral weaknesses she speculated were within Douglass's character. She took the view that the abolitionist campaign had made Douglass wealthy—"The cause has been nothing but good to Douglass, in a worldly point of view"—but with potentially damaging results. She confides, "I hope he will be strong enough to endure it when the endurance shall seem to threaten him with loss. He has uncommon abilities of practical and useful sort; I earnestly hope he may not yield to temptation."[1] On 23 January 1846, she again wrote Webb insisting on Douglass's inferiority by speculating that, "[i]f Douglass can but keep from the temptation to 'get into his own house,' (as we call being drunk with vanity) because of the general attention that his powers, circumstances and cause excite when united, he will not only do the cause great good, but receive and deserve a high place in the list of public benefactors." As she ominously concluded, "[i]f his good sense prevail, all will go well."[2]

Unfortunately for Chapman, Webb did not keep the contents of her letters to himself. Instead, he shared her views with Douglass with immediate consequences. On 29 March, Douglass wrote a letter to Chapman from Kilmarnock, Scotland, in which he expressed his hurt and anger (see Appendix B5). He stated, "I have felt som[e] what [ag]greaved to see by a letter from you to Mr R.D. Webb of Dublin that you betray a want of confidence in me as a man and an abolitionist." He was distressed to note that "[i]n that letter you were pointing out to Mr. Webb the necessity of his keeping a watch over myself and friend Mr Buffum—but as Mr Buffum was rich and I poor while there was little danger but

---

1 Maria Weston Chapman to Richard D. Webb, 29 June 1845. Boston
   Public Library Anti-Slavery Collection, https://archive.org/details/bplscas.
2 Maria Weston Chapman to Richard D. Webb, 23 January 1846. Boston
   Public Library Anti-Slavery Collection, https://archive.org/details/bplscas.

what Mr Buffum would stand firm, I might be bought up by the London committee." He denounced her criticism of his moral character—"Now Dear Madam, you do me great injustice"—to issue an ultimatum: "If you wish to drive me from the Antislavery society, put me under overseer ship and the work is done. Set some one to watch over me for evel [sic] and let them be so simple minded as to inform me of their office, and the last blow is struck" (p. 195). He is working with a deliberate use of language—"the word to be spoken by me" (*My Bondage and My Freedom* 362)—as his phrase "overseer ship" renders clear the parallels between being bought and sold in slavery and being bought and sold in abolition. Just as there were white overseers on slave plantations who sought to deny Black freedoms, so too were there white overseers on the abolitionist podium equally dedicated to circumscribing Black free will. All slanders on his character to the contrary, Douglass was insistent regarding his steadfast commitment to the cause: "I am trying to preach and practice a genuine antislavery 'life'—turning neither to the right or left and I think not without success" (Appendix B5, p. 194). While he had no doubt that he was leading a "genuine antislavery 'life,'" his implicit question to Chapman—and, by extension, to Webb and Garrison, who all at one point or another betrayed their racist assumptions—was "are you?"

The Irish and English editions were not the only publications of Douglass's *Narrative* to appear in Europe. On 29 April 1847, a journalist announced in the pages of the *National Antislavery Standard* that "the Narrative of Douglass had been translated by Miss Parkes, of Bristol, England, into French, and it was hoped that some Paris bookseller would undertake its publication." According to this same report, "Mr. Garrison also states that before he left England arrangements had been made for publishing the work in Germany." The author admitted to having read "a Review, published somewhere in the Netherlands, containing a long notice of Douglass' Narrative, which, if we rightly understood, has been published in Dutch." A few months later, on 12 November, an advertisement appeared in the *Liberator* that provided yet further confirmation of the publication of "Frederick Douglass's NARRATIVE IN FRENCH." As the reporter confirms, "We are pleased to learn, by a letter received this week from a gentleman in BRISTOL, England, that the Narrative of Frederick Douglass, translated into French by Miss S.K. Parkes, of Bristol, (Eng.,) is in the printer's hands, in PARIS, and will shortly be published." On 7 January 1848, Douglass himself printed a summary of his narrative's publishing history in his own newspaper, *The North Star*, in which he revealed, "The ELEVENTH THOUSAND of this work is just published, and may be had at this office, price 35 cents. It passed through nine editions in England, and has been translated into French and German." While an extensive investigation has as yet led to no trace of the German publication, a Dutch translation was published in Rotterdam in 1846, with the same portrait Douglass disliked, and retitled *The Story of Frederick Douglass, Formerly a Slave (Written by Himself)*. No major departure from either his British or American editions, the Dutch publication opens with Garrison's and Phillips's prefatory materials and concludes with the "extracts from newspapers" that had been included in his Irish and English editions.

Douglass's status as a fugitive slave was a source not solely of personal vulnerability but of inarguable political currency during his time spent in Britain and Ireland. On 16 April 1846, Douglass wrote a letter to Garrison from Glasgow in which he admitted to the ongoing difficulties he experienced due to the precariousness of his liberty (see Appendix B7). As he explained, "I have been frequently counselled to leave America altogether, and make Britain my home. But this I cannot do, unless it shall be absolutely necessary for my personal freedom" (p. 198). He was under no illusion that the fight for his freedom was far from over by conceding, "I doubt not that my master is in a state of mind quite favorable to attempt at re-capture." In the same letter, Douglass voiced his outrage against the public declaration of his former master, Thomas Auld, that he had never indulged in physical violence toward his former slave. Auld testified, "'I can put my hand upon my Bible, and with a clear conscience swear that I never struck him in my life, nor caused any person else to do it.'" Douglass held nothing back in his response to Auld's declaration that "he never struck me," by urging, "He has certainly forgotten when a lamp was lost for the carriage, without my knowledge, that he came to the stable with the cart-whip, and with its heavy lash beat me over the head and shoulders, to make me tell how it was lost."[1] Douglass ends the dispute by concluding, "I did not tell many things which I might have told" (p. 198). In so doing, he leaves his readers in no doubt that, if anything, his testimony

---

1 Frederick Douglass to William Lloyd Garrison, Glasgow, 16 April 1846, https://glc.yale.edu/letter-william-lloyd-garrison-april-16-1846.

falls "far short of the facts"[1] by sanitizing Auld's atrocities to suit the moral dictates of polite society.

British fears for Douglass's safety ultimately led to the end of his fugitive status and the legal procurement of his emancipation papers during his transatlantic antislavery tour. Ellen, Anna, and Henry Richardson, three white antislavery campaigners from Newcastle-upon-Tyne in England, raised the funds and orchestrated Douglass's legal sale with Thomas and Henry Auld. Since he had escaped from slavery and during his years as a "fugitive," Thomas Auld had transferred ownership of Douglass's body and soul from himself to his brother, Hugh. As Douglass himself satirically acknowledged, "[m]y master, whom I have accused of being a very mean man, and who has attempted a refutation of the truth of my narrative in a letter which he published in the United States, tried to show that he was an excellent man, and he has generously transferred his legal right in my body and soul to his brother." He adopted third-person distancing devices to register his disbelief that "[h]e has actually made his brother a present of the body and bones of Frederick Douglass," further speculating, "[h]is brother must feel exceedingly rich to-day."[2]

The correspondence between Hugh Auld and Anna Richardson in negotiating Douglass's bill of sale survives. On 6 October 1846, Hugh Auld wrote Anna Richardson from Baltimore confirming his agreement to the terms she had proposed in a letter, which is no longer extant, regarding the sale of the "body and bones of Frederick Douglass": "In reply to your letter dated Newcastle on Tyne 8th mo 17th 1846 I state that I will take 150 £ sterling for the manumission [sic] of my slave Frederick Bailey, alias, Douglass.... I am prepared to sign such papers or deed of Manumission as will forever exempt him from any claims by any person or persons, in other words the papers will render him entirely & Legally free." Auld gives his word that "[a]s soon as your agent is prepared to deliver me the money I will hand him the papers."[3]

Over a month later, Walter Lowrie, a white lawyer based in New York, addressed a letter to Hugh Auld in which he con-

---

1 Harriet Ann Jacobs, *Incidents in the Life of a Slave Girl* (1861), 5, http://docsouth.unc.edu/fpn/jacobs/jacobs.html.
2 Douglass, "Emancipation Is an Individual, a National, and an International Responsibility," London, 18 May 1846, rpt. Blassingame 252.
3 Hugh Auld to Anna Richardson, 6 October 1846, https://www.gilderlehrman.org/history-by-era/slavery-and-anti-slavery/resources/buying-frederick-douglass's-freedom-1846.

firmed that Anna's husband, "Mr. Henry Richardson of New Castle upon Tyne England has sent me, by the last Steamer, one hundred and fifty pounds sterling to purchase the freedom of Frederick Bailey alias Douglass.... At the present rate of Exchange this amounts in dollars to seven hundred and eleven 66/100 dollars." Neither he nor the Richardsons he represented chose to leave anything to chance by insisting that "[a]s Douglass, it is said was owned at one time by your brother Thomas Auld, Mr. Richardson desires that the evidence of the legal transfer of Douglass to you from Thomas Auld accompany the freedom papers, or that you both join in the Deeds of manumission." Constantly vigilant regarding the duplicitous ways of white US slaveholders, Richardson introduced further legal checks by insisting that "the freedom papers be examined by a lawyer, and be accompanied by a note from him that they are correct and legal you will please therefore to submit them to—Merideth Esqr. in Baltimore." Lowrie candidly admitted to his repugnance in this trade in bodies and souls by stipulating that "[i]n making out the papers use the name of Henry Richardson, as I do not wish my name connected with this transaction. My agency in it, as I have already stated to you, has been an unpleasant one from the first."[1]

Thomas Auld's bill of sale conferring ownership rights to his brother and the subsequent "Deed of Manumission" agreed between Auld and the Richardsons survive within Douglass's personal archive as the quintessential "chattel record." His free papers are dated 12 December 1846 and are addressed by "Hugh Auld to Frederick Baily, otherwise called Frederick Douglass." For the benefit of his readers, Douglass transcribed this original document in his *Life and Times* as follows:

> To all whom it may concern, Be it known that I, Hugh Auld of the City of Baltimore, in Baltimore County, in the State of Maryland, for divers good causes and considerations me thereunto moving, have released from slavery, liberated, manumitted, and set free, and by these presents do hereby release from slavery, liberate, manumit and set free MY NEGRO MAN named FREDERICK BAILEY, otherwise called DOUGLASS, being of the age of twenty eight years, or thereabouts and able to work and gain a sufficient liveli-

---

1 Walter Lowrie to Hugh Auld, New York, 24 November 1846, https://www.gilderlehrman.org/sites/default/files/inline-pdfs/07484_FPS.pdf.

hood and maintenance; and him the said negro man named
FREDERICK DOUGLASS, I do declare to be henceforth
free, manumitted and discharged from all manner of servitude to me, my executors, or administrators forever.
(316–17)

Despite experiencing very real fears for his own safety, Douglass adamantly maintained that he had played no instrumental
role, practical or otherwise, in securing his release from bondage.
However, a letter held in a private collection suggests otherwise.
In a letter to Anna Richardson from the "Free Trade Club" in
London written months earlier on 19 August, Douglass prefaced
his admission regarding his categorical support for her and her
husband's actions in securing his legal liberation from slavery by
revealing his distress in being away from his family. He poignantly
writes, "My Anna says 'Come home' and I have now resolved
upon going home—the day is fixed and my dear Anna will be
informed of it in a few days. I shall sail for America on the fourth
November—and hope to meet the beloved ones of my heart by
the 20th of that month." Anxious to heed his wife's plea while
ensuring that his return to the US did not in any way compromise the Richardsons' efforts on behalf of his liberation, he
urged, "Do not allow this arrangement [to] interfere in any way
with your correspondence with my owner—as whether you
succeed or fail good may come of the effort."[1] This exchange is a
powerful reminder of the necessity of researching the public life
of Douglass the political icon in close relation to the private life
of Douglass the family man.

However, despite Anna's insistence that Douglass "Come
home," he was not able to return to the US until nearly six months
after he had hoped. Garrison sheds light on the reason for his protracted stay in the UK in a letter he wrote to his wife Helen from
London a month later: "Frederick Douglass will not return till next
May, in season for our New-England Convention.... This I have
strongly advised, for many important reasons. If he and H.C.W.
[Henry Clarke Wright (1797–1870)], were both to return home
now, in the present embryo state of [the] 'Anti-Slavery League,' we
should lose a great deal of what otherwise will be permanently
secured to us" (Merrill 415). For Garrison, Douglass's private

---

1 Frederick Douglass to Anna Richardson, London, 19 August 1846,
https://www.sethkaller.com/item/283-Frederick-Douglass-to-the-
Woman-who-was-Negotiating-to-Buy-his-Freedom.

struggle was of no importance in comparison to his political value to the abolitionist cause. Douglass's personal needs came far down on a list of priorities on which securing the interests not only of abolition in general but of the American Antislavery Society in particular ranked highest. "He is really doing a great work, and the people are every where desiring his presence," noted Garrison, making only a very brief mention of his loneliness: "The poor fellow is—naturally enough—sighing to see his wife and children." Garrison believed that Douglass understood that this decision was not only advantageous to the cause but also beneficial for him and his family. He insisted that Douglass "is satisfied that it will enhance his personal safety, and be the better for them in the end, to remain here until spring" (Merrill 415).

The surviving correspondence casts doubt on the assumption that Douglass and his family were "satisfied" by Garrison's unilateral decision over his and their lives. On 22 September 1846, Douglass wrote white Irish antislavery campaigner Isabel Jennings of his own and his family's distress over this decision: "You may easily suppose the conclusion come to reluctantly when I tell you I had already written to my Anna telling her to expect me home on the 20th Nov. It will cost her some pain." Douglass took solace by observing that "[d]isappointment is the common lot of all—this may afford slight relief till I come" (McKivigan 166). Clearly, Garrison, like Chapman, was keen to put Douglass under "overseership" by seeking to control his every move, with no thought of his personal life. He also shared Chapman's determination to exaggerate Douglass's "worldly" success, which he, like Chapman, interpreted as more than ample repayment for his efforts. As Garrison observed, "In a pecuniary point of view, he is doing very well, as he sells his Narrative very readily, and receives aid in donations and presents, to some extent" (Merrill 415).

Nothing could be more different from the evidence presented by Douglass's correspondence, in which he admits to his own and his family's never-ending financial struggles. Prior to the publication of his *Narrative*, he had informed Maria Weston Chapman on 10 September 1843 of his desperate financial difficulties: "I have received a few lines from my wife asking for means to carry on household affairs. I have none to send her. Will you please see that she is provided with $25 or $30" (Foner, *Life and Writings* 112). Very little changed after the publication of his autobiography. As Douglass's later admission to Ruth Cox, an escaped enslaved woman who lived in the Douglass family household under the pseudonym Harriet Bailey, confirms, his difficulties in selling his *Narrative* exacerbated rather than eradicated his financial struggles (see Appendix D4a).

For antislavery supporters who knew only the political ideals of Douglass the public orator and author, and not the private struggles of Douglass the husband and family man, he faced a barrage of opposition regarding his sale. Writing a letter from Manchester on 22 December 1846 to one of his detractors, white campaigner Henry C. Wright, Douglass refused to concede an inch of moral ground. For Douglass, the sale of his flesh and blood represented an easy exchange: the legal purchase of his body in order to ensure his continued involvement in the antislavery cause, not just in the UK but in the US as well. He began his defense by outlining his position: "My sphere of usefulness is in the United States; my public and domestic duties are there; and there it seems my duty to go. But I am *legally* the property of Thomas Auld, and if I go to the United States, (no matter to what part, for there is no City of Refuge there, no spot sacred to freedom there)." He informed Wright what he should already have known regarding the devastating effects of the precariousness of his freedom: "Thomas Auld, *aided by the American Government,* can seize, bind and fetter, and drag me from my family, feed his cruel revenge upon me, and doomed to unending slavery" (McKivigan 166; emphasis in original). On these grounds, Douglass interpreted his sale as one that benefited both the antislavery cause and his own and his family's lives:

> In view of this simple statement of facts, a few friends, desirous of seeing me released from the terrible liability, and to relieve my wife and children from the painful trepidation, consequent upon the liability, and to place me on an equal footing of safety with all other anti-slavery lecturers in the United States, and to enhance my usefulness by enlarging the field of my labors in the United States, have nobly and generously paid Hugh Auld, the agent of Thomas Auld, £150. (McKivigan 184–85)

The key issue for Douglass was not his own personal fear but his determination to spare his wife and family from their "painful trepidation." As for his own preference if he himself had access to such funds, he was adamant regarding his opposition to giving his former slave master any financial compensation: "I am free to say, that, had I possessed one hundred and fifty pounds, I would have seen Hugh Auld *kicking*, before I would have given it to him. I would have waited till the emergency came, and only given up the money when nothing else would do" (McKivigan 188). For Douglass, there was no risk that the loss of his fugitive status would have any damaging effect on his identity or that his altered condition would do anything to remove his experience of slavery. As he maintained, his status as a formerly enslaved individual and his identification with enslaved people were lifelong realities: "I shall be Frederick Douglass still, and once a slave still," he vowed, "I shall neither be made to forget nor cease to feel the wrongs of my enslaved fellow-countrymen. My knowledge of slavery will be the same, and my hatred of it will be the same" (188).

"I have known what Slavery is": Douglass Bears Witness in His Oratory and Writings

"One day talking quietly Mr. Douglass was recalling how before speaking to the audiences who gathered at their Anti-Slavery meetings he used to ask to be alone, and his preparation was to recall the horrors and cruelties suffered by those he had left in slavery. It all would rise up before him like an actual presence, and he would go before the audience quivering with the sympathy it stirred in him" (Impey 16). So writes Catherine Impey, white British reformer and editor of *Anti-Caste*, recalling her "Visit to Cedar Hill" in an issue published just months after Douglass died. For Douglass, the burden of telling the story of Frederick Augustus Washington Bailey was intimately intertwined with the burden of bearing witness not to the story of the slave but to the stories of slaves. Douglass's ritual of meditation, in which he conjured the spirits of enslaved bodies and souls to reimagine their experiences, brought instantaneous results and undoubtedly accounts for his renown as an orator of unprecedented power. As Impey confirms, "[t]he effect on his hearers was as if they too saw what he saw inwardly. It wrought a marvellous effect on them. He could feel every being before him swayed with his emotion, and multitudes would be weeping" (16). And yet at the same time that he felt he had "no language" when writing his *Narrative*, he also experienced the anguish of being denied words when faced with delivering speeches addressing the terrible atrocities experienced by enslaved people: "Sometimes he felt unable so to speak, and often feared his quieter efforts were failures" (16).

Appearing to celebrated critical acclaim on the white abolitionist lecture circuit in the early 1840s, Douglass was no naïf.

During slavery, he had had extensive training in oratorical performance from the debating men who were members of the Baltimore Freed Men's Improvement Society, to whom he would not have had access were it not for the introductions provided by Anna Murray. Following his escape north and during his early years living in New Bedford, he had also gained renown and political sway as a preacher and political commentator within the African American community. Among his early mentors was Thomas James (1804–91), a formerly enslaved man turned radical reformer who proved to be a friend and advisor while Douglass was living in New Bedford. Writing in his autobiography in 1886, James recalled, "It was at New Bedford that I first saw Fred. Douglass. He was then, so to speak, right out of slavery, but had already begun to talk in public, though not before white people" (8). James was quick to celebrate his own role in enhancing Douglass's presence in the community by emphasizing that "[h]e had been given authority to act as an exhorter by the church before my coming, and I some time afterwards licensed him to preach." He even went so far as to insist on his instrumental role in aiding Douglass's transition from local agitator to international antislavery lecturer: "On one occasion, after I had addressed a white audience on the slavery question, I called upon Fred. Douglass, whom I saw among the auditors, to relate his story.... He did so, and in a year from that time he was in the lecture field with Parker Pillsbury and other leading abolitionist orators" (8).

In the years when Douglass lived and worked as an antislavery campaigner, first within the African American community and then on national and international stages, he repeatedly rehearsed and performed his *Narrative* in verbal form, thereby confirming the oratorical foundations not only of his first autobiography but of the majority of his writings as well. On 8 May 1845, the same month in which Douglass published his *Narrative*, Jeremiah Sanderson heard Douglass speak at the anniversary meeting of the Anti-Slavery Society in New York City. In a letter he wrote to white reformer Amy Post (1802–89), Sanderson was exultant: "Fredk. Douglass made an excellent speech. Indeed one of the best I ever heard him make" (Ripley 464). According to Sanderson's memory, Douglass delivered the following testament against his life lived in slavery: "'I shall never again tamely submit to being captured and dragged back to be manacled, and scourged. No! While I hope never to be obliged to resist any such an attempt, yet if it is made, I shall not be, will not be made a Slave tamely. I have known what Slavery is, and I now know what

Liberty is, and I love it so dearly that I will not part with it, but with Life" (464). Across his early oratory and writings, Douglass repeatedly laid claim to his irrefutable authority as a formerly enslaved individual who had experienced a condition of slavery that was alien to whites and defied the comprehension of individuals living in free Black communities.

As early as 20 October 1841, and nearly four years prior to the publication of his *Narrative*, Douglass yet again delivered a speech in which he insisted on his uncontested status as one who had "known what Slavery is" (see Appendix C1). He celebrated the reform work of white abolitionists only to endorse his insider knowledge: "though they can give you its history—though they can depict its horrors, they cannot speak as I can from *experience*" (p. 201; emphasis in original). He relied on graphic imagery to argue that "they cannot refer you to a back covered with scars, as I can; for I have felt these wounds, I have suffered under the lash without the power of resisting. Yes, my blood has sprung out as the lash embedded itself in my flesh" (p. 202). Douglass also fought to disabuse northern audiences regarding the assumed passivity and ignorance of enslaved communities. He celebrated their shared realization regarding a natural right to freedom by urging, "A large portion of the slaves *know* that they have a right to their liberty.—It is often talked about and read of, for some of us know how to read, although all our knowledge is gained in secret" (p. 202).

Douglass gave lie to claims made by Garrison and others that he was a "brand new fact" by admitting to having developed tried and tested oratorical skills among enslaved audiences long before his arrival on the abolitionist circuit (*My Bondage* 361): "I well remember getting possession of a speech by [President] John Quincy Adams [1767–1848], made in Congress about slavery and freedom, and reading it to my fellow slaves" (p. 203). At the same time, he did not hesitate to portray the north as no halcyon state of race relations by remaining candid about the discrimination he experienced beyond the plantations of the US South: "Prejudice against color is stronger north than south; it hangs around my neck like a heavy weight" (p. 203). A few months later, on 28 January 1842, Douglass contested the status of his body solely as a site of physical wounding in order to admit to the emotional damage wrought by psychological trauma: "My back is scarred by the lash—that I could show you. I would I could make visible the wounds of this system upon my soul" (Appendix C3, p. 206).

On 18 November 1842, Douglass published a public letter he addressed to Garrison on behalf of George Latimer (1819–96), a runaway slave, in the *Liberator* (see Appendix C7). As is customary among his oratory and writings, he dispensed with a prescriptive adherence to fact to work with fictional devices in order to inspire empathy among his audiences. "Hark! listen! hear the groans and cries of George Latimer, mingling with which may be heard the cry—my wife, my child—and all is still again" (p. 220). Douglass reimagined Latimer's suffering by ventriloquizing his voice: "I am to be taken back to Norfolk—must be torn from a wife and tender babe, with the threat from Mr. Gray that I am to be murdered, though not in the ordinary way" (p. 220). According to his fictional imagining, Douglass's Latimer laments: "I am to be killed by inches. I know not how; perhaps by cat-hauling until my back is torn all to pieces, my flesh is to be cut with the rugged lash, and I faint" (p. 220). For Douglass, there was no more effective a device for ensuring that audiences would "put [them]selves in the place of George Latimer" (p. 220) than by using theatrical and dramatic techniques that were designed to inspire empathy. Douglass not only deliberately created scenes "drawn from his imagination" but also bolstered his testimony by integrating examples of American laws into his oratory.

A few years later, on 3 November 1845, he delivered a speech on "Slavery and the Annexation of Texas to the United States" in which he relied on the evidence provided by US legislation to damn white slaveholding barbarities from their own statute books (see Appendix C10). "I will read you the laws of a part of the American states, regarding the relation of master and slave," he proclaimed, and then quoted as follows: "For travelling in the night without a pass, 40 lashes. Found in another person's quarters, 40 lashes. For being on horseback without a written permission, 3 lashes; for riding without leave, a slave may be whipped, cropped or branded with the letter A, in the cheek" (p. 231). He shored up his audience's sense of horror by urging, "Their whole code of justice is based on the changing basis of the color of a man's skin; for in Virginia, there are but three crimes for which a white man is hung, but in the same State, there are seventy-one crimes for which the black suffers death" (p. 232). He was careful to point his listeners to his source material so that they could see for themselves: "The laws may be found in Heywood's manual, and several other works" (p. 231). In numerous other speeches he gave during this period, Douglass repeatedly quoted from white abolitionist Theodore Weld's (1803–95) groundbreaking volume *American Slavery as It Is: Testimony of a Thousand Witnesses*, first published in 1839. Weld solely relied on the testimonies provided by white slaveholding witnesses in order to give his audiences no grounds on which to doubt the evidence they supplied regarding slavery's atrocities.

Just a week later, Douglass enhanced the effect of his presentation through the exhibition of horrifying objects. As a reporter confirms, in a speech he delivered in Limerick, Ireland, on 10 November 1845, "Mr. Douglas [sic] then proceeded to exhibit some of the implements used in torturing the slaves, among which was an iron collar taken from the neck of a young woman who had escaped from Mobile. It had so worn into her neck that her blood and flesh were found on it (sensation)."[1] "After showing the fetters used in chaining the feet of two slaves together, he exhibited a pair of hand-cuffs taken from a fugitive who escape from Maryland into Pennsylvania," the journalist recalls. For Douglass, these artifacts had an indispensable role to play by enabling him to fuse the stories of particular slaves with the story of the slave in general. As the writer observes, he "went on to exhibit a horrid whip which was made of cow hide, and whose lashes were as hard as horn. They were clotted with blood when he first got them. He saw his master tie up a young woman eighteen years of age, and beat her with that identical whip until the blood ran down her back" (85). Douglass used the "horrid whip" as the catalyst for his exposure of the barbarity suffered not only by enslaved people in general but also by one enslaved person in particular: his Aunt Hester. However, this time he chose to leave her unnamed in order to shore up her representative significance.

While there is no doubt that Douglass exhibited material proofs of slavery's atrocities, a key area of controversy surrounds whether he exposed the scars on his own back. While a newspaper account confirming that he did is yet to be found, Douglass himself insisted that he had done so. As he reminisced in *Life and Times*, "I was called upon to expose even my stripes, and with many misgivings obeyed the summons" (620). Regardless, Douglass's ready admission that he experienced "misgivings" testifies to his preferred focus on language over and above a corporeal exposure of his life as an enslaved man. For Douglass, the dehumanizing exhibition of

---

1   Douglass "Slavery and America's Bastard Republicanism: Limerick Ireland 10 November 1845," rpt. Blassingame 85.

his own body provided him with no such transformative release or sense of empowerment over his trauma. Across his works, he left his audiences in no doubt that his lifelong priority was not to indict the brutalization of enslaved bodies but to celebrate the linguistic power of enslaved peoples. In a revealing case in point, only a few months later Douglass visibilized the invisibilized agency of enslaved women and men by celebrating their authority over power. In a speech he delivered on 10 March 1846 in Scotland, he shed light on a coded system of exchange that was developed by enslaved peoples for their survival. "In the slave states we used to be afraid of using the word liberty, and we called it for safety *pig's-foot*," Douglass confides, victorious that "in this way we could speak of it even in our masters' presence, without their knowing that liberty was the subject of our discourse."[1]

A few years later, Douglass published a public letter, "To My Old Master," in the pages of his own newspaper, *The North Star* (see Appendix C12). He was undoubtedly inspired to open up correspondence with Thomas Auld after having read the dialogue between the master and slave in his treasured copy of *The Columbian Orator*. Here he pulls no punches regarding the failure of language in doing justice to both the psychological and physical traumas he experienced during slavery and in its terrible aftermath: "I have no words to describe to you the deep agony of soul which I experienced" (p. 236). In a bold departure from his decision to minimize, if not entirely omit, any details surrounding his family in his *Narrative* or his speeches, he chooses to share information regarding his personal life. As he informs Auld, "I was engaged to be married before I left you; and instead of finding my companion a burden, she was truly a helpmeet. She went to live—at service, and I to work on the wharf, and though we toiled hard the first winter, we never lived more happily" (p. 238). For the first time, he readily confides his feelings regarding his new life in freedom: "I have an industrious and neat companion, and four dear children—the oldest a girl of nine years, and three fine boys, the oldest eight, the next six, and the youngest four years old. The three oldest are now going regularly to school—two can read and write, the other can spell with tolerable correctness words of two syllables" (p. 239). He is jubilant that his family members are free: "Dear fellows! they are all in comfortable beds, and are sound asleep, perfectly secured under

---

1   Douglass, "Charges and Defence of the Free Church," rpt., Blassingame 178.

my own roof. There are no slaveholders here to rend my heart by snatching them from my arms, or blast a proud mother's dearest hopes by tearing them from her bosom" (p. 239).

And yet, in the very process of writing, Douglass's joy turns to despair. His realization regarding his own children's vulnerability soon functions as a catalyst not only for his expression of anger against slavery's injustices but also for his experiencing of emotions we would today define as post-traumatic stress disorder: "Oh! sir, a slaveholder never appears to me so completely an agent of hell, as when I think of and look upon my dear children. It is then that my feelings rise above my control" (p. 239). During his narration, he is immediately faced with uncontrollable "feelings" that defy rational explanation, given his exposure to an overwhelming sense of personal trauma: "I meant to have said more with respect to my own prosperity and happiness, but thoughts and feelings which this recital has quickened, unfits me to proceed further in that direction. The grim horrors of slavery rise in all their ghastly terror before me, the wails of millions pierce my heart, and chill my blood" (p. 239). According to this testimony, Douglass had no choice but to relive his suffering by shouldering the weight of this repressed yet resurfacing memory: "I remember the chain, the gag, the bloody whip, the deathlike gloom overshadowing the broke spirit of the fettered bondman, the appalling liability of his being torn away from wife and children and sold like a beast in the market" (p. 239).

An examination of the contents of this letter soon reveals the reason Douglass the public orator, antislavery campaigner, intellectual, and philosopher typically concealed the life of Douglass the son, the father, and the husband from view. As an individual who suffered from a daily struggle not to be overwhelmed by his body- and soul-destroying memories of his enslavement, he ran a very real risk of being overpowered by his emotions in any narration of his private suffering. As Douglass himself recognized, if he were too candid regarding his own inner turmoil, he risked not only compromising the efficacy of his antislavery arguments and putting the abolitionist cause in real jeopardy, but also doing very real harm to his psychological well-being.

Just as Douglass was mindful of the ways in which his own family had been invisibilized in the official record, he was all too aware of the very real damage that was committed against the lives of enslaved women and children and their daily fight for survival as a result of the overwhelming emphasis upon heroism as the sole domain of Black manhood throughout the pre-Civil War era.

Despite his status as a radical campaigner in the vanguard of the fight for women's rights, Douglass was also not without his complexities when it came to gender equality. Nevertheless, he was wholehearted in his endorsement of the seminal importance not only of heroic figures such as Madison Washington but of Harriet Tubman, a legendary freedom-fighter born into slavery as Araminta Ross.

A single document can be found in his body of writings in which Douglass was inspired to write a public letter of support for Tubman's life story as authored by white abolitionist Sarah Bradford (1818–1912). In a rare moment of candor, he exalts Black female exceptionalism by admitting to his own inferiority. As he confesses, "[t]he difference between us is very marked. Most that I have done and suffered in the service of our cause has been in public, and I have received much encouragement at every step of the way. You, on the other hand, have labored in a private way. I have wrought in the day—you in the night" (Appendix C13, p. 241). Nowhere is this "difference" more marked than in that between the celebrated "public" service of Frederick Douglass and the unacknowledged "private labor" of Harriet Tubman as a legendary coordinator of the Underground Railroad and an individual singlehandedly responsible for leading enslaved women, children, and men out of the American south. And yet, while Tubman has now begun to receive her due in the mass outpouring of scholarship and monuments to her heroism in the twenty-first century—including her recently announced appearance on the US $20 bill—the unsung heroism of Anna, Rosetta, Lewis Henry, Frederick Jr., Charles Remond, and Annie Douglass is still to be told.

"Struggles for the Cause of Liberty": The Lives and Works of Anna, Rosetta, Lewis Henry, Frederick Jr., Charles Remond, and Annie Douglass

Over the decades, Frederick Douglass all but erased any trace of his wife, Anna Murray (1813–82), and of his daughters and sons, Rosetta, Lewis Henry, Frederick Jr., Charles Remond, and Annie Douglass, across the various editions of his *Narrative* and the oratorical performances of his life story. Anna Murray makes a very brief appearance in his *Narrative* when he introduces her for the first time at the moment of their marriage. Following his liberty from slavery, he writes, "Anna, my intended wife, came on; for I wrote to her immediately after my arrival at New York, (notwithstanding my homeless, houseless, and helpless condition,) informing her of my successful flight, and wishing her to come on forthwith" (p. 161). He supplies undeniable proof of their union by inserting a copy of their marriage certificate into his *Narrative* alongside a note in which he provides no biographical details concerning Anna's life except to confirm that "[s]he was free" (p. 161, n. 1). He went yet further in one of his speeches in which he exalted in his own liberty by declaring, "I not only got free, but I got a wife free—the first matter a free man thinks of."[1] As the surviving records show, and in direct contrast to his self-aggrandizing rhetoric, not only was Anna already free at the time of his escape but she also in fact contributed the funds that made Douglass's own flight possible.

For information regarding Anna's life we are forced to turn to records other than those provided by Douglass. An obituary published in the *New York Globe* on 12 August 1882, immediately following her death, includes the "remarks" of "Bishop T.M.D.Ward." He informs readers that Anna Murray was born to free parents in 1813 a few years earlier than her husband. Ward writes, "She is said to have first met Mr. Douglass at a church in their native State, of the Baptist denomination, for which he had organized a choir, of which he was leader."[2] He sheds new light not only on Murray's but also on Douglass's status as a choir leader and an exemplary singer while he lived in slavery. Ward also refuses to consign Murray solely to the domestic sphere by testifying to her political knowledge: "In conversation with her on the 30th of June last, she discoursed vividly upon her home life at Rochester, and she showed that she was not unmindful of the present. She spoke approvingly of men who are striving to serve well their day and generation."

While Douglass himself remained silent about his relationship with Murray while she was alive, he held nothing back regarding his emotional turmoil following her death. He laid bare her centrality to his life by readily sharing his anguish in a letter in the *Cincinnati Commercial* on 27 August 1882: "The main pillar of my house has fallen. Four and forty years have passed away since our union. Life can not hold much for me, now that she has gone. Still I feel that the lesson taught by this death, as by all such, is silence, resignation, humility, and hope." In the same letter, Douglass ultimately found solace in his loneliness by conceding, "[w]e are all strangers and sojourners."

---

1 Douglass, "International Moral Force Can Destroy Slavery," Paisley, Scotland, 17 March 1846, rpt. Blassingame 185.
2 This newspaper clipping is in one of Lewis Henry Douglass's scrapbooks held in the private collection of Walter O. Evans.

Over their decades-long marriage, Anna Murray and Frederick Douglass had five sons and daughters, four of whom he described in his letter to his old master but does not name—Rosetta (1839–1906), Lewis Henry (1840–1908), Frederick Jr. (1842–92), Charles Remond (1844–1920)—and Annie (1849–60) born a few years later. According to the surviving letters written by Rosetta, a very different portrait of Douglass the father emerges while he was on his British abolitionist tour (see Appendix D2). Writing her father at the age of seven, on 20 October 1845, she admits to problems with her eyesight by declaring, "I was very blind," but only after reassuring him, "my eyes are almost well" (p. 248). As research into Rosetta's later life confirms, she was plagued with this condition until she died, as these health difficulties were almost certainly exacerbated by her key role as Douglass's proofreader and amanuensis. Writing Douglass following his visit to an "Asylum for the Blind" in Bristol toward the beginning of his UK trip, she empathizes with the "great many blind children" who "felt of you because they could not see you and they had heard of you before you came to see them" (p. 248). She admits, "Oh, how sorry I felt for them that they could not see you!" (p. 248). Rosetta not only confirms her profound loneliness in being away from Douglass—"My dear father, if you were here now, oh, happy, how happy, I should be!" (p. 248)—but also reveals the extent of his emotional suffering during his absence.

Just over a year later, on 23 October 1846, Rosetta confirms Douglass's own fears of being forgotten by offering him reassurance: "my dear father, how can I forget you when we talk about you every hour in the day? Oh, no, my dear father, your little Rosa can never forget you" (pp. 248–49). She also confirms the existence of an archive of letters written by her father, which no longer survives: "I have so many of your dear letters, and you tell me how you love me" (p. 249). Rosetta reveals yet more of Douglass's personal distress by paraphrasing his words: "you say that you dreamed that I did not know you when you met me; I did not smile or look pleased." She immediately offers him comfort: "That was very strange for you to dream that I did not know you, for I shall know you if I only hear you say 'Rosa,' even though you would speak to me in the dark" (p. 249).

These letters are not the only ones written by his children while they were young to have survived in the archives. We also have two letters written by his younger daughter, Annie, who was named after Anna Murray and who died tragically young at only ten years of age. Over a decade following her elder sister's correspondence, she wrote a poignant letter to her father while he was on his second transatlantic sojourn to the British Isles (see Appendix D3). This time he had made the journey to Europe not because he was on an abolitionist lecture tour but because he was on the run from US authorities following his suspected involvement in John Brown's Harpers Ferry raid, in which he sought to liberate enslaved people by capturing the US federal arsenal. In one of her letters that survive, she was at pains to inform her father of her educational achievements by sharing her prowess in the German language and also including an antislavery poem that she was preparing to recite at school. Herself a committed abolitionist and radical reformer, Annie concluded her letter by sharing her traumatized response to Brown's execution: "Poor Mr. Brown is dead. That hard hearted man said he must die and they took him in and open field and about half a mil[e] from the jail and hung him" (p. 250). By then a young adult, Rosetta had the terrible responsibility of informing her father of Annie's death only months later. While he spoke only rarely of his profound personal grief, Douglass remained inconsolable until the day he died regarding the loss of his younger daughter.

During his first transatlantic visit to the UK and Ireland and immediately following the publication of his *Narrative*, Douglass wrote a very personal series of letters to a woman he identified as his "dear sister," Harriet Bailey (see Appendices D9–12). However, a search in the archives led by researchers Tekla Ali Johnson, John R. Wunder, and Abigail B. Anderson has since proved that Harriet Bailey was the new identity Douglass gave in honor of his mother, not to his biological sister but to a fugitive slave named Ruth Cox Adams. A woman who had previously been enslaved on a plantation in Maryland that was in close proximity to Douglass's own, she succeeded in escaping north to freedom, at which point she met Douglass in circumstances that remain unknown. As Johnson, Wunder, and Anderson explain, "Douglass took her for his sister" and "gave Ruth the pseudonym Harriet Bailey" (25). And yet, as their research confirms, while she had a brother with the same surname as Douglass during slavery—he was named Leon Bailey—"Ebby Cox, Harriet's mother, did not live on the Aaron Anthony estate, but rather on an entirely separate plantation" (25). Despite this fact, Douglass named Cox after his dead mother and invited her into his home, with the result that "Adams lived with the Douglasses from about 1842 until her marriage in 1847" (124). As Adams's surviving archives confirm, she attached a note to a lock of his hair that he gave her, describing this treasured item as belonging to "My adopted Brother" (126).[1] Clearly, there are a number of unsolved mysteries regarding whether Douglass was fully aware that Cox was not his sister, and concerning his reasons for naming her after his dead mother: surely he would have honored with his dead mother's name only a person he thought to be a blood relation?

These ongoing questions notwithstanding, the series of letters that Douglass wrote to Harriet/Ruth provide no-holds-barred access to Douglass as a fallible private individual, the antithesis of Douglass the mythologized public icon. On 16 May 1846 he wrote a letter to Harriet/Ruth in which he admits to his exposure to a terrible emotional suffering. He confides in an unprecedented moment of candor, "a few days ago—quite down at the mouth. I felt worse than 'get out!' My under lip hung like that of a motherless Colt I looked so ugly that I hated to see myself in a glass. There was no living for me. I was so snappish I would have kicked my grand 'dadda'! I was in a terrible mood—dats a fac! Ole missus is you got any ting for poor nigger to eat!!!" (p. 251). Douglass's traumatized confession regarding his personal turmoil establishes the full extent of his emotional and physical wounding as a survivor of slavery. Over the decade, he suffered from repeated bouts of psychological illness that threatened his existence. Vulnerable to extended periods of depression, he experienced suicidal thoughts—"There was no living for me"—and also suffered from an extreme sense of self-hatred: "I looked so ugly that I hated to see myself in a glass."

Dramatically to the fore here is Douglass's struggle with what we would now call survivor guilt, as he was repeatedly traumatized by why he made it out of slavery when his family members—and millions more—did not. As proof of his profound trust in Harriet/Ruth, he gave vent to emotions that he repeatedly had to keep sublimated, censored, and sanitized out of view on the abolitionist podium. Nothing could be further from his staged oratorical eloquence than his reuse of idiomatic phrases from the plantation: "Ole missus is you got any ting for poor nigger to eat." Here he provides a searing indictment of an unending struggle with slavery's "grim horrors" that terrorized him even in his new life in freedom. While Douglass publicly insisted on a miraculous

---

1 Joseph L. Douglass Jr., "Harriet Bailey: Presumed Sister of Frederick Douglass," has gone in a different direction for Harriet's identity by working with Aaron Anthony's ledgers for a trace of an enslaved woman of the same name.

change from "Frederick Bailey the slave" to "Frederick Douglass the freeman," his private conflicts suggest otherwise.

According to Douglass's poignant letter to Harriet/Ruth (Appendix D4a), the antidote for his suffering was to be found only in her comfort. As he insists, "Oh, Harriet could I have seen you then. How soon I would have been relieved from that Horrible feeling" (p. 251). For Douglass, his work as an abolitionist only partly assuaged his pain, as it was to individuals he saw as family members that he turned for real emotional sustenance. A close examination of the original letter shows that Douglass was not worrying about punctuation or spelling to the same extent that he did in his correspondence with white abolitionists. While his uneven handwriting and mistakes may be a sign of personal turmoil, they are also an indication that he was able to show more of himself in his private communications. The fact that he sought out Harriet/Ruth's psychological support is confirmation of the personal toll that both his experience in slavery and his work as an abolitionist took on him. While he remains jubilant, "I am going on bravely with my antislavery work" (p. 251), he is candid in his letter to Harriet/Ruth regarding the struggles he had in selling his *Narrative*: "My book is selling slowly but I have fourteen hundred copies to dispose of before I come home." He also readily admits to his desperate desire to return home. "I wish I could see my way clear to come home in July," he explains, stating, "If I could sell what books I have on hand by that time I would come but this I do not expect so I submit to my fate and will try to make myself contented" (p. 251). He provides a rare reference to Anna by instructing Harriet/Ruth to "[r]ead the enclosed letter which I send to my dear Anna over and over again till she can fully understand its contents" (p. 251). Unfortunately, this letter to Anna no longer survives.

A few months later, on 31 January 1847, Douglass yet again admits to his profound emotional suffering by conceding, "There are many things I should like to write about—but I am not in a state of mind to write—I am miserable—unhappy—and it seems I must so live and Die" (p. 254). He remains unequivocal regarding his ongoing psychological torture by urging, "It is absolutely too bad that I should be so harassed in my feelings" (p. 254). Douglass's reference to the "many things I should like to write about," which he either was unable to do or decided not to, sounds a word of caution: there is much we will never know—and, out of respect for his privacy, *should* never know—about the life of Frederick Douglass, much less the life of Frederick Augustus Washington Bailey.

Among the posthumously published histories shedding light on Douglass and his family are "Reminiscences of Frederick Douglass," written by white author Jane Marsh Parker (1836–1913; see Appendix D5), and Rosetta Douglass Sprague's (1839–1906) printed pamphlet *My Mother as I Recall Her* (see Appendix D6). As one of their neighbors while they lived in Rochester for over twenty years, Parker provides a brief history of Douglass's family life in which she emphasizes, "Mrs. Douglass chose seclusion, and the children were models of behavior" (p. 255). More particularly, she sheds light on the hidden life of Anna Murray by observing, "Mrs. Douglass was a model housekeeper, her thrifty care of her family and her watchful supervision of expenditure making the financial venture of her husband in undertaking the 'North Star' far less hazardous than many believed" (p. 255). She also celebrated Anna's intelligence and astuteness: "She read character with marvelous accuracy, and was a wholesome check on her husband's proneness to being imposed upon" (p. 256).

According to Parker's testimony, Murray's acquisition of literacy was impossible in light of her domestic responsibilities. As she remembers, she "consented, rather reluctantly, to have a teacher in the house for herself as well as the children—an English woman, of whom she faithfully tried for a while to learn to read and write; but when it came to neglecting housewifely duties for copy-book and speller, the experiment ended; and Mrs. Douglass was glad to be released" (p. 256). Parker is also candid regarding Douglass's own struggles with written expression, referring to his "den-like upstairs study" in which he "used to keep there a list of the words he found it hard to spell" (p. 257).

Yet more revealingly, Parker provides rare insights into Douglass's early years as an orator and the risks he ran regarding his performance style and the preferred content of his speeches. In an illuminating passage, she quotes Douglass as follows: "One of the hardest things I had to learn when I was fairly under way as a public speaker was to stop telling so many funny stories. I could keep my audience in a roar of laughter—and they liked to laugh, and showed disappointment when I was not amusing" (p. 259). All too aware of the ways in which enslaved people were subjected to grotesque caricatures and dehumanized stereotypes among whites, Douglass immediately abandoned comedy in favor of tragedy. As he painfully realized, "I was convinced that I was in danger of becoming something of a clown, and that I must guard against it" (p. 259).

As published by her own daughter, Fredericka Douglass Sprague Perry, Rosetta Douglass Sprague's biography of her mother opens with a preface in which she eulogizes the hidden life of Anna Murray Douglass. She holds nothing back in her feminist critique by urging, "Too often are the facts of the great sacrifices and heroic efforts of the wives of renowned men overshadowed by the achievements of the men and the wonderful and beautiful part she has played so well is overlooked" (p. 261). Douglass Sprague borrows directly from her own father's epic rhetoric by writing of the fight for daily existence as a crucible for the formation of character: "Real life is a struggle, an activity, a will to execute" (p. 262). She also betrays her motivation for remembering her mother's life by urging, "The story of Frederick Douglass' hopes and aspirations and longing desire for freedom has been told—you all know it. It was a story made possible through the unswerving loyalty of Anna Murray, to whose memory this paper is written" (p. 263).

Across her biography of her mother's life, Rosetta takes a different view from her father's celebration that he got a "wife free" by writing of Anna's invaluable support of Douglass's life as Frederick Bailey. As Douglass Sprague confirms, Anna "as a free woman was enabled with others to make my father's life easier while he was a slave" (p. 263). She credits her mother for providing Douglass with "welcome" access into a "little circle of free people" to which "slaves were excluded" (p. 263). She also confirms that it was Anna who provided the material support for his escape by writing that she "had lived with the Wells family so long and having been able to save the greater part of her earnings was willing to share with the man she loved that he might gain the freedom he yearned to possess" (p. 264). As Douglass Sprague indicates, her mother "had previously sold one of her feather beds to assist in defraying the expenses of the flight from bondage" (p. 264).

If Harriet Tubman's work as an Underground Railroad operator has been subjected to neglect, Anna Murray Douglass's activism has been entirely invisibilized. Due to the position of their house in Rochester in upstate New York, the Douglass home was a major station that provided fugitives with lifesaving aid in their flight from bondage. As Douglass Sprague confirms, her mother was central to this enterprise: "Being herself one of the first agents of the Underground Railroad she was an untiring worker along that line" (p. 267). While Douglass himself was absent from home on his antislavery lecture tours, his daughter explains, "It was no unusual occurrence for mother to be called up at all hours of the night, cold or hot, as the case might be, to prepare supper for a hungry lot of fleeing humanity" (p. 267).

Douglass Sprague refuses to play into white racist assumptions surrounding her mother's illiteracy by insisting on the pain that a lack of education caused Anna Murray. As she declares, "[u]nfortunately an opportunity for a knowledge of books had been denied to her, the lack of which she greaty [sic] deplored" (p. 269). Across her biography, Douglass Sprague is immovable in her conviction regarding her mother's unjust neglect in the archives: "As is the condition of most wives her identity became merged into that of the husband. Thus only the few of their friends in the North really knew and appreciated the full value of the woman who presided over the Douglass home for forty-four years" (p. 264).

Rosetta Douglass Sprague's brother, Lewis H. Douglass, took the neglect not only of Douglass's wife but also of his family bitterly to task (see Appendix D7). As he argues in an unpublished and undated manuscript, there is a terrible hole in the official record regarding "the distresses, the anxieties, and the hardships that he and his family had to undergo in the struggle for the cause of liberty" (p. 270). He is categorical regarding the neglect both of Anna Murray and of him and his siblings: "The children ~~had to partake~~ partook of the ill feelings manifested on the part of the so-called superior race and were bound down to the oppression that ruled in the dark days when pro-slavery was on deck and in command" (p. 271). He does justice to a self-sacrifice that is collective rather than individual, summarizing that "[f]or years the family worked on ~~and~~ only encouraged by the thought that they were working for the cause in which their father and mother were interested—namely the emancipation of the slave" (p. 271). If examined from a comparative rather than an isolated perspective, as Lewis Henry Douglass emphasizes, Frederick Douglass's campaign for the "emancipation of the slave" was a collective and not an individual effort.

"I have on my back the marks of the lash; I have four sisters and one brother now under the galling chain. I feel it my duty to cry aloud and spare not."—Douglass repeatedly confided regarding his own and his family's lives as lived during slavery.[1] Typically unforthcoming regarding the details of his private life, he chose not to provide audiences with the names, let alone the biogra-

---

1 Douglass, "American Slavery, American Religion and the Free Church of Scotland," London, 22 May 1846, rpt. Blassingame 294.

phies, of his "four sisters and one brother" across the decades. However, there was one exception.

In an unprecedented moment of candor toward the end of his life, Douglass admitted to a desire to right these wrongs by referring to the suffering of his "one brother.": "My poor brother Perry—after a bondage of fifty-six years, deeply marked by the hardships and sorrows of that hateful condition; and after a separation from me during forty years, as complete as if he had lived on another planet—came to me two months ago, with his family of six, and took up his abode with me," he confides. Assuming the role of a younger brother determined to show his gratitude to his elder sibling for his self-sacrificing heroism, he admits, "To him—dear old fellow!—one who has carried me on his shoulders many a time (for he is older than I, though my head seems to contradict it)—one who defended me from the assaults of bigger boys when I needed defense—I have been mainly devoting myself, and gladly so." Douglass jubilantly insists that "[t]hough no longer young, he is no sluggard. Slavery got the best of his life, but he is still strong and hopeful. I wish his old master could see him now—cheerful, helpful, and 'taking care of himself.'"

In retelling his brother's history, Douglass is inspired to concede that, "[i]f slavery were not dead, and I did not in some sort wish to forget its terrible hardships, I would try to write a narrative of my brother Perry's bondage." Almost immediately, however, he dismisses the idea, proclaiming, "let the old system go! I would not call its guilty ghost from the depths into which its crimes have cast it. I turn gladly from the past to the new and better dispensation now dawning."[1]

For Frederick Douglass living with the physical and psychological wounds of Frederick Bailey, the very thought of trying "to write a narrative of my brother Perry's bondage" remained overwhelming: far better to consign the "guilty ghost" of slavery to its grave.

---

1 Douglass, n.t., n.d., n.p., Lewis Henry Douglass Scrapbook, Walter O. Evans collection.

Frederick Douglass: A Brief Chronology[1]

May 1774	Grandmother Betsey Bailey born on Skinner Plantation in Talbot County, Maryland.
28 Feb. 1792	Mother Harriet Bailey born on Skinner Plantation.
1813	Anna Murray is born to free parents in Denton, Caroline County, Maryland.
Feb. 1818	Frederick Douglass born Frederick Augustus Washington Bailey to Harriet Bailey and an unidentified white man on Holme Hill Farm, Easton, Talbot County, Maryland.
Aug. 1824	Taken to Colonel Edward Lloyd's plantation, Wye River, where his master Captain Aaron Anthony lives.
Mar. 1826	Sent to Fells Point, Baltimore, to live with Sophia and Hugh Auld and to look after their son, Thomas. Begins to learn to read and obtains a copy of Caleb Bingham's *The Columbian Orator.*
14 Nov. 1826	Aaron Anthony dies.
Oct. 1827	After the "valuation and division of the property," Douglass is given to Lucretia Auld, with the result that he returns to Baltimore.
Mar. 1833	Sent to St. Michaels to live with Thomas Auld and his second wife, Rowena. Begins teaching a Sabbath School for enslaved African Americans and immediately encounters violent opposition from white racist protesters.
1 Jan. 1834	Sent by Auld to live with Edward Covey, a white "negro breaker."
Aug. 1834	Works in Covey's treading-yard; becomes ill with a fever and collapses, with the result that he is brutally attacked by Covey. In desperation, returns to St. Michaels to appeal to

---

1 In compiling this chronology, I am indebted to the groundbreaking research of his leading biographers: David Blight, Joseph L. Douglass Jr., Leigh Fought, Dickson J. Peterson, and Benjamin Quarles.

Auld for mercy but is instead sent back to Covey. En route, encounters Sandy Jenkins, an enslaved man. Jenkins and his wife take pity on his plight and give him food to sustain him and a "root" to protect him. Inspired by such signs of Black solidarity and spiritual support, he returns to Covey with a determination to fight, and as a result is victorious.

1 Jan. 1835 — Term of service ends with Edward Covey and is hired out to William Freeland as a farm laborer.

April 1836 — Inspired by his aunt Jenny and uncle Noah's escape in 1825, devises a runaway plot. Convinces enslaved men Henry Harris, John Harris, Sandy Jenkins, Charles Roberts, and Henry Bailey to join him. Before they are able to put their plans into action, they are betrayed and incarcerated in Easton jail. Auld loses no time in sending Douglass back to Baltimore to live with his brother Hugh. Is hired out to a white shipbuilder, William Gardener, as a caulker on Fell's Point. Soon after is the victim of a terrible assault as he is attacked by white carpenters fearing the encroachment on their livelihood by Black enslaved laborers. In fear of his life, is taken out of Gardener's shipyard and allowed to hire his time. Very likely on Anna Murray's introduction, plays an active role in the East Baltimore Mental Improvement Society organized by free African American men.

3 Sept. 1838 — Borrows a friend's "sailor's protection" papers and boards a train to Wilmington, from where he takes a steamer for Philadelphia and then a train to New York. Anna Murray sells one of her feather beds to raise the funds for his flight.

15 Sept. 1838 — Sends for Anna Murray and they are married by Reverend James W.C. Pennington. On 17 September they travel to New Bedford and receive aid from Nathan Johnson and his family. Johnson convinces him to adopt

"Douglass" as his new surname as a homage to legendary freedom-fighter James Douglas, the hero of Scottish author Walter Scott's poem "Lady of the Lake." During this period, works as a manual laborer.

24 June 1839	Daughter Rosetta is born.
9 Oct. 1840	Son Lewis Henry is born.
11–12 Aug. 1841	Attends an antislavery convention in Nantucket. Delivers his first antislavery lecture to a white abolitionist audience, with the result that he is appointed as an agent of the Massachusetts Antislavery Society.
Fall 1841	Frederick, Anna, Rosetta, and Lewis Henry Douglass move to Lynn, Massachusetts.
3 Mar. 1842	Second son Frederick Jr. is born.
1843	Participates in the One Hundred Conventions Campaign. On 16 September is viciously attacked by a white racist mob in Indiana.
21 Oct. 1844	Son Charles Remond Douglass, named after his friend and antislavery campaigner Charles Remond, is born.
28 May 1845	Publishes *Narrative of the Life of Frederick Douglass, an American Slave* at the Boston Anti-Slavery Office.
16 Aug. 1845	Due to fears for his safety, travels on the steamship *Cambria* to undertake a transatlantic abolitionist tour of Britain and Ireland.
Sept. 1845	The first Dublin edition of the *Narrative* is published.
6 Oct. 1846	Hugh Auld releases Douglass's manumission papers for £150 (about $710) following his receipt of funds raised by Ellen and Anna Richardson of Newcastle-upon-Tyne, England.
3 Dec. 1847	Moves to Rochester, New York, and begins publishing *The North Star* (subsequently *Frederick Douglass's Paper* and *Douglass' Monthly*), funded by British monies. Frederick, Anna Murray, Lewis, Charles, and Frederick Jr. work together on the Underground Railroad.
19–20 July 1848	Begins his lifelong support of the women's

	liberation movement by attending the first Women's Rights Convention at Seneca Falls, New York.
22 Mar. 1849	Second daughter, Annie, is born.
9 May 1851	Breaks with William Lloyd Garrison over his conviction of the necessity for political action to oppose slavery and begins his lifelong friendship with Gerrit Smith, a Liberty Party supporter.
26 June 1851	Changes the name of *The North Star* to *Frederick Douglass's Paper* and receives financial aid from Gerrit Smith.
5 July 1852	Delivers his speech "What to the Slave is the Fourth of July?" in Corinthian Hall, Rochester, New York.
1853	Publishes his novella, *The Heroic Slave*, in white British editor Julia Griffiths's antislavery gift book, *Autographs for Freedom*.
Aug. 1855	Publishes his second autobiography, *My Bondage and My Freedom*.
Feb. 1858	John Brown stays with Douglass in preparation for his Harpers Ferry rebellion.
20 Aug. 1859	Has a clandestine meeting with Brown at a stone quarry near Chambersburg, Pennsylvania. Brown asks Douglass to participate in his raid on the federal arsenal at Harpers Ferry, West Virginia, and he refuses.
17 Oct. 1859	Escapes to Canada in the wake of John Brown's raid in order to evade arrest by Virginian governor Henry Wise.
12 Nov. 1859	Sails from Quebec to the United Kingdom. Delivers speeches in Scotland and England.
13 Mar. 1860	Annie dies and Douglass returns to the United States.
31 Dec. 1862	Speaks at a reception held at Boston's Tremont Temple to celebrate Abraham Lincoln's Emancipation Proclamation, which comes through via telegram at midnight on 1 January 1863.
Feb.–July 1863	Appointed as an agent for the US Government to recruit Black soldiers into the Union Army. On 2 March publishes his appeal, "Men of Color, To Arms," in *Douglass'*

Monthly. Lewis Henry and Charles Remond enlist in the Fifty-Fourth Massachusetts Regiment. While Lewis Henry is instantly promoted to the rank of sergeant-major and serves with commendation beside Colonel Robert Gould Shaw at Fort Wagner, Charles Remond is transferred to the Fifth Cavalry, where he acquits himself nobly. Frederick Jr. is appointed as a recruitment agent in Mississippi.

16 Aug. 1863	Ends publication of *Douglass' Monthly*.
Jan. 1870	Appointed as a corresponding editor for the *New National Era*, only to assume the role of editor and to buy the paper outright on 12 December. Lewis Henry, Charles, and Frederick Jr. play a key role in managing, typesetting, and writing articles for publication.
12 Jan. 1871	Awarded the position of assistant secretary of commission of inquiry to Santo Domingo. Endorses President General Grant's plans for the annexation of Santo Domingo to the United States.
2 June 1872	Douglass's house in Rochester is burned to the ground under suspicious circumstances.
1 July 1872	Douglass and his family move to 'A' Street NE in Washington, DC.
Mar. 1874	Appointed president of the Freedmen's Bank.
Sept. 1874	Ends publication of the *New National Era* due to ongoing financial difficulties. The Freedmen's Bank is dissolved in financial crisis and he suffers extensive personal loss.
17 Mar. 1877	Appointed by President Rutherford B. Hayes as United States Marshal for the District of Columbia.
1878	Purchases Cedar Hill, in Anacostia, Washington, DC.
Jan. 1881	Publishes his third autobiography, *Life and Times of Frederick Douglass*. Completes a final revised edition that he significantly updates a few years later in 1892.
Mar. 1881	Appointed by President James A. Garfield as Recorder of Deeds for the District of Columbia.

4 Aug. 1882	Anna Murray Douglass dies.
24 Jan. 1884	Marries white, women's rights campaigner Helen Pitts.
5 Jan. 1886	Resigns as Recorder of Deeds for District of Columbia.
1 July 1889	President Benjamin Harrison appoints Douglass as the Minister Resident and Consul General to Haiti.
Sept. 1889	Appointed as Chargé d'Affaires for Santo Domingo as well as Minister to Haiti.
30 July 1891	Resigns his position as Minister Resident and Consul General to Haiti.
26 July 1892	Frederick Jr. dies.
1892–93	Serves as Commissioner of the Haitian exhibit at the World's Fair in Chicago.
Jan. 1894	Delivers his anti-lynching speech "Lessons of the Hour."
20 Feb. 1895	Attends the National Council of Women in Washington, DC. On his return, he collapses in the hallway at Cedar Hill with Helen and dies.
25 Feb. 1895	Douglass's body is exhibited for public view at the Metropolitan African Methodist Church, Washington, DC.
26 Feb. 1895	Douglass's body is taken by train to Rochester and is on public view at the City Hall. His funeral is held in Rochester Central Presbyterian Church. Is buried beside Anna Murray and Annie Douglass in Mount Hope Cemetery, Rochester.
1903	Helen Pitts Douglass dies.
25 Nov. 1906	Rosetta Douglass Sprague dies.
9 Oct. 1908	Lewis Henry Douglass dies.
23 Nov. 1920	Charles Remond Douglass dies.

A Note on the Text

Frederick Douglass's *Narrative of the Life of Frederick Douglass, an American Slave* was a nineteenth-century publishing phenomenon, a bestselling work that went through countless American and European editions during Douglass's lifetime. This edition reprints the first imprint published at the Anti-Slavery Office in Boston in 1845. For the benefit of the reader, I have kept my editorial interventions to a minimum by silently correcting minor typographical errors and retaining the original formatting wherever possible. I have relied on only very brief explanatory notes to provide readers with further information regarding the sources of Douglass's quotations, and with very short biographies concerning individuals he chose to include in his *Narrative*. Douglass's own notes have also been reproduced with no amendments.

NARRATIVE

OF THE

LIFE

OF

FREDERICK DOUGLASS,

AN

AMERICAN SLAVE.

WRITTEN BY HIMSELF.

BOSTON:

PUBLISHED AT THE ANTI-SLAVERY OFFICE,

No. 25 CORNHILL

1845.

Frederick Douglass, Frontispiece, *Narrative of the Life of
Frederick Douglass* (Boston: Anti-Slavery Office, 1845).

PREFACE

In the month of August, 1841, I attended an anti-slavery convention in Nantucket, at which it was my happiness to become acquainted with FREDERICK DOUGLASS, the writer of the following Narrative. He was a stranger to nearly every member of that body; but, having recently made his escape from the southern prison-house of bondage, and feeling his curiosity excited to ascertain the principles and measures of the abolitionists,—of whom he had heard a somewhat vague description while he was a slave,—he was induced to give his attendance, on the occasion alluded to, though at that time a resident in New Bedford.[1]

Fortunate, most fortunate occurrence!—fortunate for the millions of his manacled brethren, yet panting for deliverance from their awful thraldom!—fortunate for the cause of negro emancipation, and of universal liberty!—fortunate for the land of his birth, which he has already done so much to save and bless!—fortunate for a large circle of friends and acquaintances, whose sympathy and affection he has strongly secured by the many sufferings he has endured, by his virtuous traits of character, by his ever-abiding remembrance of those who are in bonds, as being bound with them!—fortunate for the multitudes, in various parts of our republic, whose minds he has enlightened on the subject of slavery, and who have been melted to tears by his pathos, or roused to virtuous indignation by his stirring eloquence against the enslavers of men!—fortunate for himself, as it at once brought him into the field of public usefulness, "gave the world assurance of a MAN,"[2] quickened the slumbering energies of his soul, and consecrated him to the great work of breaking the rod of the oppressor, and letting the oppressed go free!

I shall never forget his first speech at the convention—the extraordinary emotion it excited in my own mind—the powerful impression it created upon a crowded auditory, completely taken by surprise—the applause which followed from the beginning to the end of his felicitous remarks. I think I never hated slavery so

---

1 Following his self-emancipation from slavery, Frederick Douglass lived with his wife, Anna Murray, and his children in New Bedford, Massachusetts.

2 Shakespeare, *Hamlet* 3.4.62. Theodore Parker, "Primitive Christianity," *The Critical and Miscellaneous Writings of Theodore Parker* (Boston: James Munroe Company, 1843), 244.

intensely as at that moment; certainly, my perception of the enormous outrage which is inflicted by it, on the godlike nature of its victims, was rendered far more clear than ever. There stood one, in physical proportion and stature commanding and exact—in intellect richly endowed—in natural eloquence a prodigy—in soul manifestly "created but a little lower than the angels"[1]—yet a slave, ay, a fugitive slave,—trembling for his safety, hardly daring to believe that on the American soil, a single white person could be found who would befriend him at all hazards, for the love of God and humanity! Capable of high attainments as an intellectual and moral being—needing nothing but a comparatively small amount of cultivation to make him an ornament to society and a blessing to his race—by the law of the land, by the voice of the people, by the terms of the slave code, he was only a piece of property, a beast of burden, a chattel personal, nevertheless!

A beloved friend[2] from New Bedford prevailed on Mr. DOUGLASS to address the convention: He came forward to the platform with a hesitancy and embarrassment, necessarily the attendants of a sensitive mind in such a novel position. After apologizing for his ignorance, and reminding the audience that slavery was a poor school for the human intellect and heart, he proceeded to narrate some of the facts in his own history as a slave, and in the course of his speech gave utterance to many noble thoughts and thrilling reflections. As soon as he had taken his seat, filled with hope and admiration, I rose, and declared that PATRICK HENRY,[3] of revolutionary fame, never made a speech more eloquent in the cause of liberty, than the one we had just listened to from the lips of that hunted fugitive. So I believed at that time— such is my belief now. I reminded the audience of the peril which surrounded this self-emancipated young man at the North,—even in Massachusetts, on the soil of the Pilgrim Fathers,[4] among the descendants of revolutionary sires; and I appealed to them,

---

1 Psalms 8:5; Hebrews 2:7. The original quotation reads: "For thou hast made him a little lower than the angels, and hast crowned him with glory and honour."

2 William C. Coffin, a white US antislavery campaigner and one of Douglass's keen supporters.

3 Patrick Henry (1736–99), a Founding Father and Virginia governor who delivered the renowned "Give Me Liberty or Give Me Death!" speech on 23 March 1775, which inspired Douglass's rhetoric.

4 "Pilgrim Fathers" is the collective noun given to the sixteenth-century European migrants who settled in Massachusetts prior to the region's independence from British colonial power.

whether they would ever allow him to be carried back into slavery,—law or no law, constitution or no constitution. The response was unanimous and in thunder-tones—"NO!" "Will you succor and protect him as a brother-man—a resident of the old Bay State?" "YES!" shouted the whole mass, with an energy so startling, that the ruthless tyrants south of Mason and Dixon's line might almost have heard the mighty burst of feeling, and recognized it as the pledge of an invincible determination, on the part of those who gave it, never to betray him that wanders, but to hide the outcast, and firmly to abide the consequences.

It was at once deeply impressed upon my mind, that, if Mr. DOUGLASS could be persuaded to consecrate his time and talents to the promotion of the anti-slavery enterprise, a powerful impetus would be given to it, and a stunning blow at the same time inflicted on northern prejudice against a colored complexion. I therefore endeavored to instill hope and courage into his mind, in order that he might dare to engage in a vocation so anomalous and responsible for a person in his situation; and I was seconded in this effort by warm-hearted friends, especially by the late General Agent of the Massachusetts Anti-Slavery Society, Mr. JOHN A. COLLINS,[1] whose judgment in this instance entirely coincided with my own. At first, he could give no encouragement; with unfeigned diffidence, he expressed his conviction that he was not adequate to the performance of so great a task; the path marked out was wholly an untrodden one; he was sincerely apprehensive that he should do more harm than good. After much deliberation, however, he consented to make a trial; and ever since that period, he has acted as a lecturing agent, under the auspices either of the American or the Massachusetts Anti-Slavery Society.[2] In labors he has been most abundant; and his success in combating prejudice, in gaining proselytes, in agitating the public mind, has far surpassed the most sanguine expectations that were raised at the commencement of his brilliant career. He has borne himself with gentleness and meekness, yet with true manliness of character. As a public speaker, he

---

1 John Anderson Collins (1810–79). A white US antislavery activist and social reformer, Collins was born in Vermont and educated at Middlebury College.

2 Founded in 1835, the Massachusetts Anti-Slavery Society was affiliated with the American Anti-Slavery Society and had its origins in the New England Anti-Slavery Society established by William Lloyd Garrison (1805–79) in 1831.

excels in pathos, wit, comparison, imitation, strength of reasoning, and fluency of language. There is in him that union of head and heart, which is indispensable to an enlightenment of the heads and a winning of the hearts of others. May his strength continue to be equal to his day! May he continue to "grow in grace, and in the knowledge of God,"[1] that he may be increasingly serviceable in the cause of bleeding humanity, whether at home or abroad!

It is certainly a very remarkable fact, that one of the most efficient advocates of the slave population, now before the public, is a fugitive slave, in the person of FREDERICK DOUGLASS; and that the free colored population of the United States are as ably represented by one of their own number, in the person of CHARLES LENOX REMOND,[2] whose eloquent appeals have extorted the highest applause of multitudes on both sides of the Atlantic. Let the calumniators of the colored race despise themselves for their baseness and illiberality of spirit, and henceforth cease to talk of the natural inferiority of those who require nothing but time and opportunity to attain to the highest point of human excellence.

It may, perhaps, be fairly questioned, whether any other portion of the population of the earth could have endured the privations, sufferings and horrors of slavery, without having become more degraded in the scale of humanity than the slaves of African descent. Nothing has been left undone to cripple their intellects, darken their minds, debase their moral nature, obliterate all traces of their relationship to mankind; and yet how wonderfully they have sustained the mighty load of a most frightful bondage, under which they have been groaning for centuries! To illustrate the effect of slavery on the white man,—to show that he has no powers of endurance, in such a condition, superior to those of his black brother,—DANIEL O'CONNELL,[3] the distinguished advocate of universal emancipation, and the mightiest champion of prostrate but not conquered Ireland, relates the following anecdote in a speech delivered by him in the Conciliation

---

1 2 Peter 3:18.
2 African American antislavery writer and thinker Charles Lenox Remond (1810–73) was born free in Salem, Massachusetts, and was one of Douglass's close friends in the early period.
3 Daniel O'Connell (1775–1847) was an Irish liberator, reformer, and radical. Douglass was popularly known during his transatlantic tour as the "black O'Connell."

Hall, Dublin, before the Loyal National Repeal Association, March 31, 1845. "No matter," said Mr. O'CONNELL, "under what specious term it may disguise itself, slavery is still hideous. It has a natural, an inevitable tendency to brutalize every noble faculty of man. An American sailor, who was cast away on the shore of Africa, where he was kept in slavery for three years, was, at the expiration of that period, found to be imbruted and stultified—he had lost all reasoning power; and having forgotten his native language, could only utter some savage gibberish between Arabic and English, which nobody could understand, and which even he himself found difficulty in pronouncing. So much for the humanizing influence of THE DOMESTIC INSTITUTION!" Admitting this to have been an extraordinary case of mental deterioration, it proves at least that the white slave can sink as low in the scale of humanity as the black one.

Mr. DOUGLASS has very properly chosen to write his own Narrative, in his own style, and according to the best of his ability, rather than to employ some one else. It is, therefore, entirely his own production; and, considering how long and dark was the career he had to run as a slave,—how few have been his opportunities to improve his mind since he broke his iron fetters,—it is, in my judgment, highly creditable to his head and heart. He who can peruse it without a tearful eye, a heaving breast, an afflicted spirit,—without being filled with an unutterable abhorrence of slavery and all its abettors, and animated with a determination to seek the immediate overthrow of that execrable system,—without trembling for the fate of this country in the hands of a righteous God, who is ever on the side of the oppressed, and whose arm is not shortened that it cannot save,— must have a flinty heart, and be qualified to act the part of a trafficker "in slaves and the souls of men."[1] I am confident that it is essentially true in all its statements; that nothing has been set down in malice, nothing exaggerated, nothing drawn from the imagination; that it comes short of the reality, rather than overstates a single fact in regard to SLAVERY AS IT IS.[2] The experience of FREDERICK DOUGLASS, as a slave, was not a peculiar one; his lot was not especially a hard one; his case may be regarded as a very fair specimen of the treatment of slaves in

---

1 Revelation 18:13.
2 White US abolitionist Theodore Weld (1803–95) included this phrase in his groundbreaking antislavery tract *American Slavery as It Is: Testimony of a Thousand Witnesses* (1839).

Maryland, in which State it is conceded that they are better fed and less cruelly treated than in Georgia, Alabama, or Louisiana. Many have suffered incomparably more, while very few on the plantations have suffered less, than himself. Yet how deplorable was his situation! what terrible chastisements were inflicted upon his person! what still more shocking outrages were perpetrated upon his mind! with all his noble powers and sublime aspirations, how like a brute was he treated, even by those professing to have the same mind in them that was in Christ Jesus! to what dreadful liabilities was he continually subjected! how destitute of friendly counsel and aid, even in his greatest extremities! how heavy was the midnight of woe which shrouded in blackness the last ray of hope, and filled the future with terror and gloom! what longings after freedom took possession of his breast, and how his misery augmented, in proportion as he grew reflective and intelligent,—thus demonstrating that a happy slave is an extinct man! how he thought, reasoned, felt, under the lash of the driver, with the chains upon his limbs! what perils he encountered in his endeavors to escape from his horrible doom! and how signal have been his deliverance and preservation in the midst of a nation of pitiless enemies!

This Narrative contains many affecting incidents, many passages of great eloquence and power; but I think the most thrilling one of them all is the description DOUGLASS gives of his feelings, as he stood soliloquizing respecting his fate, and the chances of his one day being a freeman, on the banks of the Chesapeake Bay—viewing the receding vessels as they flew with their white wings before the breeze, and apostrophizing them as animated by the living spirit of freedom. Who can read that passage, and be insensible to its pathos and sublimity? Compressed into it is a whole Alexandrian library[1] of thought, feeling, and sentiment— all that can, all that need be urged, in the form of expostulation, entreaty, rebuke, against that crime of crimes,—making man the property of his fellow-man! O, how accursed is that system, which entombs the godlike mind of man, defaces the divine image, reduces those who by creation were crowned with glory and honor to a level with four-footed beasts, and exalts the dealer in human flesh above all that is called God! Why should its exis-

---

1   Originating in the third century BCE, the Royal Library of Alexandria in Egypt was one of the most important libraries in the ancient world.

tence be prolonged one hour? Is it not evil, only evil, and that continually? What does its presence imply but the absence of all fear of God, all regard for man, on the part of the people of the United States? Heaven speed its eternal overthrow!

So profoundly ignorant of the nature of slavery are many persons, that they are stubbornly incredulous whenever they read or listen to any recital of the cruelties which are daily inflicted on its victims. They do not deny that the slaves are held as property; but that terrible fact seems to convey to their minds no idea of injustice, exposure to outrage, or savage barbarity. Tell them of cruel scourgings, of mutilations and brandings, of scenes of pollution and blood, of the banishment of all light and knowledge, and they affect to be greatly indignant at such enormous exaggerations, such wholesale misstatements, such abominable libels on the character of the southern planters! As if all these direful outrages were not the natural results of slavery! As if it were less cruel to reduce a human being to the condition of a thing, than to give him a severe flagellation, or to deprive him of necessary food and clothing! As if whips, chains, thumb-screws, paddles, blood-hounds, overseers, drivers, patrols, were not all indispensable to keep the slaves down, and to give protection to their ruthless oppressors! As if, when the marriage institution is abolished, concubinage, adultery, and incest, must not necessarily abound; when all the rights of humanity are annihilated, any barrier remains to protect the victim from the fury of the spoiler; when absolute power is assumed over life and liberty, it will not be wielded with destructive sway! Skeptics of this character abound in society. In some few instances, their incredulity arises from a want of reflection; but, generally, it indicates a hatred of the light, a desire to shield slavery from the assaults of its foes, a contempt of the colored race, whether bond or free. Such will try to discredit the shocking tales of slaveholding cruelty which are recorded in this truthful Narrative; but they will labor in vain. Mr. DOUGLASS has frankly disclosed the place of his birth, the names of those who claimed ownership in his body and soul, and the names also of those who committed the crimes which he has alleged against them. His statements, therefore, may easily be disproved, if they are untrue.

In the course of his Narrative, he relates two instances of murderous cruelty,—in one of which a planter deliberately shot a slave belonging to a neighboring plantation, who had unintentionally gotten within his lordly domain in quest of fish; and in the other, an overseer blew out the brains of a slave who had fled to a stream of water to escape a bloody scourging. Mr. DOUGLASS states that in neither of these instances was any thing done by way of legal arrest or judicial investigation. *The Baltimore American*, of March 17, 1845, relates a similar case of atrocity, perpetrated with similar impunity—as follows:— "Shooting a slave.—We learn, upon the authority of a letter from Charles county, Maryland, received by a gentleman of this city, that a young man, named Matthews, a nephew of General Matthews, and whose father, it is believed, holds an office at Washington, killed one of the slaves upon his father's farm by shooting him. The letter states that young Matthews had been left in charge of the farm; that he gave an order to the servant, which was disobeyed, when he proceeded to the house, obtained a gun, and, returning, shot the servant. He immediately, the letter continues, fled to his father's residence, where he still remains unmolested."—Let it never be forgotten, that no slaveholder or overseer can be convicted of any outrage perpetrated on the person of a slave, however diabolical it may be, on the testimony of colored witnesses, whether bond or free. By the slave code, they are adjudged to be as incompetent to testify against a white man, as though they were indeed a part of the brute creation. Hence, there is no legal protection in fact, whatever there may be in form, for the slave population; and any amount of cruelty may be inflicted on them with impunity. Is it possible for the human mind to conceive of a more horrible state of society?

The effect of a religious profession on the conduct of southern masters is vividly described in the following Narrative, and shown to be any thing but salutary. In the nature of the case, it must be in the highest degree pernicious. The testimony of Mr. DOUGLASS, on this point, is sustained by a cloud of witnesses, whose veracity is unimpeachable. "A slaveholder's profession of Christianity is a palpable imposture. He is a felon of the highest grade. He is a man-stealer. It is of no importance what you put in the other scale."

Reader! are you with the man-stealers in sympathy and purpose, or on the side of their down-trodden victims? If with the former, then are you the foe of God and man. If with the latter, what are you prepared to do and dare in their behalf? Be faithful, be vigilant, be untiring in your efforts to break every yoke, and let the oppressed go free. Come what may—cost what it may—inscribe on the banner which you unfurl to the breeze, as your religious and political motto—"NO COMPROMISE WITH SLAVERY! NO UNION WITH SLAVEHOLDERS!"

WM. LLOYD GARRISON.[1]

BOSTON, May 1, 1845.

LETTER FROM WENDELL PHILLIPS,[2] ESQ.

BOSTON, April 22, 1845.

My Dear Friend:

You remember the old fable of "The Man and the Lion," where the lion complained that he should not be so misrepresented "when the lions wrote history."[3]

I am glad the time has come when the "lions write history." We have been left long enough to gather the character of slavery from the involuntary evidence of the masters. One might, indeed, rest sufficiently satisfied with what, it is evident, must be, in general, the results of such a relation, without seeking farther to find whether they have followed in every instance. Indeed, those who stare at the half-peck of corn a week, and love to count the lashes on the slave's back, are seldom the "stuff" out of which reformers and abolitionists are to be made. I remember that, in 1838, many were waiting for the results of the West India experiment,[4] before they could come into our ranks. Those "results" have come long ago; but, alas! few of that number have come with them, as converts. A man must be disposed to judge of emancipation by other tests than whether it has increased the produce of sugar,—and to hate slavery for other reasons than because it starves men and whips women,—before he is ready to lay the first stone of his anti-slavery life.

I was glad to learn, in your story, how early the most neglected

---

1   William Lloyd Garrison (1805–79) was born in Newburyport, Massachusetts. A white US radical abolitionist and reformer, he was a publisher of antislavery materials and the editor of the antislavery ewspaper the *Liberator*.

2   Wendell Phillips (1811–84) was born in Boston and was a radical abolitionist, lawyer, reformer, and social activist.

3   Phillips is referring to "The Lion and the Statue," a morality tale written by enslaved Roman writer Aesop (620–564 BCE) and included in his celebrated collection *Aesop's Fables*, published after his death.

4   The British West Indies Emancipation Act took effect on 1 August 1838.

of God's children waken to a sense of their rights, and of the injustice done them. Experience is a keen teacher; and long before you had mastered your A B C, or knew where the "white sails" of the Chesapeake were bound, you began, I see, to gauge the wretchedness of the slave, not by his hunger and want, not by his lashes and toil, but by the cruel and blighting death which gathers over his soul.

In connection with this, there is one circumstance which makes your recollections peculiarly valuable, and renders your early insight the more remarkable. You come from that part of the country where we are told slavery appears with its fairest features. Let us hear, then, what it is at its best estate—gaze on its bright side, if it has one; and then imagination may task her powers to add dark lines to the picture, as she travels southward to that (for the colored man) Valley of the Shadow of Death,[1] where the Mississippi sweeps along.

Again, we have known you long, and can put the most entire confidence in your truth, candor, and sincerity. Every one who has heard you speak has felt, and, I am confident, every one who reads your book will feel, persuaded that you give them a fair specimen of the whole truth. No one-sided portrait,—no wholesale complaints,—but strict justice done, whenever individual kindliness has neutralized, for a moment, the deadly system with which it was strangely allied. You have been with us, too, some years, and can fairly compare the twilight of rights, which your race enjoy at the North, with that "noon of night" under which they labor south of Mason and Dixon's line. Tell us whether, after all, the half-free colored man of Massachusetts is worse off than the pampered slave of the rice swamps!

In reading your life, no one can say that we have unfairly picked out some rare specimens of cruelty. We know that the bitter drops, which even you have drained from the cup, are no incidental aggravations, no individual ills, but such as must mingle always and necessarily in the lot of every slave. They are the essential ingredients, not the occasional results, of the system.

After all, I shall read your book with trembling for you. Some years ago, when you were beginning to tell me your real name and birthplace, you may remember I stopped you, and preferred to remain ignorant of all. With the exception of a vague description, so I continued, till the other day, when you read me your memoirs. I hardly knew, at the time, whether to thank you or not

---

1 Psalm 23:4.

for the sight of them, when I reflected that it was still dangerous, in Massachusetts, for honest men to tell their names! They say the fathers, in 1776, signed the Declaration of Independence with the halter about their necks. You, too, publish your declaration of freedom with danger compassing you around. In all the broad lands which the Constitution of the United States overshadows, there is no single spot,—however narrow or desolate,—where a fugitive slave can plant himself and say, "I am safe." The whole armory of Northern Law has no shield for you. I am free to say that, in your place, I should throw the MS. into the fire.

You, perhaps, may tell your story in safety, endeared as you are to so many warm hearts by rare gifts, and a still rarer devotion of them to the service of others. But it will be owing only to your labors, and the fearless efforts of those who, trampling the laws and Constitution of the country under their feet, are determined that they will "hide the outcast,"[1] and that their hearths shall be, spite of the law, an asylum for the oppressed, if, some time or other, the humblest may stand in our streets, and bear witness in safety against the cruelties of which he has been the victim.

Yet it is sad to think, that these very throbbing hearts which welcome your story, and form your best safeguard in telling it, are all beating contrary to the "statute in such case made and provided." Go on, my dear friend, till you, and those who, like you, have been saved, so as by fire, from the dark prison-house, shall stereotype these free, illegal pulses into statutes; and New England, cutting loose from a blood-stained Union, shall glory in being the house of refuge for the oppressed,—till we no longer merely "hide the outcast," or make a merit of standing idly by while he is hunted in our midst; but, consecrating anew the soil of the Pilgrims as an asylum for the oppressed, proclaim our welcome to the slave so loudly, that the tones shall reach every hut in the Carolinas, and make the broken-hearted bondman leap up at the thought of old Massachusetts.

God speed the day!

Till then, and ever,

Yours truly,

WENDELL PHILLIPS

FREDERICK DOUGLASS.

---

1 Isaiah 16:3.

CHAPTER I

I was born in Tuckahoe, near Hillsborough, and about twelve miles from Easton, in Talbot county, Maryland. I have no accurate knowledge of my age, never having seen any authentic record containing it. By far the larger part of the slaves know as little of their ages as horses know of theirs, and it is the wish of most masters within my knowledge to keep their slaves thus ignorant. I do not remember to have ever met a slave who could tell of his birthday. They seldom come nearer to it than planting-time, harvest-time, cherry-time, spring-time, or fall-time. A want of information concerning my own was a source of unhappiness to me even during childhood. The white children could tell their ages. I could not tell why I ought to be deprived of the same privilege. I was not allowed to make any inquiries of my master concerning it. He deemed all such inquiries on the part of a slave improper and impertinent, and evidence of a restless spirit. The nearest estimate I can give makes me now between twenty-seven and twenty-eight years of age. I come to this, from hearing my master say, some time during 1835, I was about seventeen years old.[1]

My mother was named Harriet Bailey. She was the daughter of Isaac and Betsey Bailey, both colored, and quite dark. My mother was of a darker complexion than either my grandmother or grandfather.

My father was a white man. He was admitted to be such by all I ever heard speak of my parentage. The opinion was also whispered that my master was my father; but of the correctness of this opinion, I know nothing; the means of knowing was withheld from me. My mother and I were separated when I was but an infant—before I knew her as my mother. It is a common custom, in the part of Maryland from which I ran away, to part children from their mothers at a very early age. Frequently, before the child has reached its twelfth month, its mother is taken from it, and hired out on some farm a considerable distance off, and the child is placed under the care of an old woman, too old for field labor. For what this separation is done, I do not know, unless it

---

1 Throughout his lifetime, Frederick Douglass believed he had been born in Februrary 1817; in fact, subsequent research has categorically established that he was born in February 1818. While Douglass often celebrated Valentine's Day, 14 February, as his birthdate, his exact date of birth remains unknown.

be to hinder the development of the child's affection toward its mother, and to blunt and destroy the natural affection of the mother for the child. This is the inevitable result.

I never saw my mother, to know her as such, more than four or five times in my life; and each of these times was very short in duration, and at night. She was hired by a Mr. Stewart, who lived about twelve miles from my home. She made her journeys to see me in the night, travelling the whole distance on foot, after the performance of her day's work. She was a field hand, and a whipping is the penalty of not being in the field at sunrise, unless a slave has special permission from his or her master to the contrary—a permission which they seldom get, and one that gives to him that gives it the proud name of being a kind master. I do not recollect of ever seeing my mother by the light of day. She was with me in the night. She would lie down with me, and get me to sleep, but long before I waked she was gone. Very little communication ever took place between us. Death soon ended what little we could have while she lived, and with it her hardships and suffering. She died when I was about seven years old, on one of my master's farms, near Lee's Mill. I was not allowed to be present during her illness, at her death, or burial. She was gone long before I knew any thing about it. Never having enjoyed, to any considerable extent, her soothing presence, her tender and watchful care, I received the tidings of her death with much the same emotions I should have probably felt at the death of a stranger.

Called thus suddenly away, she left me without the slightest intimation of who my father was. The whisper that my master was my father, may or may not be true; and, true or false, it is of but little consequence to my purpose whilst the fact remains, in all its glaring odiousness, that slaveholders have ordained, and by law established, that the children of slave women shall in all cases follow the condition of their mothers; and this is done too obviously to administer to their own lusts, and make a gratification of their wicked desires profitable as well as pleasurable; for by this cunning arrangement, the slaveholder, in cases not a few, sustains to his slaves the double relation of master and father.

I know of such cases; and it is worthy of remark that such slaves invariably suffer greater hardships, and have more to contend with, than others. They are, in the first place, a constant offence to their mistress. She is ever disposed to find fault with them; they can seldom do any thing to please her; she is never better pleased than when she sees them under the lash, especially when she suspects her husband of showing to his mulatto children favors which he withholds from his black slaves. The master is frequently compelled to sell this class of his slaves, out of deference to the feelings of his white wife; and, cruel as the deed may strike any one to be, for a man to sell his own children to human flesh-mongers, it is often the dictate of humanity for him to do so; for, unless he does this, he must not only whip them himself, but must stand by and see one white son tie up his brother, of but few shades darker complexion than himself, and ply the gory lash to his naked back; and if he lisp one word of disapproval, it is set down to his parental partiality, and only makes a bad matter worse, both for himself and the slave whom he would protect and defend.

Every year brings with it multitudes of this class of slaves. It was doubtless in consequence of a knowledge of this fact, that one great statesman of the south[1] predicted the downfall of slavery by the inevitable laws of population. Whether this prophecy is ever fulfilled or not, it is nevertheless plain that a very different-looking class of people are springing up at the south, and are now held in slavery, from those originally brought to this country from Africa; and if their increase do no other good, it will do away the force of the argument, that God cursed Ham,[2] and therefore American slavery is right. If the lineal descendants of Ham are alone to be scripturally enslaved, it is certain that slavery at the south must soon become unscriptural; for thousands are ushered into the world, annually, who, like myself, owe their existence to white fathers, and those fathers most frequently their own masters.

I have had two masters. My first master's name was Anthony. I do not remember his first name. He was generally called Captain Anthony—a title which, I presume, he acquired by sailing a craft on the Chesapeake Bay. He was not considered a rich slaveholder. He owned two or three farms, and about thirty slaves. His farms and slaves were under the care of an overseer. The overseer's name was Plummer. Mr. Plummer was a miserable drunkard, a profane swearer, and a savage monster. He always went armed with a cowskin[3] and a heavy cudgel. I have

---

1 The identity of this figure is unknown.
2 Genesis 9:25.
3 A "cowskin" is a shorthand description for a whip made from the leather hide of a cow and used by white slave traders, owners, and overseers to torture, maim, and kill enslaved and free people of African descent.

known him to cut and slash the women's heads so horribly, that even master would be enraged at his cruelty, and would threaten to whip him if he did not mind himself. Master, however, was not a humane slaveholder. It required extraordinary barbarity on the part of an overseer to affect him. He was a cruel man, hardened by a long life of slaveholding. He would at times seem to take great pleasure in whipping a slave. I have often been awakened at the dawn of day by the most heart-rending shrieks of an own aunt of mine, whom he used to tie up to a joist, and whip upon her naked back till she was literally covered with blood. No words, no tears, no prayers, from his gory victim, seemed to move his iron heart from its bloody purpose. The louder she screamed, the harder he whipped; and where the blood ran fastest, there he whipped longest. He would whip her to make her scream, and whip her to make her hush; and not until overcome by fatigue, would he cease to swing the blood-clotted cowskin. I remember the first time I ever witnessed this horrible exhibition. I was quite a child, but I well remember it. I never shall forget it whilst I remember any thing. It was the first of a long series of such outrages, of which I was doomed to be a witness and a participant. It struck me with awful force. It was the blood-stained gate, the entrance to the hell of slavery, through which I was about to pass. It was a most terrible spectacle. I wish I could commit to paper the feelings with which I beheld it.

This occurrence took place very soon after I went to live with my old master, and under the following circumstances. Aunt Hester went out one night,—where or for what I do not know,—and happened to be absent when my master desired her presence. He had ordered her not to go out evenings, and warned her that she must never let him catch her in company with a young man, who was paying attention to her belonging to Colonel Lloyd. The young man's name was Ned Roberts, generally called Lloyd's Ned. Why master was so careful of her, may be safely left to conjecture. She was a woman of noble form, and of graceful proportions, having very few equals, and fewer superiors, in personal appearance, among the colored or white women of our neighborhood.

Aunt Hester had not only disobeyed his orders in going out, but had been found in company with Lloyd's Ned; which circumstance, I found, from what he said while whipping her, was the chief offence. Had he been a man of pure morals himself, he might have been thought interested in protecting the innocence of my aunt; but those who knew him will not suspect him of any such virtue. Before he commenced whipping Aunt Hester, he took her into the kitchen, and stripped her from neck to waist, leaving her neck, shoulders, and back, entirely naked. He then told her to cross her hands, calling her at the same time a d——d b——h. After crossing her hands, he tied them with a strong rope, and led her to a stool under a large hook in the joist, put in for the purpose. He made her get upon the stool, and tied her hands to the hook. She now stood fair for his infernal purpose. Her arms were stretched up at their full length, so that she stood upon the ends of her toes. He then said to her, "Now, you d——d b——h, I'll learn you how to disobey my orders!" and after rolling up his sleeves, he commenced to lay on the heavy cowskin, and soon the warm, red blood (amid heart-rending shrieks from her, and horrid oaths from him) came dripping to the floor. I was so terrified and horror-stricken at the sight, that I hid myself in a closet, and dared not venture out till long after the bloody transaction was over. I expected it would be my turn next. It was all new to me. I had never seen any thing like it before. I had always lived with my grandmother on the outskirts of the plantation, where she was put to raise the children of the younger women. I had therefore been, until now, out of the way of the bloody scenes that often occurred on the plantation.

CHAPTER II

My master's family consisted of two sons, Andrew and Richard; one daughter, Lucretia, and her husband, Captain Thomas Auld. They lived in one house, upon the home plantation of Colonel Edward Lloyd. My master was Colonel Lloyd's clerk and superintendent. He was what might be called the overseer of the overseers. I spent two years of childhood on this plantation in my old master's family. It was here that I witnessed the bloody transaction recorded in the first chapter; and as I received my first impressions of slavery on this plantation, I will give some description of it, and of slavery as it there existed. The plantation is about twelve miles north of Easton, in Talbot county, and is situated on the border of Miles River. The principal products raised upon it were tobacco, corn, and wheat. These were raised in great abundance; so that, with the products of this and the other farms belonging to him, he was able to keep in almost constant employment a large sloop, in carrying them to market at Baltimore. This sloop was named Sally Lloyd, in honor of one of the colonel's daughters. My master's son-in-law, Captain Auld, was master of the vessel; she was otherwise manned by the colonel's own slaves. Their names were Peter, Isaac, Rich, and Jake. These were esteemed very highly by the other slaves, and looked upon as the privileged ones of the plantation; for it was no small affair, in the eyes of the slaves, to be allowed to see Baltimore.

Colonel Lloyd kept from three to four hundred slaves on his home plantation, and owned a large number more on the neighboring farms belonging to him. The names of the farms nearest to the home plantation were Wye Town and New Design. "Wye Town" was under the overseership of a man named Noah Willis. New Design was under the overseership of a Mr. Townsend. The overseers of these, and all the rest of the farms, numbering over twenty, received advice and direction from the managers of the home plantation. This was the great business place. It was the seat of government for the whole twenty farms. All disputes among the overseers were settled here. If a slave was convicted of any high misdemeanor, became unmanageable, or evinced a determination to run away, he was brought immediately here, severely whipped, put on board the sloop, carried to Baltimore, and sold to Austin Woolfolk, or some other slave-trader, as a warning to the slaves remaining.

Here, too, the slaves of all the other farms received their monthly allowance of food, and their yearly clothing. The men and women slaves received, as their monthly allowance of food, eight pounds of pork, or its equivalent in fish, and one bushel of corn meal. Their yearly clothing consisted of two coarse linen shirts, one pair of linen trousers, like the shirts, one jacket, one pair of trousers for winter, made of coarse negro cloth,[1] one pair of stockings, and one pair of shoes; the whole of which could not have cost more than seven dollars. The allowance of the slave children was given to their mothers, or the old women having the care of them. The children unable to work in the field had neither shoes, stockings, jackets, nor trousers, given to them; their clothing consisted of two coarse linen shirts per year. When these failed them, they went naked until the next allowance-day. Children from seven to ten years old, of both sexes, almost naked, might be seen at all seasons of the year.

---

1 Douglass uses this term as a general description to refer to the inferior-quality fabric that was allotted to enslaved people as clothing by white slaveholders. For further information on the clothing of enslaved people see Foster.

There were no beds given the slaves, unless one coarse blanket be considered such, and none but the men and women had these. This, however, is not considered a very great privation. They find less difficulty from the want of beds, than from the want of time to sleep; for when their day's work in the field is done, the most of them having their washing, mending, and cooking to do, and having few or none of the ordinary facilities for doing either of these, very many of their sleeping hours are consumed in preparing for the field the coming day; and when this is done, old and young, male and female, married and single, drop down side by side, on one common bed,—the cold, damp floor,—each covering himself or herself with their miserable blankets; and here they sleep till they are summoned to the field by the driver's horn. At the sound of this, all must rise, and be off to the field. There must be no halting; every one must be at his or her post; and woe betides them who hear not this morning summons to the field; for if they are not awakened by the sense of hearing, they are by the sense of feeling: no age nor sex finds any favor. Mr. Severe, the overseer, used to stand by the door of the quarter, armed with a large hickory stick and heavy cowskin, ready to whip any one who was so unfortunate as not to hear, or, from any other cause, was prevented from being ready to start for the field at the sound of the horn.

Mr. Severe was rightly named: he was a cruel man. I have seen him whip a woman, causing the blood to run half an hour at the time; and this, too, in the midst of her crying children, pleading for their mother's release. He seemed to take pleasure in manifesting his fiendish barbarity. Added to his cruelty, he was a profane swearer. It was enough to chill the blood and stiffen the hair of an ordinary man to hear him talk. Scarce a sentence escaped him but that was commenced or concluded by some horrid oath. The field was the place to witness his cruelty and profanity. His presence made it both the field of blood and of blasphemy. From the rising till the going down of the sun, he was cursing, raving, cutting, and slashing among the slaves of the field, in the most frightful manner. His career was short. He died very soon after I went to Colonel Lloyd's; and he died as he lived, uttering, with his dying groans, bitter curses and horrid oaths. His death was regarded by the slaves as the result of a merciful providence.

Mr. Severe's place was filled by a Mr. Hopkins. He was a very different man. He was less cruel, less profane, and made less noise, than Mr. Severe. His course was characterized by no extraordinary demonstrations of cruelty. He whipped, but seemed to take no pleasure in it. He was called by the slaves a good overseer.

The home plantation of Colonel Lloyd wore the appearance of a country village. All the mechanical operations for all the farms were performed here. The shoemaking and mending, the blacksmithing, cartwrighting, coopering, weaving, and grain-grinding, were all performed by the slaves on the home plantation. The whole place wore a business-like aspect very unlike the neighboring farms. The number of houses, too, conspired to give it advantage over the neighboring farms. It was called by the slaves the Great House Farm. Few privileges were esteemed higher, by the slaves of the out-farms, than that of being selected to do errands at the Great House Farm. It was associated in their minds with greatness. A representative could not be prouder of his election to a seat in the American Congress, than a slave on one of the out-farms would be of his election to do errands at the Great House Farm. They regarded it as evidence of great confidence reposed in them by their overseers; and it was on this account, as well as a constant desire to be out of the field from under the driver's lash, that they esteemed it a high privilege, one worth careful living for. He was called the smartest and most trusty fellow, who had this honor conferred upon him the most frequently. The competitors for this office sought as diligently to please their overseers, as the office-seekers in the political parties seek to please and deceive the people. The same traits of character might be seen in Colonel Lloyd's slaves, as are seen in the slaves of the political parties.

The slaves selected to go to the Great House Farm, for the monthly allowance for themselves and their fellow-slaves, were peculiarly enthusiastic. While on their way, they would make the dense old woods, for miles around, reverberate with their wild songs, revealing at once the highest joy and the deepest sadness. They would compose and sing as they went along, consulting neither time nor tune. The thought that came up, came out—if not in the word, in the sound;—and as frequently in the one as in the other. They would sometimes sing the most pathetic sentiment in the most rapturous tone, and the most rapturous sentiment in the most pathetic tone. Into all of their songs they would manage to weave something of the Great House Farm. Especially would they do this, when leaving home. They would then sing most exultingly the following words:—

"I am going away to the Great House Farm!
O, yea! O, yea! O!"

This they would sing, as a chorus, to words which to many would seem unmeaning jargon, but which, nevertheless, were full of meaning to themselves. I have sometimes thought that the mere hearing of those songs would do more to impress some minds with the horrible character of slavery, than the reading of whole volumes of philosophy on the subject could do.

I did not, when a slave, understand the deep meaning of those rude and apparently incoherent songs. I was myself within the circle; so that I neither saw nor heard as those without might see and hear. They told a tale of woe which was then altogether beyond my feeble comprehension; they were tones loud, long, and deep; they breathed the prayer and complaint of souls boiling over with the bitterest anguish. Every tone was a testimony against slavery, and a prayer to God for deliverance from chains. The hearing of those wild notes always depressed my spirit, and filled me with ineffable sadness. I have frequently found myself in tears while hearing them. The mere recurrence to those songs, even now, afflicts me; and while I am writing these lines, an expression of feeling has already found its way down my cheek. To those songs I trace my first glimmering conception of the dehumanizing character of slavery. I can never get rid of that conception. Those songs still follow me, to deepen my hatred of slavery, and quicken my sympathies for my brethren in bonds. If any one wishes to be impressed with the soul-killing effects of slavery, let him go to Colonel Lloyd's plantation, and, on allowance-day, place himself in the deep pine woods, and there let him, in silence, analyze the sounds that shall pass through the chambers of his soul,—and if he is not thus impressed, it will only be because "there is no flesh in his obdurate heart."[1]

I have often been utterly astonished, since I came to the north, to find persons who could speak of the singing, among slaves, as evidence of their contentment and happiness. It is impossible to conceive of a greater mistake. Slaves sing most when they are most unhappy. The songs of the slave represent the sorrows of his heart; and he is relieved by them, only as an aching heart is

---

1   This is a direct quotation of William Cowper (1731–1800), a British
    poet who wrote *The Task: A Poem*, Book II (1784), in which the original
    appears: "There is no flesh in man's obdurate heart."

relieved by its tears. At least, such is my experience. I have often sung to drown my sorrow, but seldom to express my happiness. Crying for joy, and singing for joy, were alike uncommon to me while in the jaws of slavery. The singing of a man cast away upon a desolate island might be as appropriately considered as evidence of contentment and happiness, as the singing of a slave; the songs of the one and of the other are prompted by the same emotion.

CHAPTER III

Colonel Lloyd kept a large and finely cultivated garden, which afforded almost constant employment for four men, besides the chief gardener, (Mr. M'Durmond.) This garden was probably the greatest attraction of the place. During the summer months, people came from far and near—from Baltimore, Easton, and Annapolis—to see it. It abounded in fruits of almost every description, from the hardy apple of the north to the delicate orange of the south. This garden was not the least source of trouble on the plantation. Its excellent fruit was quite a temptation to the hungry swarms of boys, as well as the older slaves, belonging to the colonel, few of whom had the virtue or the vice to resist it. Scarcely a day passed, during the summer, but that some slave had to take the lash for stealing fruit. The colonel had to resort to all kinds of stratagems to keep his slaves out of the garden. The last and most successful one was that of tarring his fence all around; after which, if a slave was caught with any tar upon his person, it was deemed sufficient proof that he had either been into the garden, or had tried to get in. In either case, he was severely whipped by the chief gardener. This plan worked well; the slaves became as fearful of tar as of the lash. They seemed to realize the impossibility of touching tar without being defiled.

The colonel also kept a splendid riding equipage. His stable and carriage-house presented the appearance of some of our large city livery establishments. His horses were of the finest form and noblest blood. His carriage-house contained three splendid coaches, three or four gigs, besides dearborns and barouches[1] of the most fashionable style.

---

1 A gig is a light two-wheeled carriage pulled by one horse; a dearborn is a light carriage with four wheels; a barouche is a four-wheeled horse-drawn carriage.

This establishment was under the care of two slaves—old Barney and young Barney—father and son. To attend to this establishment was their sole work. But it was by no means an easy employment; for in nothing was Colonel Lloyd more particular than in the management of his horses. The slightest inattention to these was unpardonable, and was visited upon those, under whose care they were placed, with the severest punishment; no excuse could shield them, if the colonel only suspected any want of attention to his horses—a supposition which he frequently indulged, and one which, of course, made the office of old and young Barney a very trying one. They never knew when they were safe from punishment. They were frequently whipped when least deserving, and escaped whipping when most deserving it. Every thing depended upon the looks of the horses, and the state of Colonel Lloyd's own mind when his horses were brought to him for use. If a horse did not move fast enough, or hold his head high enough, it was owing to some fault of his keepers. It was painful to stand near the stable-door, and hear the various complaints against the keepers when a horse was taken out for use. "This horse has not had proper attention. He has not been sufficiently rubbed and curried, or he has not been properly fed; his food was too wet or too dry; he got it too soon or too late; he was too hot or too cold; he had too much hay, and not enough of grain; or he had too much grain, and not enough of hay; instead of old Barney's attending to the horse, he had very improperly left it to his son." To all these complaints, no matter how unjust, the slave must answer never a word. Colonel Lloyd could not brook any contradiction from a slave. When he spoke, a slave must stand, listen, and tremble; and such was literally the case. I have seen Colonel Lloyd make old Barney, a man between fifty and sixty years of age, uncover his bald head, kneel down upon the cold, damp ground, and receive upon his naked and toil-worn shoulders more than thirty lashes at the time. Colonel Lloyd had three sons—Edward, Murray, and Daniel,— and three sons-in-law, Mr. Winder, Mr. Nicholson, and Mr. Lowndes. All of these lived at the Great House Farm, and enjoyed the luxury of whipping the servants when they pleased, from old Barney down to William Wilkes, the coach-driver. I have seen Winder make one of the house-servants stand off from him a suitable distance to be touched with the end of his whip, and at every stroke raise great ridges upon his back.

To describe the wealth of Colonel Lloyd would be almost equal to describing the riches of Job.[1] He kept from ten to fifteen

1 Job 1:1–3.

house-servants. He was said to own a thousand slaves, and I think this estimate quite within the truth. Colonel Lloyd owned so many that he did not know them when he saw them; nor did all the slaves of the out-farms know him. It is reported of him, that, while riding along the road one day, he met a colored man, and addressed him in the usual manner of speaking to colored people on the public highways of the south: "Well, boy, whom do you belong to?" "To Colonel Lloyd," replied the slave. "Well, does the colonel treat you well?" "No, sir," was the ready reply. "What, does he work you too hard?" "Yes, sir." "Well, don't he give you enough to eat?" "Yes, sir, he gives me enough, such as it is."

The colonel, after ascertaining where the slave belonged, rode on; the man also went on about his business, not dreaming that he had been conversing with his master. He thought, said, and heard nothing more of the matter, until two or three weeks afterwards. The poor man was then informed by his overseer that, for having found fault with his master, he was now to be sold to a Georgia trader. He was immediately chained and handcuffed; and thus, without a moment's warning, he was snatched away, and forever sundered, from his family and friends, by a hand more unrelenting than death. This is the penalty of telling the truth, of telling the simple truth, in answer to a series of plain questions.

It is partly in consequence of such facts, that slaves, when inquired of as to their condition and the character of their masters, almost universally say they are contented, and that their masters are kind. The slaveholders have been known to send in spies among their slaves, to ascertain their views and feelings in regard to their condition. The frequency of this has had the effect to establish among the slaves the maxim, that a still tongue makes a wise head. They suppress the truth rather than take the consequences of telling it, and in so doing prove themselves a part of the human family. If they have any thing to say of their masters, it is generally in their masters' favor, especially when speaking to an untried man. I have been frequently asked, when a slave, if I had a kind master, and do not remember ever to have given a negative answer; nor did I, in pursuing this course, consider myself as uttering what was absolutely false; for I always measured the kindness of my master by the standard of kindness set up among slaveholders around us. Moreover, slaves are like other people, and imbibe prejudices quite common to others. They think their own better than that of others. Many, under the influence of this prejudice, think their own masters are better than the masters of other slaves; and this, too, in some cases, when the very reverse is true. Indeed, it is not uncommon for slaves even to fall out and quarrel among themselves about the relative goodness of their masters, each contending for the superior goodness of his own over that of the others. At the very same time, they mutually execrate their masters when viewed separately. It was so on our plantation. When Colonel Lloyd's slaves met the slaves of Jacob Jepson, they seldom parted without a quarrel about their masters; Colonel Lloyd's slaves contending that he was the richest, and Mr. Jepson's slaves that he was the smartest, and most of a man. Colonel Lloyd's slaves would boast his ability to buy and sell Jacob Jepson. Mr. Jepson's slaves would boast his ability to whip Colonel Lloyd. These quarrels would almost always end in a fight between the parties, and those that whipped were supposed to have gained the point at issue. They seemed to think that the greatness of their masters was transferable to themselves. It was considered as being bad enough to be a slave; but to be a poor man's slave was deemed a disgrace indeed!

CHAPTER IV

Mr. Hopkins remained but a short time in the office of overseer. Why his career was so short, I do not know, but suppose he lacked the necessary severity to suit Colonel Lloyd. Mr. Hopkins was succeeded by Mr. Austin Gore, a man possessing, in an eminent degree, all those traits of character indispensable to what is called a first-rate overseer. Mr. Gore had served Colonel Lloyd, in the capacity of overseer, upon one of the out-farms, and had shown himself worthy of the high station of overseer upon the home or Great House Farm.

Mr. Gore was proud, ambitious, and persevering. He was artful, cruel, and obdurate. He was just the man for such a place, and it was just the place for such a man. It afforded scope for the full exercise of all his powers, and he seemed to be perfectly at home in it. He was one of those who could torture the slightest look, word, or gesture, on the part of the slave, into impudence, and would treat it accordingly. There must be no answering back to him; no explanation was allowed a slave, showing himself to have been wrongfully accused. Mr. Gore acted fully up to the maxim laid down by slaveholders,—"It is better that a dozen slaves should suffer under the lash, than that the overseer should be convicted, in the presence of the slaves, of having been at fault." No matter how innocent a slave might be—it availed him nothing, when accused by Mr. Gore of any misdemeanor. To be accused was to be convicted, and to be convicted was to be punished; the one always following the other with immutable certainty. To escape punishment was to escape accusation; and few slaves had the fortune to do either, under the overseership of Mr. Gore. He was just proud enough to demand the most debasing homage of the slave, and quite servile enough to crouch, himself, at the feet of the master. He was ambitious enough to be contented with nothing short of the highest rank of overseers, and persevering enough to reach the height of his ambition. He was cruel enough to inflict the severest punishment, artful enough to descend to the lowest trickery, and obdurate enough to be insensible to the voice of a reproving conscience. He was, of all the overseers, the most dreaded by the slaves. His presence was painful; his eye flashed confusion; and seldom was his sharp, shrill voice heard, without producing horror and trembling in their ranks.

Mr. Gore was a grave man, and, though a young man, he indulged in no jokes, said no funny words, seldom smiled. His words were in perfect keeping with his looks, and his looks were in perfect keeping with his words. Overseers will sometimes indulge in a witty word, even with the slaves; not so with Mr. Gore. He spoke but to command, and commanded but to be obeyed; he dealt sparingly with his words, and bountifully with his whip, never using the former where the latter would answer as well. When he whipped, he seemed to do so from a sense of duty, and feared no consequences. He did nothing reluctantly, no matter how disagreeable; always at his post, never inconsistent. He never promised but to fulfil. He was, in a word, a man of the most inflexible firmness and stone-like coolness.

His savage barbarity was equalled only by the consummate coolness with which he committed the grossest and most savage deeds upon the slaves under his charge. Mr. Gore once undertook to whip one of Colonel Lloyd's slaves, by the name of Demby. He had given Demby but few stripes, when, to get rid of the scourging, he ran and plunged himself into a creek, and stood there at the depth of his shoulders, refusing to come out. Mr. Gore told him that he would give him three calls, and that, if he did not come out at the third call, he would shoot him. The first call was given. Demby made no response, but stood his ground. The second and third calls were given with the same result. Mr. Gore then, without consultation or deliberation with any one, not even giving Demby an additional call, raised his musket to his face, taking deadly aim at his standing victim, and in an instant poor Demby was no more. His mangled body sank out of sight, and blood and brains marked the water where he had stood.

A thrill of horror flashed through every soul upon the plantation, excepting Mr. Gore. He alone seemed cool and collected. He was asked by Colonel Lloyd and my old master, why he resorted to this extraordinary expedient. His reply was, (as well as I can remember,) that Demby had become unmanageable. He was setting a dangerous example to the other slaves,—one which, if suffered to pass without some such demonstration on his part, would finally lead to the total subversion of all rule and order upon the plantation. He argued that if one slave refused to be corrected, and escaped with his life, the other slaves would soon copy the example; the result of which would be, the freedom of the slaves, and the enslavement of the whites. Mr. Gore's defence was satisfactory. He was continued in his station as overseer upon the home plantation. His fame as an overseer went abroad. His horrid crime was not even submitted to judicial investigation. It was committed in the presence of slaves, and they of course could neither institute a suit, nor testify against him; and thus the guilty perpetrator of one of the bloodiest and most foul murders goes unwhipped of justice, and uncensured by the community in which he lives. Mr. Gore lived in St. Michael's, Talbot county, Maryland, when I left there; and if he is still alive, he very probably lives there now; and if so, he is now, as he was then, as highly esteemed and as much respected as though his guilty soul had not been stained with his brother's blood.

I speak advisedly when I say this,—that killing a slave, or any colored person, in Talbot county, Maryland, is not treated as a crime, either by the courts or the community. Mr. Thomas Lanman, of St. Michael's, killed two slaves, one of whom he killed with a hatchet, by knocking his brains out. He used to boast of the commission of the awful and bloody deed. I have heard him do so laughingly, saying, among other things, that he was the only benefactor of his country in the company, and that when others would do as much as he had done, we should be relieved of "the d——d niggers."

The wife of Mr. Giles Hicks, living but a short distance from where I used to live, murdered my wife's cousin, a young girl between fifteen and sixteen years of age, mangling her person in the most horrible manner, breaking her nose and breastbone with a stick, so that the poor girl expired in a few hours afterward. She was immediately buried, but had not been in her untimely grave but a few hours before she was taken up and examined by the coroner, who decided that she had come to her death by severe beating. The offence for which this girl was thus murdered was this:—She had been set that night to mind Mrs. Hicks's baby, and during the night she fell asleep, and the baby cried. She, having lost her rest for several nights previous, did not hear the crying. They were both in the room with Mrs. Hicks. Mrs. Hicks, finding the girl slow to move, jumped from her bed, seized an oak stick of wood by the fireplace, and with it broke the girl's nose and breastbone, and thus ended her life. I will not say that this most horrid murder produced no sensation in the community. It did produce sensation, but not enough to bring the murderess to punishment. There was a warrant issued for her arrest, but it was never served. Thus she escaped not only punishment, but even the pain of being arraigned before a court for her horrid crime.

Whilst I am detailing bloody deeds which took place during my stay on Colonel Lloyd's plantation, I will briefly narrate another, which occurred about the same time as the murder of Demby by Mr. Gore.

Colonel Lloyd's slaves were in the habit of spending a part of their nights and Sundays in fishing for oysters, and in this way made up the deficiency of their scanty allowance. An old man belonging to Colonel Lloyd, while thus engaged, happened to get beyond the limits of Colonel Lloyd's, and on the premises of Mr. Beal Bondly. At this trespass, Mr. Bondly took offence, and with his musket came down to the shore, and blew its deadly contents into the poor old man.

Mr. Bondly came over to see Colonel Lloyd the next day, whether to pay him for his property, or to justify himself in what he had done, I know not. At any rate, this whole fiendish trans- action was soon hushed up. There was very little said about it at all, and nothing done. It was a common saying, even among little white boys, that it was worth a half-cent to kill a "nigger," and a half-cent to bury one.

CHAPTER V

As to my own treatment while I lived on Colonel Lloyd's planta- tion, it was very similar to that of the other slave children. I was not old enough to work in the field, and there being little else than field work to do, I had a great deal of leisure time. The most I had to do was to drive up the cows at evening, keep the fowls out of the garden, keep the front yard clean, and run errands for my old master's daughter, Mrs. Lucretia Auld. The most of my leisure time I spent in helping Master Daniel Lloyd in finding his birds, after he had shot them. My connection with Master Daniel was of some advantage to me. He became quite attached to me, and was a sort of protector of me. He would not allow the older boys to impose upon me, and would divide his cakes with me.

I was seldom whipped by my old master, and suffered little from any thing else than hunger and cold. I suffered much from hunger, but much more from cold. In hottest summer and coldest winter, I was kept almost naked—no shoes, no stockings, no jacket, no trousers, nothing on but a coarse tow linen shirt, reaching only to my knees. I had no bed. I must have perished with cold, but that, the coldest nights, I used to steal a bag which was used for carrying corn to the mill. I would crawl into this bag, and there sleep on the cold, damp, clay floor, with my head in and feet out. My feet have been so cracked with the frost, that the pen with which I am writing might be laid in the gashes.

We were not regularly allowanced. Our food was coarse corn meal boiled. This was called mush. It was put into a large wooden tray or trough, and set down upon the ground. The children were then called, like so many pigs, and like so many pigs they would come and devour the mush; some with oyster-shells, others with pieces of shingle, some with naked hands, and none with spoons. He that ate fastest got most; he that was strongest secured the best place; and few left the trough satisfied.

I was probably between seven and eight years old when I left Colonel Lloyd's plantation. I left it with joy. I shall never forget the ecstasy with which I received the intelligence that my old master (Anthony) had determined to let me go to Baltimore, to live with Mr. Hugh Auld, brother to my old master's son-in-law, Captain Thomas Auld. I received this information about three days before my departure. They were three of the happiest days I ever enjoyed. I spent the most part of all these three days in the creek, washing off the plantation scurf, and preparing myself for my departure.

The pride of appearance which this would indicate was not my own. I spent the time in washing, not so much because I wished to, but because Mrs. Lucretia had told me I must get all the dead skin off my feet and knees before I could go to Baltimore; for the people in Baltimore were very cleanly, and would laugh at me if I looked dirty. Besides, she was going to give me a pair of trousers, which I should not put on unless I got all the dirt off me. The thought of owning a pair of trousers was great indeed! It was almost a sufficient motive, not only to make me take off what would be called by pig-drovers the mange, but the skin itself. I went at it in good earnest, working for the first time with the hope of reward.

The ties that ordinarily bind children to their homes were all suspended in my case. I found no severe trial in my departure. My home was charmless; it was not home to me; on parting from it, I could not feel that I was leaving any thing which I could have enjoyed by staying. My mother was dead, my grandmother lived far off, so that I seldom saw her. I had two sisters and one brother, that lived in the same house with me; but the early separation of us from our mother had well nigh blotted the fact of our relationship from our memories. I looked for home elsewhere, and was confident of finding none which I should relish less than the one which I was leaving. If, however, I found in my new home hardship, hunger, whipping, and nakedness, I had the consolation that I should not have escaped any one of them by staying. Having already had more than a taste of them in the house of my old master, and having endured them there, I very naturally inferred my ability to endure them elsewhere, and especially at Baltimore; for I had something of the feeling about Baltimore that is expressed in the proverb, that "being hanged in England is preferable to dying a natural death in Ireland." I had the strongest desire to see Baltimore. Cousin Tom, though not fluent in speech, had inspired me with that desire by his eloquent description of the place. I could never point out any thing at the Great House, no matter how beautiful or powerful, but that he had seen something at Baltimore far exceeding, both in beauty and strength, the object which I pointed out to him. Even the Great House itself, with all its pictures, was far inferior to many buildings in Baltimore. So strong was my desire, that I thought a gratification of it would fully compensate for whatever loss of comforts I should sustain by the exchange. I left without a regret, and with the highest hopes of future happiness.

We sailed out of Miles River for Baltimore on a Saturday morning. I remember only the day of the week, for at that time I had no knowledge of the days of the month, nor the months of the year. On setting sail, I walked aft, and gave to Colonel Lloyd's plantation what I hoped would be the last look. I then placed myself in the bows of the sloop, and there spent the remainder of the day in looking ahead, interesting myself in what was in the distance rather than in things near by or behind.

In the afternoon of that day, we reached Annapolis, the capital of the State. We stopped but a few moments, so that I had no time to go on shore. It was the first large town that I had ever seen, and though it would look small compared with some of our New England factory villages, I thought it a wonderful place for its size—more imposing even than the Great House Farm!

We arrived at Baltimore early on Sunday morning, landing at Smith's Wharf, not far from Bowley's Wharf. We had on board the sloop a large flock of sheep; and after aiding in driving them to the slaughterhouse of Mr. Curtis on Louden Slater's Hill, I was conducted by Rich, one of the hands belonging on board of the sloop, to my new home in Alliciana Street, near Mr. Gardner's ship-yard, on Fells Point.

Mr. and Mrs. Auld were both at home, and met me at the door with their little son Thomas, to take care of whom I had been given. And here I saw what I had never seen before; it was a white face beaming with the most kindly emotions; it was the face of my new mistress, Sophia Auld. I wish I could describe the rapture that flashed through my soul as I beheld it. It was a new and strange sight to me, brightening up my pathway with the light of happiness. Little Thomas was told, there was his Freddy,—and I was told to take care of little Thomas; and thus I entered upon the duties of my new home with the most cheering prospect ahead.

I look upon my departure from Colonel Lloyd's plantation as one of the most interesting events of my life. It is possible, and even quite probable, that but for the mere circumstance of being removed from that plantation to Baltimore, I should have to-day, instead of being here seated by my own table, in the enjoyment of freedom and the happiness of home, writing this Narrative, been confined in the galling chains of slavery. Going to live at Baltimore laid the foundation, and opened the gateway, to all my subsequent prosperity. I have ever regarded it as the first plain manifestation of that kind providence which has ever since attended me, and marked my life with so many favors. I regarded the selection of myself as being somewhat remarkable. There were a number of slave children that might have been sent from the plantation to Baltimore. There were those younger, those older, and those of the same age. I was chosen from among them all, and was the first, last, and only choice.

I may be deemed superstitious, and even egotistical, in regarding this event as a special interposition of divine Providence in my favor. But I should be false to the earliest sentiments of my soul, if I suppressed the opinion. I prefer to be true to myself, even at the hazard of incurring the ridicule of others, rather than to be false, and incur my own abhorrence. From my earliest recollection, I date the entertainment of a deep conviction that slavery would not always be able to hold me within its foul embrace; and in the darkest hours of my career in slavery, this living word of faith and spirit of hope departed not from me, but remained like ministering angels to cheer me through the gloom. This good spirit was from God, and to him I offer thanksgiving and praise.

CHAPTER VI

My new mistress proved to be all she appeared when I first met her at the door,—a woman of the kindest heart and finest feelings. She had never had a slave under her control previously to myself, and prior to her marriage she had been dependent upon her own industry for a living. She was by trade a weaver; and by constant application to her business, she had been in a good degree preserved from the blighting and dehumanizing effects of slavery. I was utterly astonished at her goodness. I scarcely knew how to behave towards her. She was entirely unlike any other white woman I had ever seen. I could not approach her as I was accustomed to approach other white ladies. My early instruction was all out of place. The crouching servility, usually so acceptable a quality in a slave, did not answer when manifested toward her. Her favor was not gained by it; she seemed to be disturbed by it. She did not deem it impudent or unmannerly for a slave to look her in the face. The meanest slave was put fully at ease in her presence, and none left without feeling better for having seen her. Her face was made of heavenly smiles, and her voice of tranquil music.

But, alas! this kind heart had but a short time to remain such. The fatal poison of irresponsible power was already in her hands, and soon commenced its infernal work. That cheerful eye, under the influence of slavery, soon became red with rage; that voice, made all of sweet accord, changed to one of harsh and horrid discord; and that angelic face gave place to that of a demon.

Very soon after I went to live with Mr. and Mrs. Auld, she very kindly commenced to teach me the A, B, C. After I had learned this, she assisted me in learning to spell words of three or four letters. Just at this point of my progress, Mr. Auld found out what was going on, and at once forbade Mrs. Auld to instruct me further, telling her, among other things, that it was unlawful, as well as unsafe, to teach a slave to read. To use his own words, further, he said, "If you give a nigger an inch, he will take an ell. A nigger should know nothing but to obey his master—to do as he is told to do. Learning would spoil the best nigger in the world. Now," said he, "if you teach that nigger (speaking of myself) how to read, there would be no keeping him. It would forever unfit him to be a slave. He would at once become unmanageable, and of no value to his master. As to himself, it could do him no good, but a great deal of harm. It would make him discontented and unhappy." These words sank deep into my heart, stirred up sentiments within that lay slumbering, and called into existence an entirely new train of thought. It was a new and special revelation, explaining dark and mysterious things, with which my youthful understanding had struggled, but struggled in vain. I now understood what had been to me a most perplexing difficulty—to wit, the white man's power to enslave the black man. It was a grand achievement, and I prized it highly. From that moment, I understood the pathway from slavery to freedom. It was just what I wanted, and I got it at a time when I the least expected it. Whilst I was saddened by the thought of losing the aid of my kind mistress, I was gladdened by the invaluable instruction which, by the merest accident, I had gained from my master. Though conscious of the difficulty of learning without a teacher, I set out with high hope, and a fixed purpose, at whatever cost of trouble, to learn how to read. The very decided manner with which he spoke, and strove to impress his wife with the evil consequences of giving me instruction, served to convince me that he was deeply sensible of the truths he was uttering. It gave me the best assurance that I might rely with the utmost confidence on the results which, he said, would flow from teaching me to read. What he most dreaded, that I most desired. What he most loved, that I most hated. That which to him was a great evil, to be carefully shunned, was to me a great good, to be diligently sought; and the argument which he so warmly urged, against my learning to read, only served to inspire me with a desire and determination to learn. In learning to read, I owe almost as much to the bitter opposition of my master, as to the kindly aid of my mistress. I acknowledge the benefit of both.

I had resided but a short time in Baltimore before I observed a marked difference, in the treatment of slaves, from that which I had witnessed in the country. A city slave is almost a freeman, compared with a slave on the plantation. He is much better fed and clothed, and enjoys privileges altogether unknown to the slave on the plantation. There is a vestige of decency, a sense of shame, that does much to curb and check those outbreaks of atrocious cruelty so commonly enacted upon the plantation. He is a desperate slaveholder, who will shock the humanity of his non-slaveholding neighbors with the cries of his lacerated slave. Few are willing to incur the odium attaching to the reputation of being a cruel master; and above all things, they would not be known as not giving a slave enough to eat. Every city slaveholder is anxious to have it known of him, that he feeds his slaves well; and it is due to them to say, that most of them do give their slaves enough to eat. There are, however, some painful exceptions to this rule. Directly opposite to us, on Philpot Street, lived Mr. Thomas Hamilton. He owned two slaves. Their names were Henrietta and Mary. Henrietta was about twenty-two years of age, Mary was about fourteen; and of all the mangled and emaciated creatures I ever looked upon, these two were the most so. His heart must be harder than stone, that could look upon these unmoved. The head, neck, and shoulders of Mary were literally cut to pieces. I have frequently felt her head, and found it nearly covered with festering sores, caused by the lash of her cruel mistress. I do not know that her master ever whipped her, but I have been an eye-witness to the cruelty of Mrs. Hamilton. I used to be in Mr. Hamilton's house nearly every day. Mrs. Hamilton used to sit in a large chair in the middle of the room, with a heavy cowskin always by her side, and scarce an hour passed during the day but was marked by the blood of one of these slaves. The girls seldom passed her without her saying, "Move faster, you black gip!" at the same time giving them a blow with the cowskin over the head or shoulders, often drawing the blood. She would then say, "Take that, you black gip!" continuing, "If you don't move faster, I'll move you!" Added to the cruel lashings to which these slaves were subjected, they were kept nearly half-starved. They seldom knew what it was to eat a full meal. I have seen Mary contending with the pigs for the offal thrown into the street. So much was Mary kicked and cut to pieces, that she was oftener called "pecked" than by her name.

CHAPTER VII

I lived in Master Hugh's family about seven years. During this time, I succeeded in learning to read and write. In accomplishing this, I was compelled to resort to various stratagems. I had no regular teacher. My mistress, who had kindly commenced to instruct me, had, in compliance with the advice and direction of her husband, not only ceased to instruct, but had set her face against my being instructed by any one else. It is due, however, to my mistress to say of her, that she did not adopt this course of treatment immediately. She at first lacked the depravity indispensable to shutting me up in mental darkness. It was at least necessary for her to have some training in the exercise of irresponsible power, to make her equal to the task of treating me as though I were a brute.

My mistress was, as I have said, a kind and tender-hearted woman; and in the simplicity of her soul she commenced, when I first went to live with her, to treat me as she supposed one human being ought to treat another. In entering upon the duties of a slaveholder, she did not seem to perceive that I sustained to her the relation of a mere chattel, and that for her to treat me as a human being was not only wrong, but dangerously so. Slavery proved as injurious to her as it did to me. When I went there, she was a pious, warm, and tender-hearted woman. There was no sorrow or suffering for which she had not a tear. She had bread for the hungry, clothes for the naked, and comfort for every mourner that came within her reach. Slavery soon proved its ability to divest her of these heavenly qualities. Under its influence, the tender heart became stone, and the lamblike disposition gave way to one of tiger-like fierceness. The first step in her downward course was in her ceasing to instruct me. She now commenced to practise her husband's precepts. She finally became even more violent in her opposition than her husband himself. She was not satisfied with simply doing as well as he had commanded; she seemed anxious to do better. Nothing seemed to make her more angry than to see me with a newspaper. She seemed to think that here lay the danger. I have had her rush at me with a face made all up of fury, and snatch from me a newspaper, in a manner that fully revealed her apprehension. She was an apt woman; and a little experience soon demonstrated, to her satisfaction, that education and slavery were incompatible with each other.

From this time I was most narrowly watched. If I was in a separate room any considerable length of time, I was sure to be suspected of having a book, and was at once called to give an account of myself. All this, however, was too late. The first step had been taken. Mistress, in teaching me the alphabet, had given me the inch, and no precaution could prevent me from taking the ell.

The plan which I adopted, and the one by which I was most successful, was that of making friends of all the little white boys whom I met in the street. As many of these as I could, I converted into teachers. With their kindly aid, obtained at different times and in different places, I finally succeeded in learning to read. When I was sent of errands, I always took my book with me, and by going one part of my errand quickly, I found time to get a lesson before my return. I used also to carry bread with me, enough of which was always in the house, and to which I was always welcome; for I was much better off in this regard than many of the poor white children in our neighborhood. This bread I used to bestow upon the hungry little urchins, who, in return, would give me that more valuable bread of knowledge. I am strongly tempted to give the names of two or three of those little boys, as a testimonial of the gratitude and affection I bear them; but prudence forbids;—not that it would injure me, but it might embarrass them; for it is almost an unpardonable offence to teach slaves to read in this Christian country. It is enough to say of the dear little fellows, that they lived on Philpot Street, very near Durgin and Bailey's ship-yard. I used to talk this matter of slavery over with them. I would sometimes say to them, I wished I could be as free as they would be when they got to be men. "You will be free as soon as you are twenty-one, but I am a slave for life! Have not I as good a right to be free as you have?" These words used to trouble them; they would express for me the liveliest sympathy, and console me with the hope that something would occur by which I might be free.

I was now about twelve years old, and the thought of being a slave for life began to bear heavily upon my heart. Just about this time, I got hold of a book entitled "The Columbian Orator."[1] Every opportunity I got, I used to read this book. Among much

1 Caleb Bingham (1757–1817) was a white US author of educational tracts including *The Columbian Orator*, an anthology of speeches and essays first published in 1797 that went through multiple editions due to its popularity.

of other interesting matter, I found in it a dialogue between a master and his slave.[1] The slave was represented as having run away from his master three times. The dialogue represented the conversation which took place between them, when the slave was retaken the third time. In this dialogue, the whole argument in behalf of slavery was brought forward by the master, all of which was disposed of by the slave. The slave was made to say some very smart as well as impressive things in reply to his master—things which had the desired though unexpected effect; for the conversation resulted in the voluntary emancipation of the slave on the part of the master.

In the same book, I met with one of Sheridan's mighty speeches on and in behalf of Catholic emancipation.[2] These were choice documents to me. I read them over and over again with unabated interest. They gave tongue to interesting thoughts of my own soul, which had frequently flashed through my mind, and died away for want of utterance. The moral which I gained from the dialogue was the power of truth over the conscience of even a slaveholder. What I got from Sheridan was a bold denunciation of slavery, and a powerful vindication of human rights. The reading of these documents enabled me to utter my thoughts, and to meet the arguments brought forward to sustain slavery; but while they relieved me of one difficulty, they brought on another even more painful than the one of which I was relieved. The more I read, the more I was led to abhor and detest my enslavers. I could regard them in no other light than a band of successful robbers, who had left their homes, and gone to Africa, and stolen us from our homes, and in a strange land reduced us to slavery. I loathed them as being the meanest as well as the most wicked of men. As I read and contemplated the subject, behold! that very discontentment which Master Hugh had predicted would follow my learning to read had already come, to torment and sting my soul to unutterable anguish. As I writhed under it, I would at times feel that learning to read had been a curse rather than a blessing. It had given me a view of my wretched condition, without the remedy. It opened my eyes to the horrible pit, but to no ladder upon which to get out. In moments of agony, I envied my fellow-slaves for their stupidity. I have often wished myself a

---

1 Douglass is referring to the "Dialogue between a Master and Slave" that Bingham included in *The Columbian Orator.*
2 Bingham included Richard Brinsley Sheridan's (1751–1816) "Speech in the British Parliament" in *The Columbian Orator.*

beast. I preferred the condition of the meanest reptile to my own. Any thing, no matter what, to get rid of thinking! It was this ever-lasting thinking of my condition that tormented me. There was no getting rid of it. It was pressed upon me by every object within sight or hearing, animate or inanimate. The silver trump of freedom had roused my soul to eternal wakefulness. Freedom now appeared, to disappear no more forever. It was heard in every sound, and seen in every thing. It was ever present to torment me with a sense of my wretched condition. I saw nothing without seeing it, I heard nothing without hearing it, and felt nothing without feeling it. It looked from every star, it smiled in every calm, breathed in every wind, and moved in every storm.

I often found myself regretting my own existence, and wishing myself dead; and but for the hope of being free, I have no doubt but that I should have killed myself, or done something for which I should have been killed. While in this state of mind, I was eager to hear any one speak of slavery. I was a ready listener. Every little while, I could hear something about the abolitionists. It was some time before I found what the word meant. It was always used in such connections as to make it an interesting word to me. If a slave ran away and succeeded in getting clear, or if a slave killed his master, set fire to a barn, or did any thing very wrong in the mind of a slaveholder, it was spoken of as the fruit of abolition. Hearing the word in this connection very often, I set about learning what it meant. The dictionary afforded me little or no help. I found it was "the act of abolishing;" but then I did not know what was to be abolished. Here I was perplexed. I did not dare to ask any one about its meaning, for I was satisfied that it was something they wanted me to know very little about. After a patient waiting, I got one of our city papers, containing an account of the number of petitions from the north, praying for the abolition of slavery in the District of Columbia, and of the slave trade between the States. From this time I understood the words abolition and abolitionist, and always drew near when that word was spoken, expecting to hear something of importance to myself and fellow-slaves. The light broke in upon me by degrees. I went one day down on the wharf of Mr. Waters; and seeing two Irishmen unloading a scow of stone, I went, unasked, and helped them. When we had finished, one of them came to me and asked me if I were a slave. I told him I was. He asked, "Are ye a slave for life?" I told him that I was. The good Irishman seemed to be deeply affected by the statement. He said to the other that it was a pity so fine a little fellow as myself should be a slave for life. He said it was a shame to hold me. They both advised me to run away to the north; that I should find friends there, and that I should be free. I pretended not to be interested in what they said, and treated them as if I did not understand them; for I feared they might be treacherous. White men have been known to encourage slaves to escape, and then, to get the reward, catch them and return them to their masters. I was afraid that these seemingly good men might use me so; but I nevertheless remembered their advice, and from that time I resolved to run away. I looked forward to a time at which it would be safe for me to escape. I was too young to think of doing so immediately; besides, I wished to learn how to write, as I might have occasion to write my own pass. I consoled myself with the hope that I should one day find a good chance. Meanwhile, I would learn to write.

The idea as to how I might learn to write was suggested to me by being in Durgin and Bailey's ship-yard, and frequently seeing the ship carpenters, after hewing, and getting a piece of timber ready for use, write on the timber the name of that part of the ship for which it was intended. When a piece of timber was intended for the larboard side, it would be marked thus—"L." When a piece was for the starboard side, it would be marked thus—"S." A piece for the larboard side forward, would be marked thus—"L. F." When a piece was for starboard side forward, it would be marked thus—"S. F." For larboard aft, it would be marked thus—"L. A." For starboard aft, it would be marked thus—"S. A." I soon learned the names of these letters, and for what they were intended when placed upon a piece of timber in the ship-yard. I immediately commenced copying them, and in a short time was able to make the four letters named. After that, when I met with any boy who I knew could write, I would tell him I could write as well as he. The next word would be, "I don't believe you. Let me see you try it." I would then make the letters which I had been so fortunate as to learn, and ask him to beat that. In this way I got a good many lessons in writing, which it is quite possible I should never have gotten in any other way. During this time, my copybook was the board fence, brick wall, and pavement; my pen and ink was a lump of chalk. With these, I learned mainly how to write. I then commenced and continued copying the Italics in Webster's Spelling Book,[1] until I could make them all without looking on

---

1 Noah Webster (1758–1842) was a white US educator and author of dictionaries and spelling books including *The American Spelling Book*, first published in 1783.

the book. By this time, my little Master Thomas had gone to school, and learned how to write, and had written over a number of copy-books. These had been brought home, and shown to some of our near neighbors, and then laid aside. My mistress used to go to class meeting at the Wilk Street meetinghouse every Monday afternoon, and leave me to take care of the house. When left thus, I used to spend the time in writing in the spaces left in Master Thomas's copy-book, copying what he had written. I continued to do this until I could write a hand very similar to that of Master Thomas. Thus, after a long, tedious effort for years, I finally succeeded in learning how to write.

CHAPTER VIII

In a very short time after I went to live at Baltimore, my old master's youngest son Richard died; and in about three years and six months after his death, my old master, Captain Anthony, died, leaving only his son, Andrew, and daughter, Lucretia, to share his estate. He died while on a visit to see his daughter at Hillsborough. Cut off thus unexpectedly, he left no will as to the disposal of his property. It was therefore necessary to have a valuation of the property, that it might be equally divided between Mrs. Lucretia and Master Andrew. I was immediately sent for, to be valued with the other property. Here again my feelings rose up in detestation of slavery. I had now a new conception of my degraded condition. Prior to this, I had become, if not insensible to my lot, at least partly so. I left Baltimore with a young heart overborne with sadness, and a soul full of apprehension. I took passage with Captain Rowe, in the schooner Wild Cat, and, after a sail of about twenty-four hours, I found myself near the place of my birth. I had now been absent from it almost, if not quite, five years. I, however, remembered the place very well. I was only about five years old when I left it, to go and live with my old master on Colonel Lloyd's plantation; so that I was now between ten and eleven years old.

We were all ranked together at the valuation. Men and women, old and young, married and single, were ranked with horses, sheep, and swine. There were horses and men, cattle and women, pigs and children, all holding the same rank in the scale of being, and were all subjected to the same narrow examination. Silvery-headed age and sprightly youth, maids and matrons, had to undergo the same indelicate inspection. At this moment, I saw more clearly than ever the brutalizing effects of slavery upon both slave and slaveholder.

After the valuation, then came the division. I have no language to express the high excitement and deep anxiety which were felt among us poor slaves during this time. Our fate for life was now to be decided. We had no more voice in that decision than the brutes among whom we were ranked. A single word from the white men was enough—against all our wishes, prayers, and entreaties—to sunder forever the dearest friends, dearest kindred, and strongest ties known to human beings. In addition to the pain of separation, there was the horrid dread of falling into the hands of Master Andrew. He was known to us all as being a most cruel wretch,—a common drunkard, who had, by his reckless mismanagement and profligate dissipation, already wasted a large portion of his father's property. We all felt that we might as well be sold at once to the Georgia traders, as to pass into his hands; for we knew that that would be our inevitable condition,—a condition held by us all in the utmost horror and dread.

I suffered more anxiety than most of my fellow-slaves. I had known what it was to be kindly treated; they had known nothing of the kind. They had seen little or nothing of the world. They were in very deed men and women of sorrow, and acquainted with grief. Their backs had been made familiar with the bloody lash, so that they had become callous; mine was yet tender; for while at Baltimore I got few whippings, and few slaves could boast of a kinder master and mistress than myself; and the thought of passing out of their hands into those of Master Andrew—a man who, but a few days before, to give me a sample of his bloody disposition, took my little brother by the throat, threw him on the ground, and with the heel of his boot stamped upon his head till the blood gushed from his nose and ears—was well calculated to make me anxious as to my fate. After he had committed this savage outrage upon my brother, he turned to me, and said that was the way he meant to serve me one of these days,—meaning, I suppose, when I came into his possession.

Thanks to a kind Providence, I fell to the portion of Mrs. Lucretia, and was sent immediately back to Baltimore, to live again in the family of Master Hugh. Their joy at my return equalled their sorrow at my departure. It was a glad day to me. I had escaped a worse than lion's jaws. I was absent from Baltimore, for the purpose of valuation and division, just about one month, and it seemed to have been six.

Very soon after my return to Baltimore, my mistress, Lucretia, died, leaving her husband and one child, Amanda; and in a very short time after her death, Master Andrew died. Now all the property of my old master, slaves included, was in the hands of strangers,—strangers who had had nothing to do with accumulating it. Not a slave was left free. All remained slaves, from the youngest to the oldest. If any one thing in my experience, more than another, served to deepen my conviction of the infernal character of slavery, and to fill me with unutterable loathing of slaveholders, it was their base ingratitude to my poor old grandmother. She had served my old master faithfully from youth to old age. She had been the source of all his wealth; she had peopled his plantation with slaves; she had become a great grandmother in his service. She had rocked him in infancy, attended him in childhood, served him through life, and at his death wiped from his icy brow the cold death-sweat, and closed his eyes forever. She was nevertheless left a slave—a slave for life—a slave in the hands of strangers; and in their hands she saw her children, her grandchildren, and her great-grandchildren, divided, like so many sheep, without being gratified with the small privilege of a single word, as to their or her own destiny. And, to cap the climax of their base ingratitude and fiendish barbarity, my grandmother, who was now very old, having outlived my old master and all his children, having seen the beginning and end of all of them, and her present owners finding she was of but little value, her frame already racked with the pains of old age, and complete helplessness fast stealing over her once active limbs, they took her to the woods, built her a little hut, put up a little mud-chimney, and then made her welcome to the privilege of supporting herself there in perfect loneliness; thus virtually turning her out to die! If my poor old grandmother now lives, she lives to suffer in utter loneliness; she lives to remember and mourn over the loss of children, the loss of grandchildren, and the loss of great-grandchildren. They are, in the language of the slave's poet, Whittier,—

"Gone, gone, sold and gone
    To the rice swamp dank and lone,
Where the slave-whip ceaseless swings,
Where the noisome insect stings,
Where the fever-demon strews
Poison with the falling dews,
Where the sickly sunbeams glare
Through the hot and misty air:—

Gone, gone, sold and gone
To the rice swamp dank and lone,
From Virginia hills and waters—
Woe is me, my stolen daughters!"[1]

The hearth is desolate. The children, the unconscious children, who once sang and danced in her presence, are gone. She gropes her way, in the darkness of age, for a drink of water. Instead of the voices of her children, she hears by day the moans of the dove, and by night the screams of the hideous owl. All is gloom. The grave is at the door. And now, when weighed down by the pains and aches of old age, when the head inclines to the feet, when the beginning and ending of human existence meet, and helpless infancy and painful old age combine together—at this time, this most needful time, the time for the exercise of that tenderness and affection which children only can exercise towards a declining parent—my poor old grandmother, the devoted mother of twelve children, is left all alone, in yonder little hut, before a few dim embers. She stands—she sits—she staggers—she falls—she groans—she dies—and there are none of her children or grandchildren present, to wipe from her wrinkled brow the cold sweat of death, or to place beneath the sod her fallen remains. Will not a righteous God visit for these things?

In about two years after the death of Mrs. Lucretia, Master Thomas married his second wife. Her name was Rowena Hamilton. She was the eldest daughter of Mr. William Hamilton. Master now lived in St. Michael's. Not long after his marriage, a misunderstanding took place between himself and Master Hugh; and as a means of punishing his brother, he took me from him to live with himself at St. Michael's. Here I underwent another most painful separation. It, however, was not so severe as the one I dreaded at the division of property; for, during this interval, a great change had taken place in Master Hugh and his once kind and affectionate wife. The influence of brandy upon him, and of slavery upon her, had effected a disastrous change in the characters of both; so that, as far as they were concerned, I thought I had little to lose by the change. But it was not to them that I was

---

1 From John Greenleaf Whittier, "The Farewell of a Virginia Slave
   Mother to Her Daughters Sold into Southern Bondage," *Anti-Slavery
   Poems: Songs of Labor and Reform* (Cambridge, MA: Riverside Press,
   1888). Whittier (1807–92) was a white US poet, radical reformer, and
   prolific author of antislavery writings.

attached. It was to those little Baltimore boys that I felt the strongest attachment. I had received many good lessons from them, and was still receiving them, and the thought of leaving them was painful indeed. I was leaving, too, without the hope of ever being allowed to return. Master Thomas had said he would never let me return again. The barrier betwixt himself and brother he considered impassable.

I then had to regret that I did not at least make the attempt to carry out my resolution to run away; for the chances of success are tenfold greater from the city than from the country.

I sailed from Baltimore for St. Michael's in the sloop Amanda, Captain Edward Dodson. On my passage, I paid particular attention to the direction which the steamboats took to go to Philadelphia. I found, instead of going down, on reaching North Point they went up the bay, in a north-easterly direction. I deemed this knowledge of the utmost importance. My determination to run away was again revived. I resolved to wait only so long as the offering of a favorable opportunity. When that came, I was determined to be off.

CHAPTER IX

I have now reached a period of my life when I can give dates. I left Baltimore, and went to live with Master Thomas Auld, at St. Michael's, in March, 1832. It was now more than seven years since I lived with him in the family of my old master, on Colonel Lloyd's plantation. We of course were now almost entire strangers to each other. He was to me a new master, and I to him a new slave. I was ignorant of his temper and disposition; he was equally so of mine. A very short time, however, brought us into full acquaintance with each other. I was made acquainted with his wife not less than with himself. They were well matched, being equally mean and cruel. I was now, for the first time during a space of more than seven years, made to feel the painful gnawings of hunger—a something which I had not experienced before since I left Colonel Lloyd's plantation. It went hard enough with me then, when I could look back to no period at which I had enjoyed a sufficiency. It was tenfold harder after living in Master Hugh's family, where I had always had enough to eat, and of that which was good. I have said Master Thomas was a mean man. He was so. Not to give a slave enough to eat, is regarded as the most aggravated development of meanness even among slaveholders. The rule is, no matter how coarse the food, only let there be enough of it. This is the theory; and in the part of Maryland from which I came, it is the general practice,—though there are many exceptions. Master Thomas gave us enough of neither coarse nor fine food. There were four slaves of us in the kitchen—my sister Eliza, my aunt Priscilla, Henny, and myself; and we were allowed less than a half of a bushel of corn-meal per week, and very little else, either in the shape of meat or vegetables. It was not enough for us to subsist upon. We were therefore reduced to the wretched necessity of living at the expense of our neighbors. This we did by begging and stealing, whichever came handy in the time of need, the one being considered as legitimate as the other. A great many times have we poor creatures been nearly perishing with hunger, when food in abundance lay mouldering in the safe and smoke-house, and our pious mistress was aware of the fact; and yet that mistress and her husband would kneel every morning, and pray that God would bless them in basket and store!

Bad as all slaveholders are, we seldom meet one destitute of every element of character commanding respect. My master was one of this rare sort. I do not know of one single noble act ever performed by him. The leading trait in his character was meanness; and if there were any other element in his nature, it was made subject to this. He was mean; and, like most other mean men, he lacked the ability to conceal his meanness. Captain Auld was not born a slaveholder. He had been a poor man, master only of a Bay craft. He came into possession of all his slaves by marriage; and of all men, adopted slaveholders are the worst. He was cruel, but cowardly. He commanded without firmness. In the enforcement of his rules, he was at times rigid, and at times lax. At times, he spoke to his slaves with the firmness of Napoleon[1] and the fury of a demon; at other times, he might well be mistaken for an inquirer who had lost his way. He did nothing of himself. He might have passed for a lion, but for his ears. In all things noble which he attempted, his own meanness shone most conspicuous. His airs, words, and actions, were the airs, words, and actions of born slave-

---

1 Napoleon Bonaparte (1769–1821) was a French statesman and military general who ascended to political power to become the first emperor of France in 1804. He is infamous for incarcerating Toussaint Louverture (1743–1803), revolutionary leader of Haiti as the first Black republic in the western hemisphere, in the prison Fort-de-Joux in France in August 1802, which resulted in his death eight months later.

holders, and, being assumed, were awkward enough. He was not even a good imitator. He possessed all the disposition to deceive, but wanted the power. Having no resources within himself, he was compelled to be the copyist of many, and being such, he was forever the victim of inconsistency; and of consequence he was an object of contempt, and was held as such even by his slaves. The luxury of having slaves of his own to wait upon him was something new and unprepared for. He was a slaveholder without the ability to hold slaves. He found himself incapable of managing his slaves either by force, fear, or fraud. We seldom called him "master;" we generally called him "Captain Auld," and were hardly disposed to title him at all. I doubt not that our conduct had much to do with making him appear awkward, and of consequence fretful. Our want of reverence for him must have perplexed him greatly. He wished to have us call him master, but lacked the firmness necessary to command us to do so. His wife used to insist upon our calling him so, but to no purpose. In August, 1832, my master attended a Methodist camp-meeting held in the Bay-side, Talbot county, and there experienced religion. I indulged a faint hope that his conversion would lead him to emancipate his slaves, and that, if he did not do this, it would, at any rate, make him more kind and humane. I was disappointed in both these respects. It neither made him to be humane to his slaves, nor to emancipate them. If it had any effect on his character, it made him more cruel and hateful in all his ways; for I believe him to have been a much worse man after his conversion than before. Prior to his conversion, he relied upon his own depravity to shield and sustain him in his savage barbarity; but after his conversion, he found religious sanction and support for his slaveholding cruelty. He made the greatest pretensions to piety. His house was the house of prayer. He prayed morning, noon, and night. He very soon distinguished himself among his brethren, and was soon made a class-leader and exhorter. His activity in revivals was great, and he proved himself an instrument in the hands of the church in converting many souls. His house was the preachers' home. They used to take great pleasure in coming there to put up; for while he starved us, he stuffed them. We have had three or four preachers there at a time. The names of those who used to come most frequently while I lived there, were Mr. Storks, Mr. Ewery, Mr. Humphry, and Mr. Hickey. I have also seen Mr. George Cookman at our house. We slaves loved Mr. Cookman. We believed him to be a good man. We thought him instrumental in getting Mr. Samuel Harrison, a very rich slaveholder, to emancipate his slaves; and by some means got the impression that he was laboring to effect the emancipation of all the slaves. When he was at our house, we were sure to be called in to prayers. When the others were there, we were sometimes called in and sometimes not. Mr. Cookman took more notice of us than either of the other ministers. He could not come among us without betraying his sympathy for us, and, stupid as we were, we had the sagacity to see it.

While I lived with my master in St. Michael's, there was a white young man, a Mr. Wilson, who proposed to keep a Sabbath school for the instruction of such slaves as might be disposed to learn to read the New Testament. We met but three times, when Mr. West and Mr. Fairbanks, both class-leaders, with many others, came upon us with sticks and other missiles, drove us off, and forbade us to meet again. Thus ended our little Sabbath school in the pious town of St. Michael's.

I have said my master found religious sanction for his cruelty. As an example, I will state one of many facts going to prove the charge. I have seen him tie up a lame young woman, and whip her with a heavy cowskin upon her naked shoulders, causing the warm red blood to drip; and, in justification of the bloody deed, he would quote this passage of Scripture—"He that knoweth his master's will, and doeth it not, shall be beaten with many stripes."[1]

Master would keep this lacerated young woman tied up in this horrid situation four or five hours at a time. I have known him to tie her up early in the morning, and whip her before breakfast; leave her, go to his store, return at dinner, and whip her again, cutting her in the places already made raw with his cruel lash. The secret of master's cruelty toward "Henny" is found in the fact of her being almost helpless. When quite a child, she fell into the fire, and burned herself horribly. Her hands were so burnt that she never got the use of them. She could do very little but bear heavy burdens. She was to master a bill of expense; and as he was a mean man, she was a constant offence to him. He seemed desirous of getting the poor girl out of existence. He gave her away once to his sister; but, being a poor gift, she was not disposed to keep her. Finally, my benevolent master, to use his own words, "set her adrift to take care of herself." Here was a recently-converted man, holding on upon the mother, and at the same time turning out her helpless child, to starve and die! Master Thomas was one of the many pious slaveholders who hold slaves for the very charitable purpose of taking care of them.

1 Luke 12:47.

My master and myself had quite a number of differences. He found me unsuitable to his purpose. My city life, he said, had had a very pernicious effect upon me. It had almost ruined me for every good purpose, and fitted me for every thing which was bad. One of my greatest faults was that of letting his horse run away, and go down to his father-in-law's farm, which was about five miles from St. Michael's. I would then have to go after it. My reason for this kind of carelessness, or carefulness, was, that I could always get something to eat when I went there. Master William Hamilton, my master's father-in-law, always gave his slaves enough to eat. I never left there hungry, no matter how great the need of my speedy return. Master Thomas at length said he would stand it no longer. I had lived with him nine months, during which time he had given me a number of severe whippings, all to no good purpose. He resolved to put me out, as he said, to be broken; and, for this purpose, he let me for one year to a man named Edward Covey. Mr. Covey was a poor man, a farm-renter. He rented the place upon which he lived, as also the hands with which he tilled it. Mr. Covey had acquired a very high reputation for breaking young slaves, and this reputation was of immense value to him. It enabled him to get his farm tilled with much less expense to himself than he could have had it done without such a reputation. Some slaveholders thought it not much loss to allow Mr. Covey to have their slaves one year, for the sake of the training to which they were subjected, without any other compensation. He could hire young help with great ease, in consequence of this reputation. Added to the natural good qualities of Mr. Covey, he was a professor of religion—a pious soul— a member and a class-leader in the Methodist church. All of this added weight to his reputation as a "nigger-breaker." I was aware of all the facts, having been made acquainted with them by a young man who had lived there. I nevertheless made the change gladly; for I was sure of getting enough to eat, which is not the smallest consideration to a hungry man.

CHAPTER X

I had left Master Thomas's house, and went to live with Mr. Covey, on the 1st of January, 1833. I was now, for the first time in my life, a field hand. In my new employment, I found myself even more awkward than a country boy appeared to be in a large city. I had been at my new home but one week before Mr. Covey gave me a very severe whipping, cutting my back, causing the blood to run, and raising ridges on my flesh as large as my little finger. The details of this affair are as follows: Mr. Covey sent me, very early in the morning of one of our coldest days in the month of January, to the woods, to get a load of wood. He gave me a team of unbroken oxen. He told me which was the in-hand ox, and which the off-hand one. He then tied the end of a large rope around the horns of the in-hand ox, and gave me the other end of it, and told me, if the oxen started to run, that I must hold on upon the rope. I had never driven oxen before, and of course I was very awkward. I, however, succeeded in getting to the edge of the woods with little difficulty; but I had got a very few rods into the woods, when the oxen took fright, and started full tilt, carrying the cart against trees, and over stumps, in the most frightful manner. I expected every moment that my brains would be dashed out against the trees. After running thus for a considerable distance, they finally upset the cart, dashing it with great force against a tree, and threw themselves into a dense thicket. How I escaped death, I do not know. There I was, entirely alone, in a thick wood, in a place new to me. My cart was upset and shattered, my oxen were entangled among the young trees, and there was none to help me. After a long spell of effort, I succeeded in getting my cart righted, my oxen disentangled, and again yoked to the cart. I now proceeded with my team to the place where I had, the day before, been chopping wood, and loaded my cart pretty heavily, thinking in this way to tame my oxen. I then proceeded on my way home. I had now consumed one half of the day. I got out of the woods safely, and now felt out of danger. I stopped my oxen to open the woods gate; and just as I did so, before I could get hold of my ox-rope, the oxen again started, rushed through the gate, catching it between the wheel and the body of the cart, tearing it to pieces, and coming within a few inches of crushing me against the gate-post. Thus twice, in one short day, I escaped death by the merest chance. On my return, I told Mr. Covey what had happened, and how it happened. He ordered me to return to the woods again immediately. I did so, and he followed on after me. Just as I got into the woods, he came up and told me to stop my cart, and that he would teach me how to trifle away my time, and break gates. He then went to a large gum-tree, and with his axe cut three large switches, and, after trimming them up neatly with his pocketknife, he ordered me to take off my clothes. I made him no answer, but stood with my clothes on. He repeated his order. I still made him no answer, nor did I move to strip myself. Upon this he rushed at me with the fierceness of a tiger, tore off my clothes, and lashed me till he had worn out his switches, cutting me so savagely as to leave the marks visible for a long time after. This whipping was the first of a number just like it, and for similar offences.

I lived with Mr. Covey one year. During the first six months, of that year, scarce a week passed without his whipping me. I was seldom free from a sore back. My awkwardness was almost always his excuse for whipping me. We were worked fully up to the point of endurance. Long before day we were up, our horses fed, and by the first approach of day we were off to the field with our hoes and ploughing teams. Mr. Covey gave us enough to eat, but scarce time to eat it. We were often less than five minutes taking our meals. We were often in the field from the first approach of day till its last lingering ray had left us; and at saving-fodder time, midnight often caught us in the field binding blades.

Covey would be out with us. The way he used to stand it, was this. He would spend the most of his afternoons in bed. He would then come out fresh in the evening, ready to urge us on with his words, example, and frequently with the whip. Mr. Covey was one of the few slaveholders who could and did work with his hands. He was a hard-working man. He knew by himself just what a man or a boy could do. There was no deceiving him. His work went on in his absence almost as well as in his presence; and he had the faculty of making us feel that he was ever present with us. This he did by surprising us. He seldom approached the spot where we were at work openly, if he could do it secretly. He always aimed at taking us by surprise. Such was his cunning, that we used to call him, among ourselves, "the snake." When we were at work in the cornfield, he would sometimes crawl on his hands and knees to avoid detection, and all at once he would rise nearly in our midst, and scream out, "Ha, ha! Come, come! Dash on, dash on!" This being his mode of attack, it was never safe to stop a single minute. His comings were like a thief in the night. He appeared to us as being ever at hand. He was under every tree, behind every stump, in every bush, and at every window, on the plantation. He would sometimes mount his horse, as if bound to St. Michael's, a distance of seven miles, and in half an hour afterwards you would see him coiled up in the corner of the wood-fence, watching every motion of the slaves. He would, for this purpose, leave his horse tied up in the woods. Again, he would sometimes walk up to us, and give us orders as though he was upon the point of starting on a long journey, turn his back upon us, and make as though he was going to the house to get ready; and, before he would get half way thither, he would turn short and crawl into a fence-corner, or behind some tree, and there watch us till the going down of the sun.

Mr. Covey's forte consisted in his power to deceive. His life was devoted to planning and perpetrating the grossest deceptions. Every thing he possessed in the shape of learning or religion, he made conform to his disposition to deceive. He seemed to think himself equal to deceiving the Almighty. He would make a short prayer in the morning, and a long prayer at night; and, strange as it may seem, few men would at times appear more devotional than he. The exercises of his family devotions were always commenced with singing; and, as he was a very poor singer himself, the duty of raising the hymn generally came upon me. He would read his hymn, and nod at me to commence. I would at times do so; at others, I would not. My non-compliance would almost always produce much confusion. To show himself independent of me, he would start and stagger through with his hymn in the most discordant manner. In this state of mind, he prayed with more than ordinary spirit. Poor man! such was his disposition, and success at deceiving, I do verily believe that he sometimes deceived himself into the solemn belief, that he was a sincere worshipper of the most high God; and this, too, at a time when he may be said to have been guilty of compelling his woman slave to commit the sin of adultery. The facts in the case are these: Mr. Covey was a poor man; he was just commencing in life; he was only able to buy one slave; and, shocking as is the fact, he bought her, as he said, for a breeder. This woman was named Caroline. Mr. Covey bought her from Mr. Thomas Lowe, about six miles from St. Michael's. She was a large, able-bodied woman, about twenty years old. She had already given birth to one child, which proved her to be just what he wanted. After buying her, he hired a married man of Mr. Samuel Harrison, to live with him one year; and him he used to fasten up with her every night! The result was, that, at the end of the year, the miserable woman gave birth to twins. At this result Mr. Covey seemed to be highly pleased, both with the man and the wretched woman. Such was his joy, and that of his wife, that nothing they could do for Caroline during her confinement was too good, or too hard, to be done. The children were regarded as being quite an addition to his wealth.

If at any one time of my life more than another, I was made to drink the bitterest dregs of slavery, that time was during the first six months of my stay with Mr. Covey. We were worked in all weathers. It was never too hot or too cold; it could never rain, blow, hail, or snow, too hard for us to work in the field. Work, work, work, was scarcely more the order of the day than of the night. The longest days were too short for him, and the shortest nights too long for him. I was somewhat unmanageable when I first went there, but a few months of this discipline tamed me. Mr. Covey succeeded in breaking me. I was broken in body, soul, and spirit. My natural elasticity was crushed, my intellect languished, the disposition to read departed, the cheerful spark that lingered about my eye died; the dark night of slavery closed in upon me; and behold a man transformed into a brute!

Sunday was my only leisure time. I spent this in a sort of beast-like stupor, between sleep and wake, under some large tree. At times I would rise up, a flash of energetic freedom would dart through my soul, accompanied with a faint beam of hope, that flickered for a moment, and then vanished. I sank down again, mourning over my wretched condition. I was sometimes prompted to take my life, and that of Covey, but was prevented by a combination of hope and fear. My sufferings on this plantation seem now like a dream rather than a stern reality.

Our house stood within a few rods of the Chesapeake Bay, whose broad bosom was ever white with sails from every quarter of the habitable globe. Those beautiful vessels, robed in purest white, so delightful to the eye of freemen, were to me so many shrouded ghosts, to terrify and torment me with thoughts of my wretched condition. I have often, in the deep stillness of a summer's Sabbath, stood all alone upon the lofty banks of that noble bay, and traced, with saddened heart and tearful eye, the countless number of sails moving off to the mighty ocean. The sight of these always affected me powerfully. My thoughts would compel utterance; and there, with no audience but the Almighty, I would pour out my soul's complaint, in my rude way, with an apostrophe to the moving multitude of ships:—

"You are loosed from your moorings, and are free; I am fast in my chains, and am a slave! You move merrily before the gentle gale, and I sadly before the bloody whip! You are freedom's swift-winged angels, that fly round the world; I am confined in bands of iron! O that I were free! O, that I were on one of your gallant decks, and under your protecting wing! Alas! betwixt me and you, the turbid waters roll. Go on, go on. O that I could also go!

Could I but swim! If I could fly! O, why was I born a man, of whom to make a brute! The glad ship is gone; she hides in the dim distance. I am left in the hottest hell of unending slavery. O God, save me! God, deliver me! Let me be free! Is there any God? Why am I a slave? I will run away. I will not stand it. Get caught, or get clear, I'll try it. I had as well die with ague as the fever. I have only one life to lose. I had as well be killed running as die standing. Only think of it; one hundred miles straight north, and I am free! Try it? Yes! God helping me, I will. It cannot be that I shall live and die a slave. I will take to the water. This very bay shall yet bear me into freedom. The steamboats steered in a north-east course from North Point. I will do the same; and when I get to the head of the bay, I will turn my canoe adrift, and walk straight through Delaware into Pennsylvania. When I get there, I shall not be required to have a pass; I can travel without being disturbed. Let but the first opportunity offer, and, come what will, I am off. Meanwhile, I will try to bear up under the yoke. I am not the only slave in the world. Why should I fret? I can bear as much as any of them. Besides, I am but a boy, and all boys are bound to some one. It may be that my misery in slavery will only increase my happiness when I get free. There is a better day coming."

Thus I used to think, and thus I used to speak to myself; goaded almost to madness at one moment, and at the next reconciling myself to my wretched lot.

I have already intimated that my condition was much worse, during the first six months of my stay at Mr. Covey's, than in the last six. The circumstances leading to the change in Mr. Covey's course toward me form an epoch in my humble history. You have seen how a man was made a slave; you shall see how a slave was made a man. On one of the hottest days of the month of August, 1833, Bill Smith, William Hughes, a slave named Eli, and myself, were engaged in fanning wheat. Hughes was clearing the fanned wheat from before the fan. Eli was turning, Smith was feeding, and I was carrying wheat to the fan. The work was simple, requiring strength rather than intellect; yet, to one entirely unused to such work, it came very hard. About three o'clock of that day, I broke down; my strength failed me; I was seized with a violent aching of the head, attended with extreme dizziness; I trembled in every limb. Finding what was coming, I nerved myself up, feeling it would never do to stop work. I stood as long as I could stagger to the hopper with grain. When I could stand no longer, I fell, and felt as if held down by an immense weight. The fan of course stopped; every one had his own work to do; and no one could do the work of the other, and have his own go on at the same time.

Mr. Covey was at the house, about one hundred yards from the treading-yard where we were fanning. On hearing the fan stop, he left immediately, and came to the spot where we were. He hastily inquired what the matter was. Bill answered that I was sick, and there was no one to bring wheat to the fan. I had by this time crawled away under the side of the post and rail-fence by which the yard was enclosed, hoping to find relief by getting out of the sun. He then asked where I was. He was told by one of the hands. He came to the spot, and, after looking at me awhile, asked me what was the matter. I told him as well as I could, for I scarce had strength to speak. He then gave me a savage kick in the side, and told me to get up. I tried to do so, but fell back in the attempt. He gave me another kick, and again told me to rise. I again tried, and succeeded in gaining my feet; but, stooping to get the tub with which I was feeding the fan, I again staggered and fell. While down in this situation, Mr. Covey took up the hickory slat with which Hughes had been striking off the half-bushel measure, and with it gave me a heavy blow upon the head, making a large wound, and the blood ran freely; and with this again told me to get up. I made no effort to comply, having now made up my mind to let him do his worst. In a short time after receiving this blow, my head grew better. Mr. Covey had now left me to my fate. At this moment I resolved, for the first time, to go to my master, enter a complaint, and ask his protection. In order to do this, I must that afternoon walk seven miles; and this, under the circumstances, was truly a severe undertaking. I was exceedingly feeble; made so as much by the kicks and blows which I received, as by the severe fit of sickness to which I had been subjected. I, however, watched my chance, while Covey was looking in an opposite direction, and started for St. Michael's. I succeeded in getting a considerable distance on my way to the woods, when Covey discovered me, and called after me to come back, threatening what he would do if I did not come. I disregarded both his calls and his threats, and made my way to the woods as fast as my feeble state would allow; and thinking I might be overhauled by him if I kept the road, I walked through the woods, keeping far enough from the road to avoid detection, and near enough to prevent losing my way. I had not gone far before my little strength again failed me. I could go no farther. I fell down, and lay for a considerable time. The blood was yet oozing from the wound on my head. For a time I thought I should bleed to death; and think now that I should have done so, but that the blood so matted my hair as to stop the wound. After lying there about three quarters of an hour, I nerved myself up again, and started on my way, through bogs and briers, barefooted and bareheaded, tearing my feet sometimes at nearly every step; and after a journey of about seven miles, occupying some five hours to perform it, I arrived at master's store. I then presented an appearance enough to affect any but a heart of iron. From the crown of my head to my feet, I was covered with blood. My hair was all clotted with dust and blood; my shirt was stiff with blood. I suppose I looked like a man who had escaped a den of wild beasts, and barely escaped them. In this state I appeared before my master, humbly entreating him to interpose his authority for my protection. I told him all the circumstances as well as I could, and it seemed, as I spoke, at times to affect him. He would then walk the floor, and seek to justify Covey by saying he expected I deserved it. He asked me what I wanted. I told him, to let me get a new home; that as sure as I lived with Mr. Covey again, I should live with but to die with him; that Covey would surely kill me; he was in a fair way for it. Master Thomas ridiculed the idea that there was any danger of Mr. Covey's killing me, and said that he knew Mr. Covey; that he was a good man, and that he could not think of taking me from him; that, should he do so, he would lose the whole year's wages; that I belonged to Mr. Covey for one year, and that I must go back to him, come what might; and that I must not trouble him with any more stories, or that he would himself get hold of me. After threatening me thus, he gave me a very large dose of salts, telling me that I might remain in St. Michael's that night, (it being quite late,) but that I must be off back to Mr. Covey's early in the morning; and that if I did not, he would get hold of me, which meant that he would whip me. I remained all night, and, according to his orders, I started off to Covey's in the morning, (Saturday morning,) wearied in body and broken in spirit. I got no supper that night, or breakfast that morning. I reached Covey's about nine o'clock; and just as I was getting over the fence that divided Mrs. Kemp's fields from ours, out ran Covey with his cowskin, to give me another whipping. Before he could reach me, I succeeded in getting to the cornfield; and as the corn was very high, it afforded me the means of hiding. He seemed very angry, and searched for me a long time. My behavior was altogether unaccountable. He finally gave up the chase, thinking, I suppose, that I must come home for something to eat; he would give himself no further trouble in looking for me. I spent that day mostly in the woods, having the alternative before me,—to go home and be whipped to death, or stay in the woods and be starved to death. That night, I fell in with Sandy Jenkins, a slave with whom I was somewhat acquainted. Sandy had a free wife who lived about four miles from Mr. Covey's; and it being Saturday, he was on his way to see her. I told him my circumstances, and he very kindly invited me to go home with him. I went home with him, and talked this whole matter over, and got his advice as to what course it was best for me to pursue. I found Sandy an old adviser. He told me, with great solemnity, I must go back to Covey; but that before I went, I must go with him into another part of the woods, where there was a certain root, which, if I would take some of it with me, carrying it always on my right side, would render it impossible for Mr. Covey, or any other white man, to whip me. He said he had carried it for years; and since he had done so, he had never received a blow, and never expected to while he carried it. I at first rejected the idea, that the simple carrying of a root in my pocket would have any such effect as he had said, and was not disposed to take it; but Sandy impressed the necessity with much earnestness, telling me it could do no harm, if it did no good. To please him, I at length took the root, and, according to his direction, carried it upon my right side. This was Sunday morning. I immediately started for home; and upon entering the yard gate, out came Mr. Covey on his way to meeting. He spoke to me very kindly, bade me drive the pigs from a lot near by, and passed on towards the church. Now, this singular conduct of Mr. Covey really made me begin to think that there was something in the root which Sandy had given me; and had it been on any other day than Sunday, I could have attributed the conduct to no other cause than the influence of that root; and as it was, I was half inclined to think the root to be something more than I at first had taken it to be. All went well till Monday morning. On this morning, the virtue of the root was fully tested. Long before daylight, I was called to go and rub, curry, and feed, the horses. I obeyed, and was glad to obey. But whilst thus engaged, whilst in the act of throwing down some blades from the loft, Mr. Covey entered the stable with a long rope; and just as I was half out of the loft, he caught hold of my legs, and was about tying me. As soon as I found what he was up to, I gave a sudden spring, and as I did so, he holding to my legs, I was brought sprawling on the stable floor. Mr. Covey seemed now to think he had me, and could do what he pleased; but at this moment—from whence came the spirit I don't know—I resolved to fight; and, suiting my action to the resolution, I seized Covey hard by the throat; and as I did so, I rose. He held on to me, and I to him. My resistance was so entirely unexpected that Covey seemed taken all aback. He trembled like a leaf. This gave me assurance, and I held him uneasy, causing the blood to run where I touched him with the ends of my fingers. Mr. Covey soon called out to Hughes for help. Hughes came, and, while Covey held me, attempted to tie my right hand. While he was in the act of doing so, I watched my chance, and gave him a heavy kick close under the ribs. This kick fairly sickened Hughes, so that he left me in the hands of Mr. Covey. This kick had the effect of not only weakening Hughes, but Covey also. When he saw Hughes bending over with pain, his courage quailed. He asked me if I meant to persist in my resistance. I told him I did, come what might; that he had used me like a brute for six months, and that I was determined to be used so no longer. With that, he strove to drag me to a stick that was lying just out of the stable door. He meant to knock me down. But just as he was leaning over to get the stick, I seized him with both hands by his collar, and brought him by a sudden snatch to the ground. By this time, Bill came. Covey called upon him for assistance. Bill wanted to know what he could do. Covey said, "Take hold of him, take hold of him!" Bill said his master hired him out to work, and not to help to whip me; so he left Covey and myself to fight our own battle out. We were at it for nearly two hours. Covey at length let me go, puffing and blowing at a great rate, saying that if I had not resisted, he would not have whipped me half so much. The truth was, that he had not whipped me at all. I considered him as getting entirely the worst end of the bargain; for he had drawn no blood from me, but I had from him. The whole six months afterwards, that I spent with Mr. Covey, he never laid the weight of his finger upon me in anger. He would occasionally say, he didn't want to get hold of me again. "No," thought I, "you need not; for you will come off worse than you did before."

This battle with Mr. Covey was the turning-point in my career as a slave. It rekindled the few expiring embers of freedom, and revived within me a sense of my own manhood. It recalled the departed self-confidence, and inspired me again with a determination to be free. The gratification afforded by the triumph was a full compensation for whatever else might follow, even death itself. He only can understand the deep satisfaction which I experienced, who has himself repelled by force the bloody arm of slavery. I felt as I never felt before. It was a glorious resurrection, from the tomb of slavery, to the heaven of freedom. My long-crushed spirit rose, cowardice departed, bold defiance took its place; and I now resolved that, however long I might remain a slave in form, the day had passed forever when I could be a slave in fact. I did not hesitate to let it be known of me, that the white man who expected to succeed in whipping, must also succeed in killing me.

From this time I was never again what might be called fairly whipped, though I remained a slave four years afterwards. I had several fights, but was never whipped.

It was for a long time a matter of surprise to me why Mr. Covey did not immediately have me taken by the constable to the whipping-post, and there regularly whipped for the crime of raising my hand against a white man in defence of myself. And the only explanation I can now think of does not entirely satisfy me; but such as it is, I will give it. Mr. Covey enjoyed the most unbounded reputation for being a first-rate overseer and negro-breaker. It was of considerable importance to him. That reputation was at stake; and had he sent me—a boy about sixteen years old—to the public whipping-post, his reputation would have been lost; so, to save his reputation, he suffered me to go unpunished.

My term of actual service to Mr. Edward Covey ended on Christmas day, 1833. The days between Christmas and New Year's day are allowed as holidays; and, accordingly, we were not required to perform any labor, more than to feed and take care of the stock. This time we regarded as our own, by the grace of our masters; and we therefore used or abused it nearly as we pleased. Those of us who had families at a distance, were generally allowed to spend the whole six days in their society. This time, however, was spent in various ways. The staid, sober, thinking and industrious ones of our number would employ themselves in making corn-brooms, mats, horse-collars, and baskets; and another class of us would spend the time in hunting opossums, hares, and coons. But by far the larger part engaged in such sports and merriments as playing ball, wrestling, running foot-races, fiddling, dancing, and drinking whisky; and this latter mode of spending the time was by far the most agreeable to the feelings of our masters. A slave who would work during the holidays was considered by our masters as scarcely deserving them. He was regarded as one who rejected the favor of his master. It was deemed a disgrace not to get drunk at Christmas; and he was regarded as lazy indeed, who had not provided himself with the necessary means, during the year, to get whisky enough to last him through Christmas.

From what I know of the effect of these holidays upon the slave, I believe them to be among the most effective means in the hands of the slaveholder in keeping down the spirit of insurrection. Were the slaveholders at once to abandon this practice, I have not the slightest doubt it would lead to an immediate insurrection among the slaves. These holidays serve as conductors, or safety-valves, to carry off the rebellious spirit of enslaved humanity. But for these, the slave would be forced up to the wildest desperation; and woe betide the slaveholder, the day he ventures to remove or hinder the operation of those conductors! I warn him that, in such an event, a spirit will go forth in their midst, more to be dreaded than the most appalling earthquake.

The holidays are part and parcel of the gross fraud, wrong, and inhumanity of slavery. They are professedly a custom established by the benevolence of the slaveholders; but I undertake to say, it is the result of selfishness, and one of the grossest frauds committed upon the down-trodden slave. They do not give the slaves this time because they would not like to have their work during its continuance, but because they know it would be unsafe to deprive them of it. This will be seen by the fact, that the slaveholders like to have their slaves spend those days just in such a manner as to make them as glad of their ending as of their beginning. Their object seems to be, to disgust their slaves with freedom, by plunging them into the lowest depths of dissipation. For instance, the slaveholders not only like to see the slave drink of his own accord, but will adopt various plans to make him drunk. One plan is, to make bets on their slaves, as to who can drink the most whisky without getting drunk; and in this way they succeed in getting whole multitudes to drink to excess. Thus, when the slave asks for virtuous freedom, the cunning slaveholder, knowing his ignorance, cheats him with a dose of vicious dissipation, artfully labelled with the name of liberty. The most of us used to drink it down, and the result was just what might be supposed; many of us were led to think that there was little to choose between liberty and slavery. We felt, and very properly too, that we had almost as well be slaves to man as to rum. So, when the holidays ended, we staggered up from the filth of our wallowing, took a long breath, and marched to the field,— feeling, upon the whole, rather glad to go, from what our master had deceived us into a belief was freedom, back to the arms of slavery.

I have said that this mode of treatment is a part of the whole system of fraud and inhumanity of slavery. It is so. The mode here adopted to disgust the slave with freedom, by allowing him to see only the abuse of it, is carried out in other things. For instance, a slave loves molasses; he steals some. His master, in many cases, goes off to town, and buys a large quantity; he returns, takes his whip, and commands the slave to eat the molasses, until the poor fellow is made sick at the very mention of it. The same mode is sometimes adopted to make the slaves refrain from asking for more food than their regular allowance. A slave runs through his allowance, and applies for more. His master is enraged at him; but, not willing to send him off without food, gives him more than is necessary, and compels him to eat it within a given time. Then, if he complains that he cannot eat it, he is said to be satisfied neither full nor fasting, and is whipped for being hard to please! I have an abundance of such illustrations of the same principle, drawn from my own observation, but think the cases I have cited sufficient. The practice is a very common one.

On the first of January, 1834, I left Mr. Covey, and went to live with Mr. William Freeland, who lived about three miles from St. Michael's. I soon found Mr. Freeland a very different man from Mr. Covey. Though not rich, he was what would be called an educated southern gentleman. Mr. Covey, as I have shown, was a well-trained negro-breaker and slave-driver. The former (slaveholder though he was) seemed to possess some regard for honor, some reverence for justice, and some respect for humanity. The latter seemed totally insensible to all such sentiments. Mr. Freeland had many of the faults peculiar to slaveholders, such as being very passionate and fretful; but I must do him the justice to say, that he was exceedingly free from those degrading vices to which Mr. Covey was constantly addicted. The one was open and frank, and we always knew where to find him. The other was a most artful deceiver, and could be understood only by such as were skilful enough to detect his cunningly-devised frauds. Another advantage I gained in my new master was, he made no pretensions to, or profession of, religion; and this, in my opinion, was truly a great advantage. I assert most unhesitatingly, that the religion of the south is a mere covering for the most horrid crimes,—a justifier of the most appalling barbarity,—a sanctifier of the most hateful frauds,—and a dark shelter under, which the darkest, foulest, grossest, and most infernal deeds of slaveholders find the strongest protection. Were I to be again reduced to the chains of slavery, next to that enslavement, I should regard being the slave of a religious master the greatest calamity that could befall me. For of all slaveholders with whom I have ever met, religious slaveholders are the worst. I have ever found them the meanest and basest, the most cruel and cowardly, of all others. It was my unhappy lot not only to belong to a religious slaveholder, but to live in a community of such religionists. Very near Mr. Freeland lived the Rev. Daniel Weeden, and in the same neighborhood lived the Rev. Rigby Hopkins. These were members and ministers in the Reformed Methodist Church. Mr. Weeden owned, among others, a woman slave, whose name I have forgotten. This woman's back, for weeks, was kept literally raw, made so by the lash of this merciless, religious wretch. He used to hire hands. His maxim was, Behave well or behave ill, it is the duty of a master occasionally to whip a slave, to remind him of his master's authority. Such was his theory, and such his practice.

Mr. Hopkins was even worse than Mr. Weeden. His chief boast was his ability to manage slaves. The peculiar feature of his government was that of whipping slaves in advance of deserving it. He always managed to have one or more of his slaves to whip every Monday morning. He did this to alarm their fears, and strike terror into those who escaped. His plan was to whip for the smallest offences, to prevent the commission of large ones. Mr. Hopkins could always find some excuse for whipping a slave. It would astonish one, unaccustomed to a slaveholding life, to see with what wonderful ease a slaveholder can find things, of which to make occasion to whip a slave. A mere look, word, or motion,—a mistake, accident, or want of power,—are all matters for which a slave may be whipped at any time. Does a slave look dissatisfied? It is said, he has the devil in him, and it must be whipped out. Does he speak loudly when spoken to by his master? Then he is getting high-minded, and should be taken down a button-hole lower. Does he forget to pull off his hat at the approach of a white person? Then he is wanting in reverence, and should be whipped for it. Does he ever venture to vindicate his conduct, when censured for it? Then he is guilty of impudence,— one of the greatest crimes of which a slave can be guilty. Does he ever venture to suggest a different mode of doing things from that pointed out by his master? He is indeed presumptuous, and getting above himself; and nothing less than a flogging will do for him. Does he, while ploughing, break a plough,—or, while hoeing, break a hoe? It is owing to his carelessness, and for it a slave must always be whipped. Mr. Hopkins could always find something of this sort to justify the use of the lash, and he seldom failed to embrace such opportunities. There was not a man in the whole county, with whom the slaves who had the getting their own home, would not prefer to live, rather than with this Rev. Mr. Hopkins. And yet there was not a man any where round, who made higher professions of religion, or was more active in revivals,—more attentive to the class, love-feast, prayer and preaching meetings, or more devotional in his family,—that prayed earlier, later, louder, and longer,—than this same reverend slave-driver, Rigby Hopkins.

But to return to Mr. Freeland, and to my experience while in his employment. He, like Mr. Covey, gave us enough to eat; but, unlike Mr. Covey, he also gave us sufficient time to take our meals. He worked us hard, but always between sunrise and sunset. He required a good deal of work to be done, but gave us good tools with which to work. His farm was large, but he employed hands enough to work it, and with ease, compared with many of his neighbors. My treatment, while in his employment, was heavenly, compared with what I experienced at the hands of Mr. Edward Covey.

Mr. Freeland was himself the owner of but two slaves. Their names were Henry Harris and John Harris. The rest of his hands he hired. These consisted of myself, Sandy Jenkins,[1] and Handy Caldwell. Henry and John were quite intelligent, and in a very little while after I went there, I succeeded in creating in them a strong desire to learn how to read. This desire soon sprang up in the others also. They very soon mustered up some old spelling-books, and nothing would do but that I must keep a Sabbath school. I agreed to do so, and accordingly devoted my Sundays to teaching these my loved fellow-slaves how to read. Neither of them knew his letters when I went there. Some of the slaves of the neighboring farms found what was going on, and also availed themselves of this little opportunity to learn to read. It was understood, among all who came, that there must be as little display about it as possible. It was necessary to keep our religious

---

1 [Douglass's note:] This is the same man who gave me the roots to prevent my being whipped by Mr. Covey. He was "a clever soul." We used frequently to talk about the fight with Covey, and as often as we did so, he would claim my success as the result of the roots which he gave me. This superstition is very common among the more ignorant slaves. A slave seldom dies but that his death is attributed to trickery.

masters at St. Michael's unacquainted with the fact, that, instead of spending the Sabbath in wrestling, boxing, and drinking whisky, we were trying to learn how to read the will of God; for they had much rather see us engaged in those degrading sports, than to see us behaving like intellectual, moral, and accountable beings. My blood boils as I think of the bloody manner in which Messrs. Wright Fairbanks and Garrison West, both class-leaders, in connection with many others, rushed in upon us with sticks and stones, and broke up our virtuous little Sabbath school, at St. Michael's—all calling themselves Christians! humble followers of the Lord Jesus Christ! But I am again digressing.

I held my Sabbath school at the house of a free colored man, whose name I deem it imprudent to mention; for should it be known, it might embarrass him greatly, though the crime of holding the school was committed ten years ago. I had at one time over forty scholars, and those of the right sort, ardently desiring to learn. They were of all ages, though mostly men and women. I look back to those Sundays with an amount of pleasure not to be expressed. They were great days to my soul. The work of instructing my dear fellow-slaves was the sweetest engagement with which I was ever blessed. We loved each other, and to leave them at the close of the Sabbath was a severe cross indeed. When I think that these precious souls are to-day shut up in the prison-house of slavery, my feelings overcome me, and I am almost ready to ask, "Does a righteous God govern the universe? and for what does he hold the thunders in his right hand, if not to smite the oppressor, and deliver the spoiled out of the hand of the spoiler?" These dear souls came not to Sabbath school because it was popular to do so, nor did I teach them because it was reputable to be thus engaged. Every moment they spent in that school, they were liable to be taken up, and given thirty-nine lashes. They came because they wished to learn. Their minds had been starved by their cruel masters. They had been shut up in mental darkness. I taught them, because it was the delight of my soul to be doing something that looked like bettering the condition of my race. I kept up my school nearly the whole year I lived with Mr. Freeland; and, beside my Sabbath school, I devoted three evenings in the week, during the winter, to teaching the slaves at home. And I have the happiness to know, that several of those who came to Sabbath school learned how to read; and that one, at least, is now free through my agency.

The year passed off smoothly. It seemed only about half as long as the year which preceded it. I went through it without receiving a single blow. I will give Mr. Freeland the credit of being the best master I ever had, till I became my own master. For the ease with which I passed the year, I was, however, somewhat indebted to the society of my fellow-slaves. They were noble souls; they not only possessed loving hearts, but brave ones. We were linked and interlinked with each other. I loved them with a love stronger than any thing I have experienced since. It is sometimes said that we slaves do not love and confide in each other. In answer to this assertion, I can say, I never loved any or confided in any people more than my fellow-slaves, and especially those with whom I lived at Mr. Freeland's. I believe we would have died for each other. We never undertook to do any thing, of any importance, without a mutual consultation. We never moved separately. We were one; and as much so by our tempers and dispositions, as by the mutual hardships to which we were necessarily subjected by our condition as slaves.

At the close of the year 1834, Mr. Freeland again hired me of my master, for the year 1835. But, by this time, I began to want to live upon free land as well as with Freeland; and I was no longer content, therefore, to live with him or any other slaveholder. I began, with the commencement of the year, to prepare myself for a final struggle, which should decide my fate one way or the other. My tendency was upward. I was fast approaching manhood, and year after year had passed, and I was still a slave. These thoughts roused me—I must do something. I therefore resolved that 1835 should not pass without witnessing an attempt, on my part, to secure my liberty. But I was not willing to cherish this determination alone. My fellow-slaves were dear to me. I was anxious to have them participate with me in this, my life-giving determination. I therefore, though with great prudence, commenced early to ascertain their views and feelings in regard to their condition, and to imbue their minds with thoughts of freedom. I bent myself to devising ways and means for our escape, and meanwhile strove, on all fitting occasions, to impress them with the gross fraud and inhumanity of slavery. I went first to Henry, next to John, then to the others. I found, in them all, warm hearts and noble spirits. They were ready to hear, and ready to act when a feasible plan should be proposed. This was what I wanted. I talked to them of our want of manhood, if we submitted to our enslavement without at least one noble effort to be free. We met often, and consulted frequently, and told our hopes and fears, recounted the difficulties, real and imagined, which we should be called on to meet. At times we were almost disposed to give up, and try to content ourselves with our wretched lot; at others, we were firm and unbending in our determination to go. Whenever we suggested any plan, there was shrinking—the odds were fearful. Our path was beset with the greatest obstacles; and if we succeeded in gaining the end of it, our right to be free was yet questionable—we were yet liable to be returned to bondage. We could see no spot, this side of the ocean, where we could be free. We knew nothing about Canada. Our knowledge of the north did not extend farther than New York; and to go there, and be forever harassed with the frightful liability of being returned to slavery—with the certainty of being treated tenfold worse than before—the thought was truly a horrible one, and one which it was not easy to overcome. The case sometimes stood thus: At every gate through which we were to pass, we saw a watchman—at every ferry a guard—on every bridge a sentinel—and in every wood a patrol. We were hemmed in upon every side. Here were the difficulties, real or imagined—the good to be sought, and the evil to be shunned. On the one hand, there stood slavery, a stern reality, glaring frightfully upon us,—its robes already crimsoned with the blood of millions, and even now feasting itself greedily upon our own flesh. On the other hand, away back in the dim distance, under the flickering light of the north star, behind some craggy hill or snow-covered mountain, stood a doubtful freedom—half frozen—beckoning us to come and share its hospitality. This in itself was sometimes enough to stagger us; but when we permitted ourselves to survey the road, we were frequently appalled. Upon either side we saw grim death, assuming the most horrid shapes. Now it was starvation, causing us to eat our own flesh;—now we were contending with the waves, and were drowned;—now we were overtaken, and torn to pieces by the fangs of the terrible bloodhound. We were stung by scorpions, chased by wild beasts, bitten by snakes, and finally, after having nearly reached the desired spot,—after swimming rivers, encountering wild beasts, sleeping in the woods, suffering hunger and nakedness,—we were overtaken by our pursuers, and, in our resistance, we were shot dead upon the spot! I say, this picture sometimes appalled us, and made us

> "rather bear those ills we had,
> Than fly to others, that we knew not of."[1]

---

1 *Hamlet* 3.1.81–82.

In coming to a fixed determination to run away, we did more than Patrick Henry, when he resolved upon liberty or death. With us it was a doubtful liberty at most, and almost certain death if we failed. For my part, I should prefer death to hopeless bondage.

Sandy, one of our number, gave up the notion, but still encouraged us. Our company then consisted of Henry Harris, John Harris, Henry Bailey, Charles Roberts, and myself. Henry Bailey was my uncle, and belonged to my master. Charles married my aunt: he belonged to my master's father-in-law, Mr. William Hamilton.

The plan we finally concluded upon was, to get a large canoe belonging to Mr. Hamilton, and upon the Saturday night previous to Easter holidays, paddle directly up the Chesapeake Bay. On our arrival at the head of the bay, a distance of seventy or eighty miles from where we lived, it was our purpose to turn our canoe adrift, and follow the guidance of the north star till we got beyond the limits of Maryland. Our reason for taking the water route was, that we were less liable to be suspected as runaways; we hoped to be regarded as fishermen; whereas, if we should take the land route, we should be subjected to interruptions of almost every kind. Any one having a white face, and being so disposed, could stop us, and subject us to examination.

The week before our intended start, I wrote several protections, one for each of us. As well as I can remember, they were in the following words, to wit:—

"This is to certify that I, the undersigned, have given the bearer, my servant, full liberty to go to Baltimore, and spend the Easter holidays. Written with mine own hand, &c., 1835.

"WILLIAM HAMILTON,

"Near St. Michael's, in Talbot county, Maryland."

We were not going to Baltimore; but, in going up the bay, we went toward Baltimore, and these protections were only intended to protect us while on the bay.

As the time drew near for our departure, our anxiety became more and more intense. It was truly a matter of life and death with us. The strength of our determination was about to be fully tested. At this time, I was very active in explaining every difficulty, removing every doubt, dispelling every fear, and inspiring all with the firmness indispensable to success in our undertaking; assuring them that half was gained the instant we made the move;

we had talked long enough; we were now ready to move; if not now, we never should be; and if we did not intend to move now, we had as well fold our arms, sit down, and acknowledge ourselves fit only to be slaves. This, none of us were prepared to acknowledge. Every man stood firm; and at our last meeting, we pledged ourselves afresh, in the most solemn manner, that, at the time appointed, we would certainly start in pursuit of freedom. This was in the middle of the week, at the end of which we were to be off. We went, as usual, to our several fields of labor, but with bosoms highly agitated with thoughts of our truly hazardous undertaking. We tried to conceal our feelings as much as possible; and I think we succeeded very well.

After a painful waiting, the Saturday morning, whose night was to witness our departure, came. I hailed it with joy, bring what of sadness it might. Friday night was a sleepless one for me. I probably felt more anxious than the rest, because I was, by common consent, at the head of the whole affair. The responsibility of success or failure lay heavily upon me. The glory of the one, and the confusion of the other, were alike mine. The first two hours of that morning were such as I never experienced before, and hope never to again. Early in the morning, we went, as usual, to the field. We were spreading manure; and all at once, while thus engaged, I was overwhelmed with an indescribable feeling, in the fulness of which I turned to Sandy, who was near by, and said, "We are betrayed!" "Well," said he, "that thought has this moment struck me." We said no more. I was never more certain of any thing.

The horn was blown as usual, and we went up from the field to the house for breakfast. I went for the form, more than for want of any thing to eat that morning. Just as I got to the house, in looking out at the lane gate, I saw four white men, with two colored men. The white men were on horseback, and the colored ones were walking behind, as if tied. I watched them a few moments till they got up to our lane gate. Here they halted, and tied the colored men to the gate-post. I was not yet certain as to what the matter was. In a few moments, in rode Mr. Hamilton, with a speed betokening great excitement. He came to the door, and inquired if Master William was in. He was told he was at the barn. Mr. Hamilton, without dismounting, rode up to the barn with extraordinary speed. In a few moments, he and Mr. Freeland returned to the house. By this time, the three constables rode up, and in great haste dismounted, tied their horses, and met Master William and Mr. Hamilton returning from the barn;

and after talking awhile, they all walked up to the kitchen door. There was no one in the kitchen but myself and John. Henry and Sandy were up at the barn. Mr. Freeland put his head in at the door, and called me by name, saying, there were some gentlemen at the door who wished to see me. I stepped to the door, and inquired what they wanted. They at once seized me, and, without giving me any satisfaction, tied me—lashing my hands closely together. I insisted upon knowing what the matter was. They at length said, that they had learned I had been in a "scrape," and that I was to be examined before my master; and if their information proved false, I should not be hurt.

In a few moments, they succeeded in tying John. They then turned to Henry, who had by this time returned, and commanded him to cross his hands. "I won't!" said Henry, in a firm tone, indicating his readiness to meet the consequences of his refusal. "Won't you?" said Tom Graham, the constable. "No, I won't!" said Henry, in a still stronger tone. With this, two of the constables pulled out their shining pistols, and swore, by their Creator, that they would make him cross his hands or kill him. Each cocked his pistol, and, with fingers on the trigger, walked up to Henry, saying, at the same time, if he did not cross his hands, they would blow his damned heart out. "Shoot me, shoot me!" said Henry; "you can't kill me but once. Shoot, shoot,—and be damned! I won't be tied!" This he said in a tone of loud defiance; and at the same time, with a motion as quick as lightning, he with one single stroke dashed the pistols from the hand of each constable. As he did this, all hands fell upon him, and, after beating him some time, they finally overpowered him, and got him tied.

During the scuffle, I managed, I know not how, to get my pass out, and, without being discovered, put it into the fire. We were all now tied; and just as we were to leave for Easton jail, Betsy Freeland, mother of William Freeland, came to the door with her hands full of biscuits, and divided them between Henry and John. She then delivered herself of a speech, to the following effect:—addressing herself to me, she said, "You devil! You yellow devil! it was you that put it into the heads of Henry and John to run away. But for you, you long-legged mulatto devil! Henry nor John would never have thought of such a thing." I made no reply, and was immediately hurried off towards St. Michael's. Just a moment previous to the scuffle with Henry, Mr. Hamilton suggested the propriety of making a search for the protections which he had understood Frederick had written for himself and the rest. But, just at the moment he was about carrying his proposal into effect, his aid was needed in helping to tie Henry; and the excitement attending the scuffle caused them either to forget, or to deem it unsafe, under the circumstances, to search. So we were not yet convicted of the intention to run away.

When we got about half way to St. Michael's, while the constables having us in charge were looking ahead, Henry inquired of me what he should do with his pass. I told him to eat it with his biscuit, and own nothing; and we passed the word around, "Own nothing;" and "Own nothing!" said we all. Our confidence in each other was unshaken. We were resolved to succeed or fail together, after the calamity had befallen us as much as before. We were now prepared for any thing. We were to be dragged that morning fifteen miles behind horses, and then to be placed in the Easton jail. When we reached St. Michael's, we underwent a sort of examination. We all denied that we ever intended to run away. We did this more to bring out the evidence against us, than from any hope of getting clear of being sold; for, as I have said, we were ready for that. The fact was, we cared but little where we went, so we went together. Our greatest concern was about separation. We dreaded that more than any thing this side of death. We found the evidence against us to be the testimony of one person; our master would not tell who it was; but we came to a unanimous decision among ourselves as to who their informant was. We were sent off to the jail at Easton. When we got there, we were delivered up to the sheriff, Mr. Joseph Graham, and by him placed in jail. Henry, John, and myself, were placed in one room together—Charles, and Henry Bailey, in another. Their object in separating us was to hinder concert.

We had been in jail scarcely twenty minutes, when a swarm of slave traders, and agents for slave traders, flocked into jail to look at us, and to ascertain if we were for sale. Such a set of beings I never saw before! I felt myself surrounded by so many fiends from perdition. A band of pirates never looked more like their father, the devil. They laughed and grinned over us, saying, "Ah, my boys! we have got you, haven't we?" And after taunting us in various ways, they one by one went into an examination of us, with intent to ascertain our value. They would impudently ask us if we would not like to have them for our masters. We would make them no answer, and leave them to find out as best they could. Then they would curse and swear at us, telling us that they could take the devil out of us in a very little while, if we were only in their hands.

While in jail, we found ourselves in much more comfortable quarters than we expected when we went there. We did not get much to eat, nor that which was very good; but we had a good clean room, from the windows of which we could see what was going on in the street, which was very much better than though we had been placed in one of the dark, damp cells. Upon the whole, we got along very well, so far as the jail and its keeper were concerned. Immediately after the holidays were over, contrary to all our expectations, Mr. Hamilton and Mr. Freeland came up to Easton, and took Charles, the two Henrys, and John, out of jail, and carried them home, leaving me alone. I regarded this separation as a final one. It caused me more pain than any thing else in the whole transaction. I was ready for any thing rather than separation. I supposed that they had consulted together, and had decided that, as I was the whole cause of the intention of the others to run away, it was hard to make the innocent suffer with the guilty; and that they had, therefore, concluded to take the others home, and sell me, as a warning to the others that remained. It is due to the noble Henry to say, he seemed almost as reluctant at leaving the prison as at leaving home to come to the prison. But we knew we should, in all probability, be separated, if we were sold; and since he was in their hands, he concluded to go peaceably home.

I was now left to my fate. I was all alone, and within the walls of a stone prison. But a few days before, and I was full of hope. I expected to have been safe in a land of freedom; but now I was covered with gloom, sunk down to the utmost despair. I thought the possibility of freedom was gone. I was kept in this way about one week, at the end of which, Captain Auld, my master, to my surprise and utter astonishment, came up, and took me out, with the intention of sending me, with a gentleman of his acquaintance, into Alabama. But, from some cause or other, he did not send me to Alabama, but concluded to send me back to Baltimore, to live again with his brother Hugh, and to learn a trade.

Thus, after an absence of three years and one month, I was once more permitted to return to my old home at Baltimore. My master sent me away, because there existed against me a very great prejudice in the community, and he feared I might be killed.

In a few weeks after I went to Baltimore, Master Hugh hired me to Mr. William Gardner, an extensive ship-builder, on Fell's Point. I was put there to learn how to calk. It, however, proved a very unfavorable place for the accomplishment of this object. Mr.

Gardner was engaged that spring in building two large man-of-war brigs, professedly for the Mexican government. The vessels were to be launched in the July of that year, and in failure thereof, Mr. Gardner was to lose a considerable sum; so that when I entered, all was hurry. There was no time to learn any thing. Every man had to do that which he knew how to do. In entering the shipyard, my orders from Mr. Gardner were, to do whatever the carpenters commanded me to do. This was placing me at the beck and call of about seventy-five men. I was to regard all these as masters. Their word was to be my law. My situation was a most trying one. At times I needed a dozen pair of hands. I was called a dozen ways in the space of a single minute. Three or four voices would strike my ear at the same moment. It was—"Fred., come help me to cant this timber here."—"Fred., come carry this timber yonder."—"Fred., bring that roller here."—"Fred., go get a fresh can of water."—"Fred., come help saw off the end of this timber."—"Fred., go quick, and get the crowbar."—"Fred., hold on the end of this fall."—"Fred., go to the blacksmith's shop, and get a new punch."—"Hurra, Fred! run and bring me a cold chisel."—"I say, Fred., bear a hand, and get up a fire as quick as lightning under that steam-box."—"Halloo, nigger! come, turn this grindstone."—"Come, come! move, move! and bowse this timber forward."—"I say, darky, blast your eyes, why don't you heat up some pitch?"—"Halloo! halloo! halloo!" (Three voices at the same time.) "Come here!—Go there!—Hold on where you are! Damn you, if you move, I'll knock your brains out!"

This was my school for eight months; and I might have remained there longer, but for a most horrid fight I had with four of the white apprentices, in which my left eye was nearly knocked out, and I was horribly mangled in other respects. The facts in the case were these: Until a very little while after I went there, white and black ship-carpenters worked side by side, and no one seemed to see any impropriety in it. All hands seemed to be very well satisfied. Many of the black carpenters were freemen. Things seemed to be going on very well. All at once, the white carpenters knocked off, and said they would not work with free colored workmen. Their reason for this, as alleged, was, that if free colored carpenters were encouraged, they would soon take the trade into their own hands, and poor white men would be thrown out of employment. They therefore felt called upon at once to put a stop to it. And, taking advantage of Mr. Gardner's necessities, they broke off, swearing they would work no longer, unless he would discharge his black carpenters. Now, though this did not extend to me in form, it did reach me in fact. My fellow-apprentices very soon began to feel it degrading to them to work with me. They began to put on airs, and talk about the "niggers" taking the country, saying we all ought to be killed; and, being encouraged by the journeymen, they commenced making my condition as hard as they could, by hectoring me around, and sometimes striking me. I, of course, kept the vow I made after the fight with Mr. Covey, and struck back again, regardless of consequences; and while I kept them from combining, I succeeded very well; for I could whip the whole of them, taking them separately. They, however, at length combined, and came upon me, armed with sticks, stones, and heavy handspikes. One came in front with a half brick. There was one at each side of me, and one behind me. While I was attending to those in front, and on either side, the one behind ran up with the handspike, and struck me a heavy blow upon the head. It stunned me. I fell, and with this they all ran upon me, and fell to beating me with their fists. I let them lay on for a while, gathering strength. In an instant, I gave a sudden surge, and rose to my hands and knees. Just as I did that, one of their number gave me, with his heavy boot, a powerful kick in the left eye. My eyeball seemed to have burst. When they saw my eye closed, and badly swollen, they left me. With this I seized the handspike, and for a time pursued them. But here the carpenters interfered, and I thought I might as well give it up. It was impossible to stand my hand against so many. All this took place in sight of not less than fifty white ship-carpenters, and not one interposed a friendly word; but some cried, "Kill the damned nigger! Kill him! kill him! He struck a white person." I found my only chance for life was in flight. I succeeded in getting away without an additional blow, and barely so; for to strike a white man is death by Lynch law,—and that was the law in Mr. Gardner's ship-yard; nor is there much of any other out of Mr. Gardner's ship-yard.

I went directly home, and told the story of my wrongs to Master Hugh; and I am happy to say of him, irreligious as he was, his conduct was heavenly, compared with that of his brother Thomas under similar circumstances. He listened attentively to my narration of the circumstances leading to the savage outrage, and gave many proofs of his strong indignation at it. The heart of my once overkind mistress was again melted into pity. My puffed-out eye and blood-covered face moved her to tears. She took a chair by me, washed the blood from my face, and, with a mother's tenderness, bound up my head, covering the wounded eye with a lean piece of fresh beef. It was almost compensation for my suffering to witness, once more, a manifestation of kindness from this, my once affectionate old mistress. Master Hugh was very much enraged. He gave expression to his feelings by pouring out curses upon the heads of those who did the deed. As soon as I got a little the better of my bruises, he took me with him to Esquire Watson's, on Bond Street, to see what could be done about the matter. Mr. Watson inquired who saw the assault committed. Master Hugh told him it was done in Mr. Gardner's shipyard at midday, where there were a large company of men at work. "As to that," he said, "the deed was done, and there was no question as to who did it." His answer was, he could do nothing in the case, unless some white man would come forward and testify. He could issue no warrant on my word. If I had been killed in the presence of a thousand colored people, their testimony combined would have been insufficient to have arrested one of the murderers. Master Hugh, for once, was compelled to say this state of things was too bad. Of course, it was impossible to get any white man to volunteer his testimony in my behalf, and against the white young men. Even those who may have sympathized with me were not prepared to do this. It required a degree of courage unknown to them to do so; for just at that time, the slightest manifestation of humanity toward a colored person was denounced as abolitionism, and that name subjected its bearer to frightful liabilities. The watchwords of the bloody-minded in that region, and in those days, were, "Damn the abolitionists!" and "Damn the niggers!" There was nothing done, and probably nothing would have been done if I had been killed. Such was, and such remains, the state of things in the Christian city of Baltimore.

Master Hugh, finding he could get no redress, refused to let me go back again to Mr. Gardner. He kept me himself, and his wife dressed my wound till I was again restored to health. He then took me into the ship-yard of which he was foreman, in the employment of Mr. Walter Price. There I was immediately set to calking, and very soon learned the art of using my mallet and irons. In the course of one year from the time I left Mr. Gardner's, I was able to command the highest wages given to the most experienced caulkers. I was now of some importance to my master. I was bringing him from six to seven dollars per week. I sometimes brought him nine dollars per week: my wages were a dollar and a half a day. After learning how to calk, I sought my own employment, made my own contracts, and collected the money which I earned. My pathway became much more smooth than before; my condition was now much more comfortable. When I could get no calking to do, I did nothing. During these leisure times, those old notions about freedom would steal over me again. When in Mr. Gardner's employment, I was kept in such a perpetual whirl of excitement, I could think of nothing, scarcely, but my life; and in thinking of my life, I almost forgot my liberty. I have observed this in my experience of slavery,—that whenever my condition was improved, instead of its increasing my contentment, it only increased my desire to be free, and set me to thinking of plans to gain my freedom. I have found that, to make a contented slave, it is necessary to make a thoughtless one. It is necessary to darken his moral and mental vision, and, as far as possible, to annihilate the power of reason. He must be able to detect no inconsistencies in slavery; he must be made to feel that slavery is right; and he can be brought to that only when he ceases to be a man.

I was now getting, as I have said, one dollar and fifty cents per day. I contracted for it; I earned it; it was paid to me; it was rightfully my own; yet, upon each returning Saturday night, I was compelled to deliver every cent of that money to Master Hugh. And why? Not because he earned it,—not because he had any hand in earning it,—not because I owed it to him,—nor because he possessed the slightest shadow of a right to it; but solely because he had the power to compel me to give it up. The right of the grim-visaged pirate upon the high seas is exactly the same.

CHAPTER XI

I now come to that part of my life during which I planned, and finally succeeded in making, my escape from slavery. But before narrating any of the peculiar circumstances, I deem it proper to make known my intention not to state all the facts connected with the transaction. My reasons for pursuing this course may be understood from the following: First, were I to give a minute statement of all the facts, it is not only possible, but quite probable, that others would thereby be involved in the most embarrassing difficulties. Secondly, such a statement would most undoubtedly induce greater vigilance on the part of slaveholders than has existed heretofore among them; which would, of course, be the means of guarding a door whereby some dear brother bondman might escape his galling chains. I deeply regret the necessity that impels me to suppress any thing of importance connected with my experience in slavery. It would afford me great pleasure indeed, as well as materially add to the interest of my narrative, were I at liberty to gratify a curiosity, which I know exists in the minds of many, by an accurate statement of all the facts pertaining to my most fortunate escape. But I must deprive myself of this pleasure, and the curious of the gratification which such a statement would afford. I would allow myself to suffer under the greatest imputations which evil-minded men might suggest, rather than exculpate myself, and thereby run the hazard of closing the slightest avenue by which a brother slave might clear himself of the chains and fetters of slavery.

I have never approved of the very public manner in which some of our western friends have conducted what they call the underground railroad, but which I think, by their open declarations, has been made most emphatically the upper-ground railroad.[1] I honor those good men and women for their noble daring, and applaud them for willingly subjecting themselves to bloody persecution, by openly avowing their participation in the escape of slaves. I, however, can see very little good resulting from such a course, either to themselves or the slaves escaping; while, upon the other hand, I see and feel assured that those open declarations are a positive evil to the slaves remaining, who are seeking to escape. They do nothing towards enlightening the slave, whilst they do much towards enlightening the master. They stimulate him to greater watchfulness, and enhance his power to capture his slave. We owe something to the slave south of the line as well as to those north of it; and in aiding the latter on their way to freedom, we should be careful to do nothing which would be likely to hinder the former from escaping from slavery. I would keep the merciless slaveholder profoundly ignorant of the means of flight adopted by the slave. I would leave him to imagine himself surrounded by myriads of invisible tormentors, ever ready to snatch from his infernal grasp his trembling prey. Let

---

1   In his second autobiography, *My Bondage and My Freedom*, Douglass names names in his denunciation of the sensationalized publicity of the Underground Railroad that in his view cost lives: "Had not Henry Box Brown [c. 1816–97] and his friends attracted slaveholding attention to the manner of his escape, we might have had a thousand Box Browns per annum. The singularly original plan adopted by William [1824–1900] and Ellen [1826–91] Crafts [sic], perished with the first using, because every slaveholder in the land was apprised of it" (323).

him be left to feel his way in the dark; let darkness commensurate with his crime hover over him; and let him feel that at every step he takes, in pursuit of the flying bondman, he is running the frightful risk of having his hot brains dashed out by an invisible agency. Let us render the tyrant no aid; let us not hold the light by which he can trace the footprints of our flying brother. But enough of this. I will now proceed to the statement of those facts, connected with my escape, for which I am alone responsible, and for which no one can be made to suffer but myself.

In the early part of the year 1838, I became quite restless. I could see no reason why I should, at the end of each week, pour the reward of my toil into the purse of my master. When I carried to him my weekly wages, he would, after counting the money, look me in the face with a robber-like fierceness, and ask, "Is this all?" He was satisfied with nothing less than the last cent. He would, however, when I made him six dollars, sometimes give me six cents, to encourage me. It had the opposite effect. I regarded it as a sort of admission of my right to the whole. The fact that he gave me any part of my wages was proof, to my mind, that he believed me entitled to the whole of them. I always felt worse for having received any thing; for I feared that the giving me a few cents would ease his conscience, and make him feel himself to be a pretty honorable sort of robber. My discontent grew upon me. I was ever on the look-out for means of escape; and, finding no direct means, I determined to try to hire my time, with a view of getting money with which to make my escape. In the spring of 1838, when Master Thomas came to Baltimore to purchase his spring goods, I got an opportunity, and applied to him to allow me to hire my time. He unhesitatingly refused my request, and told me this was another stratagem by which to escape. He told me I could go nowhere but that he could get me; and that, in the event of my running away, he should spare no pains in his efforts to catch me. He exhorted me to content myself, and be obedient. He told me, if I would be happy, I must lay out no plans for the future. He said, if I behaved myself properly, he would take care of me. Indeed, he advised me to complete thoughtlessness of the future, and taught me to depend solely upon him for happiness. He seemed to see fully the pressing necessity of setting aside my intellectual nature, in order to contentment in slavery. But in spite of him, and even in spite of myself, I continued to think, and to think about the injustice of my enslavement, and the means of escape.

About two months after this, I applied to Master Hugh for the privilege of hiring my time. He was not acquainted with the fact that I had applied to Master Thomas, and had been refused. He too, at first, seemed disposed to refuse; but, after some reflection, he granted me the privilege, and proposed the following terms: I was to be allowed all my time, make all contracts with those for whom I worked, and find my own employment; and, in return for this liberty, I was to pay him three dollars at the end of each week; find myself in calking tools, and in board and clothing. My board was two dollars and a half per week. This, with the wear and tear of clothing and calking tools, made my regular expenses about six dollars per week. This amount I was compelled to make up, or relinquish the privilege of hiring my time. Rain or shine, work or no work, at the end of each week the money must be forthcoming, or I must give up my privilege. This arrangement, it will be perceived, was decidedly in my master's favor. It relieved him of all need of looking after me. His money was sure. He received all the benefits of slaveholding without its evils; while I endured all the evils of a slave, and suffered all the care and anxiety of a freeman. I found it a hard bargain. But, hard as it was, I thought it better than the old mode of getting along. It was a step towards freedom to be allowed to bear the responsibilities of a freeman, and I was determined to hold on upon it. I bent myself to the work of making money. I was ready to work at night as well as day, and by the most untiring perseverance and indus-try, I made enough to meet my expenses, and lay up a little money every week. I went on thus from May till August. Master Hugh then refused to allow me to hire my time longer. The ground for his refusal was a failure on my part, one Saturday night, to pay him for my week's time. This failure was occasioned by my attending a camp meeting about ten miles from Baltimore. During the week, I had entered into an engagement with a number of young friends to start from Baltimore to the camp ground early Saturday evening; and being detained by my employer, I was unable to get down to Master Hugh's without disappointing the company. I knew that Master Hugh was in no special need of the money that night. I therefore decided to go to camp meeting, and upon my return pay him the three dollars. I staid at the camp meeting one day longer than I intended when I left. But as soon as I returned, I called upon him to pay him what he considered his due. I found him very angry; he could scarce restrain his wrath. He said he had a great mind to give me a severe whipping. He wished to know how I dared go out of the city without asking his permission. I told him I hired my time and while I paid him the price which he asked for it, I did not know that I was bound to ask him when and where I should go. This reply troubled him; and, after reflecting a few moments, he turned to me, and said I should hire my time no longer; that the next thing he should know of, I would be running away. Upon the same plea, he told me to bring my tools and clothing home forthwith. I did so; but instead of seeking work, as I had been accustomed to do previously to hiring my time, I spent the whole week without the performance of a single stroke of work. I did this in retaliation. Saturday night, he called upon me as usual for my week's wages. I told him I had no wages; I had done no work that week. Here we were upon the point of coming to blows. He raved, and swore his determination to get hold of me. I did not allow myself a single word; but was resolved, if he laid the weight of his hand upon me, it should be blow for blow. He did not strike me, but told me that he would find me in constant employment in future. I thought the matter over during the next day, Sunday, and finally resolved upon the third day of September, as the day upon which I would make a second attempt to secure my freedom. I now had three weeks during which to prepare for my journey. Early on Monday morning, before Master Hugh had time to make any engagement for me, I went out and got employment of Mr. Butler, at his ship-yard near the drawbridge, upon what is called the City Block, thus making it unnecessary for him to seek employment for me. At the end of the week, I brought him between eight and nine dollars. He seemed very well pleased, and asked why I did not do the same the week before. He little knew what my plans were. My object in working steadily was to remove any suspicion he might entertain of my intent to run away; and in this I succeeded admirably. I suppose he thought I was never better satisfied with my condition than at the very time during which I was planning my escape. The second week passed, and again I carried him my full wages; and so well pleased was he, that he gave me twenty-five cents, (quite a large sum for a slaveholder to give a slave,) and bade me to make a good use of it. I told him I would.

Things went on without very smoothly indeed, but within there was trouble. It is impossible for me to describe my feelings as the time of my contemplated start drew near. I had a number of warmhearted friends in Baltimore,—friends that I loved almost as I did my life,—and the thought of being separated from them forever was painful beyond expression. It is my opinion that thousands would escape from slavery, who now remain, but for the strong cords of affection that bind them to their friends. The thought of leaving my friends was decidedly the most painful thought with which I had to contend. The love of them was my tender point, and shook my decision more than all things else. Besides the pain of separation, the dread and apprehension of a failure exceeded what I had experienced at my first attempt. The appalling defeat I then sustained returned to torment me. I felt assured that, if I failed in this attempt, my case would be a hopeless one—it would seal my fate as a slave forever. I could not hope to get off with any thing less than the severest punishment, and being placed beyond the means of escape. It required no very vivid imagination to depict the most frightful scenes through which I should have to pass, in case I failed. The wretchedness of slavery, and the blessedness of freedom, were perpetually before me. It was life and death with me. But I remained firm, and, according to my resolution, on the third day of September, 1838, I left my chains, and succeeded in reaching New York without the slightest interruption of any kind. How I did so,—what means I adopted,—what direction I travelled, and by what mode of conveyance,—I must leave unexplained, for the reasons before mentioned.

I have been frequently asked how I felt when I found myself in a free State. I have never been able to answer the question with any satisfaction to myself. It was a moment of the highest excitement I ever experienced. I suppose I felt as one may imagine the unarmed mariner to feel when he is rescued by a friendly man-of-war from the pursuit of a pirate. In writing to a dear friend, immediately after my arrival at New York, I said I felt like one who had escaped a den of hungry lions. This state of mind, however, very soon subsided; and I was again seized with a feeling of great insecurity and loneliness. I was yet liable to be taken back, and subjected to all the tortures of slavery. This in itself was enough to damp the ardor of my enthusiasm. But the loneliness overcame me. There I was in the midst of thousands, and yet a perfect stranger; without home and without friends, in the midst of thousands of my own brethren—children of a common Father, and yet I dared not to unfold to any one of them my sad condition. I was afraid to speak to any one for fear of speaking to the wrong one, and thereby falling into the hands of money-loving kidnappers, whose business it was to lie in wait for the panting fugitive, as the ferocious beasts of the forest lie in wait for their prey. The motto which I adopted when I started from slavery was this—"Trust no man!" I saw in every white man an enemy, and in almost every colored man cause for distrust. It was a most painful situation; and, to understand it, one must needs experience it, or imagine himself in similar circumstances. Let him be a fugitive slave in a strange land—a land given up to be the hunting-ground for slaveholders—whose inhabitants are legalized kidnappers—where he is every moment subjected to the terrible liability of being seized upon by his fellowmen, as the hideous crocodile seizes upon his prey!—I say, let him place himself in my situation—without home or friends—without money or credit—wanting shelter, and no one to give it—wanting bread, and no money to buy it,—and at the same time let him feel that he is pursued by merciless men-hunters, and in total darkness as to what to do, where to go, or where to stay,—perfectly helpless both as to the means of defence and means of escape,—in the midst of plenty, yet suffering the terrible gnawings of hunger,—in the midst of houses, yet having no home,—among fellow-men, yet feeling as if in the midst of wild beasts, whose greediness to swallow up the trembling and half-famished fugitive is only equalled by that with which the monsters of the deep swallow up the helpless fish upon which they subsist,—I say, let him be placed in this most trying situation,—the situation in which I was placed,—then, and not till then, will he fully appreciate the hardships of, and know how to sympathize with, the toil-worn and whip-scarred fugitive slave.

Thank Heaven, I remained but a short time in this distressed situation. I was relieved from it by the humane hand of Mr. David Ruggles,[1] whose vigilance, kindness, and perseverance, I shall never forget. I am glad of an opportunity to express, as far as words can, the love and gratitude I bear him. Mr. Ruggles is now afflicted with blindness, and is himself in need of the same kind offices which he was once so forward in the performance of toward others. I had been in New York but a few days, when Mr. Ruggles sought me out, and very kindly took me to his boarding-house at the corner of Church and Lespenard Streets. Mr. Ruggles was then very deeply engaged in the memorable Darg[2] case, as well as attending to a number of other fugitive slaves,

---

1 David Ruggles (1810–49) was born in Lyme, Connecticut. He was an African American abolitionist, Underground Railroad coordinator, and member of the Vigilance Committee in New York.

2 Ruggles played a leading role in the infamous Darg case, that occurred in 1838 at the time of Douglass's escape and which involved Ruggles's participation in the struggle to liberate an enslaved man, Thomas Hughes, from his white slaveholder, John P. Darg.

devising ways and means for their successful escape; and, though watched and hemmed in on almost every side, he seemed to be more than a match for his enemies.

Very soon after I went to Mr. Ruggles, he wished to know of me where I wanted to go; as he deemed it unsafe for me to remain in New York. I told him I was a caulker, and should like to go where I could get work. I thought of going to Canada; but he decided against it, and in favor of my going to New Bedford, thinking I should be able to get work there at my trade. At this time, Anna,[1] my intended wife, came on; for I wrote to her immediately after my arrival at New York, (notwithstanding my homeless, houseless, and helpless condition,) informing her of my successful flight, and wishing her to come on forthwith. In a few days after her arrival, Mr. Ruggles called in the Rev. J.W.C. Pennington,[2] who, in the presence of Mr. Ruggles, Mrs. Michaels, and two or three others, performed the marriage ceremony, and gave us a certificate, of which the following is an exact copy:—

"This may certify, that I joined together in holy matrimony Frederick Johnson[3] and Anna Murray, as man and wife, in the presence of Mr. David Ruggles and Mrs. Michaels.

"JAMES W.C. PENNINGTON
"New York, Sept. 15, 1838"

Upon receiving this certificate, and a five-dollar bill from Mr. Ruggles, I shouldered one part of our baggage, and Anna took up the other, and we set out forthwith to take passage on board of the steamboat John W. Richmond for Newport, on our way to New Bedford. Mr. Ruggles gave me a letter to a Mr. Shaw in Newport, and told me, in case my money did not serve me to New Bedford, to stop in Newport and obtain further assistance; but upon our arrival at Newport, we were so anxious to get to a place of safety, that, notwithstanding we lacked the necessary money to pay our fare, we decided to take seats in the stage, and promise to pay when we got to New Bedford. We were encouraged to do this by two excellent gentlemen, residents of New

---

1 [Douglass's note:] She was free.
2 James W.C. Pennington (1807–70) was an African American abolitionist, minister, historian, essayist, editor, and author.
3 [Douglass's note:] I had changed my name from Frederick *Bailey* to that of *Johnson*.

Bedford, whose names I afterward ascertained to be Joseph Ricketson and William C. Taber. They seemed at once to understand our circumstances, and gave us such assurance of their friendliness as put us fully at ease in their presence. It was good indeed to meet with such friends, at such a time. Upon reaching New Bedford, we were directed to the house of Mr. Nathan Johnson, by whom we were kindly received, and hospitably provided for. Both Mr. and Mrs. Johnson took a deep and lively interest in our welfare. They proved themselves quite worthy of the name of abolitionists. When the stage-driver found us unable to pay our fare, he held on upon our baggage as security for the debt. I had but to mention the fact to Mr. Johnson, and he forthwith advanced the money.

We now began to feel a degree of safety, and to prepare ourselves for the duties and responsibilities of a life of freedom. On the morning after our arrival at New Bedford, while at the breakfast-table, the question arose as to what name I should be called by. The name given me by my mother was, "Frederick Augustus Washington Bailey." I, however, had dispensed with the two middle names long before I left Maryland so that I was generally known by the name of "Frederick Bailey." I started from Baltimore bearing the name of "Stanley." When I got to New York, I again changed my name to "Frederick Johnson," and thought that would be the last change. But when I got to New Bedford, I found it necessary again to change my name. The reason of this necessity was, that there were so many Johnsons in New Bedford, it was already quite difficult to distinguish between them. I gave Mr. Johnson the privilege of choosing me a name, but told him he must not take from me the name of "Frederick." I must hold on to that, to preserve a sense of my identity. Mr. Johnson had just been reading the "Lady of the Lake,"[1] and at once suggested that my name be "Douglass." From that time until now I have been called "Frederick Douglass;" and as I am more widely known by that name than by either of the others, I shall continue to use it as my own.

I was quite disappointed at the general appearance of things in New Bedford. The impression which I had received respecting the character and condition of the people of the north, I found to

---

1 The Lady of the Lake by Sir Walter Scott (1771–1832) was published in 1810. Johnson is named Douglass after James Douglas (c. 1286–1330), a knight and lord who played a key role in the wars for independence in Scotland.

be singularly erroneous. I had very strangely supposed, while in slavery, that few of the comforts, and scarcely any of the luxuries, of life were enjoyed at the north, compared with what were enjoyed by the slaveholders of the south. I probably came to this conclusion from the fact that northern people owned no slaves. I supposed that they were about upon a level with the non-slaveholding population of the south. I knew they were exceedingly poor, and I had been accustomed to regard their poverty as the necessary consequence of their being non-slaveholders. I had somehow imbibed the opinion that, in the absence of slaves, there could be no wealth, and very little refinement. And upon coming to the north, I expected to meet with a rough, hard-handed, and uncultivated population, living in the most Spartan-like simplicity, knowing nothing of the ease, luxury, pomp, and grandeur of southern slaveholders. Such being my conjectures, any one acquainted with the appearance of New Bedford may very readily infer how palpably I must have seen my mistake.

In the afternoon of the day when I reached New Bedford, I visited the wharves, to take a view of the shipping. Here I found myself surrounded with the strongest proofs of wealth. Lying at the wharves, and riding in the stream, I saw many ships of the finest model, in the best order, and of the largest size. Upon the right and left, I was walled in by granite warehouses of the widest dimensions, stowed to their utmost capacity with the necessaries and comforts of life. Added to this, almost every body seemed to be at work, but noiselessly so, compared with what I had been accustomed to in Baltimore. There were no loud songs heard from those engaged in loading and unloading ships. I heard no deep oaths or horrid curses on the laborer. I saw no whipping of men; but all seemed to go smoothly on. Every man appeared to understand his work, and went at it with a sober, yet cheerful earnestness, which betokened the deep interest which he felt in what he was doing, as well as a sense of his own dignity as a man. To me this looked exceedingly strange. From the wharves I strolled around and over the town, gazing with wonder and admiration at the splendid churches, beautiful dwellings, and finely-cultivated gardens; evincing an amount of wealth, comfort, taste, and refinement, such as I had never seen in any part of slaveholding Maryland.

Every thing looked clean, new, and beautiful. I saw few or no dilapidated houses, with poverty-stricken inmates; no half-naked children and barefooted women, such as I had been accustomed to see in Hillsborough, Easton, St. Michael's, and Baltimore. The people looked more able, stronger, healthier, and happier, than those of Maryland. I was for once made glad by a view of extreme wealth, without being saddened by seeing extreme poverty. But the most astonishing as well as the most interesting thing to me was the condition of the colored people, a great many of whom, like myself, had escaped thither as a refuge from the hunters of men. I found many, who had not been seven years out of their chains, living in finer houses, and evidently enjoying more of the comforts of life, than the average of slaveholders in Maryland. I will venture to assert, that my friend Mr. Nathan Johnson (of whom I can say with a grateful heart, "I was hungry, and he gave me meat; I was thirsty, and he gave me drink; I was a stranger, and he took me in"[1]) lived in a neater house; dined at a better table; took, paid for, and read, more newspapers; better understood the moral, religious, and political character of the nation,— than nine tenths of the slaveholders in Talbot county Maryland. Yet Mr. Johnson was a working man. His hands were hardened by toil, and not his alone, but those also of Mrs. Johnson. I found the colored people much more spirited than I had supposed they would be. I found among them a determination to protect each other from the blood-thirsty kidnapper, at all hazards. Soon after my arrival, I was told of a circumstance which illustrated their spirit. A colored man and a fugitive slave were on unfriendly terms. The former was heard to threaten the latter with informing his master of his whereabouts. Straightway a meeting was called among the colored people, under the stereotyped notice, "Business of importance!" The betrayer was invited to attend. The people came at the appointed hour, and organized the meeting by appointing a very religious old gentleman as president, who, I believe, made a prayer, after which he addressed the meeting as follows: "Friends, we have got him here, and I would recommend that you young men just take him outside the door, and kill him!" With this, a number of them bolted at him; but they were intercepted by some more timid than themselves, and the betrayer escaped their vengeance, and has not been seen in New Bedford since. I believe there have been no more such threats, and should there be hereafter, I doubt not that death would be the consequence.

I found employment, the third day after my arrival, in stowing a sloop with a load of oil. It was new, dirty, and hard work for me; but I went at it with a glad heart and a willing hand. I was now

---

1 Matthew 25:35.

my own master. It was a happy moment, the rapture of which can be understood only by those who have been slaves. It was the first work, the reward of which was to be entirely my own. There was no Master Hugh standing ready, the moment I earned the money, to rob me of it. I worked that day with a pleasure I had never before experienced. I was at work for myself and newly-married wife. It was to me the starting-point of a new existence. When I got through with that job, I went in pursuit of a job of calking; but such was the strength of prejudice against color, among the white caulkers, that they refused to work with me, and of course I could get no employment.[1] Finding my trade of no immediate benefit, I threw off my calking habiliments, and prepared myself to do any kind of work I could get to do. Mr. Johnson kindly let me have his wood-horse and saw, and I very soon found myself a plenty of work. There was no work too hard—none too dirty. I was ready to saw wood, shovel coal, carry wood, sweep the chimney, or roll oil casks,—all of which I did for nearly three years in New Bedford, before I became known to the anti-slavery world.

In about four months after I went to New Bedford, there came a young man to me, and inquired if I did not wish to take the "Liberator."[2] I told him I did; but, just having made my escape from slavery, I remarked that I was unable to pay for it then. I, however, finally became a subscriber to it. The paper came, and I read it from week to week with such feelings as it would be quite idle for me to attempt to describe. The paper became my meat and my drink. My soul was set all on fire. Its sympathy for my brethren in bonds—its scathing denunciations of slaveholders—its faithful exposures of slavery—and its powerful attacks upon the upholders of the institution—sent a thrill of joy through my soul, such as I had never felt before!

I had not long been a reader of the "Liberator," before I got a pretty correct idea of the principles, measures and spirit of the anti-slavery reform. I took right hold of the cause. I could do but little; but what I could, I did with a joyful heart, and never felt happier than when in an anti-slavery meeting. I seldom had much to say at the meetings, because what I wanted to say was said so much better by others. But, while attending an anti-

---

1 [Douglass's note:] I am told that colored persons can now get employment at calking in New Bedford—a result of anti-slavery effort.

2 The *Liberator* was an abolitionist newspaper published by William Lloyd Garrison.

slavery convention at Nantucket, on the 11th of August, 1841, I felt strongly moved to speak, and was at the same time much urged to do so by Mr. William C. Coffin,[1] a gentleman who had heard me speak in the colored people's meeting at New Bedford. It was a severe cross, and I took it up reluctantly. The truth was, I felt myself a slave, and the idea of speaking to white people weighed me down. I spoke but a few moments, when I felt a degree of freedom, and said what I desired with considerable ease. From that time until now, I have been engaged in pleading the cause of my brethren—with what success, and with what devotion, I leave those acquainted with my labors to decide.

APPENDIX

I find, since reading over the foregoing Narrative, that I have, in several instances, spoken in such a tone and manner, respecting religion, as may possibly lead those unacquainted with my religious views to suppose me an opponent of all religion. To remove the liability of such misapprehension, I deem it proper to append the following brief explanation. What I have said respecting and against religion, I mean strictly to apply to the slaveholding religion of this land, and with no possible reference to Christianity proper; for, between the Christianity of this land, and the Christianity of Christ, I recognize the widest possible difference—so wide, that to receive the one as good, pure, and holy, is of necessity to reject the other as bad, corrupt, and wicked. To be the friend of the one, is of necessity to be the enemy of the other. I love the pure, peaceable, and impartial Christianity of Christ: I therefore hate the corrupt, slaveholding, women-whipping, cradle-plundering, partial and hypocritical Christianity of this land. Indeed, I can see no reason, but the most deceitful one, for calling the religion of this land Christianity. I look upon it as the climax of all misnomers, the boldest of all frauds, and the grossest of all libels. Never was there a clearer case of "stealing the livery of the court of heaven to serve the devil in."[2] I am filled

---

1 William C. Coffin (b. 1816) was a white radical abolitionist and reformer who met Douglass while they were both living in New Bedford, Massachusetts.
2 From Scottish poet Robert Pollok (1798–1827), *The Course of Time: A Poem* (Boston, 1843), Book 8.

with unutterable loathing when I contemplate the religious pomp and show, together with the horrible inconsistencies, which every where surround me. We have men-stealers for ministers, women-whippers for missionaries, and cradle-plunderers for church members. The man who wields the blood-clotted cowskin during the week fills the pulpit on Sunday, and claims to be a minister of the meek and lowly Jesus. The man who robs me of my earnings at the end of each week meets me as a class-leader on Sunday morning, to show me the way of life, and the path of salvation. He who sells my sister, for purposes of prostitution, stands forth as the pious advocate of purity. He who proclaims it a religious duty to read the Bible denies me the right of learning to read the name of the God who made me. He who is the religious advocate of marriage robs whole millions of its sacred influence, and leaves them to the ravages of wholesale pollution. The warm defender of the sacredness of the family relation is the same that scatters whole families,—sundering husbands and wives, parents and children, sisters and brothers,—leaving the hut vacant, and the hearth desolate. We see the thief preaching against theft, and the adulterer against adultery. We have men sold to build churches, women sold to support the gospel, and babes sold to purchase Bibles for the Poor Heathen! All For The Glory Of God And The Good Of Souls! The slave auctioneer's bell and the church-going bell chime in with each other, and the bitter cries of the heart-broken slave are drowned in the religious shouts of his pious master. Revivals of religion and revivals in the slave-trade go hand in hand together. The slave prison and the church stand near each other. The clanking of fetters and the rattling of chains in the prison, and the pious psalm and solemn prayer in the church, may be heard at the same time. The dealers in the bodies and souls of men erect their stand in the presence of the pulpit, and they mutually help each other. The dealer gives his blood-stained gold to support the pulpit, and the pulpit, in return, covers his infernal business with the garb of Christianity. Here we have religion and robbery the allies of each other—devils dressed in angels' robes, and hell presenting the semblance of paradise.

> "Just God! and these are they,
> Who minister at thine altar, God of right!
> Men who their hands, with prayer and blessing, lay
> On Israel's ark of light.

"What! preach, and kidnap men?
        Give thanks, and rob thy own afflicted poor?
Talk of thy glorious liberty, and then
        Bolt hard the captive's door?

"What! servants of thy own
        Merciful Son, who came to seek and save
The homeless and the outcast, fettering down
        The tasked and plundered slave!

"Pilate and Herod friends!
        Chief priests and rulers, as of old, combine!
Just God and holy! is that church which lends
        Strength to the spoiler thine?"[1]

The Christianity of America is a Christianity, of whose votaries it may be as truly said, as it was of the ancient scribes and Pharisees, "They bind heavy burdens, and grievous to be borne, and lay them on men's shoulders, but they themselves will not move them with one of their fingers. All their works they do for to be seen of men.—They love the uppermost rooms at feasts, and the chief seats in the synagogues, ... and to be called of men, Rabbi, Rabbi.—But woe unto you, scribes and Pharisees, hypocrites! for ye shut up the kingdom of heaven against men; for ye neither go in yourselves, neither suffer ye them that are entering to go in. Ye devour widows' houses, and for a pretence make long prayers; therefore ye shall receive the greater damnation. Ye compass sea and land to make one proselyte, and when he is made, ye make him twofold more the child of hell than yourselves.—Woe unto you, scribes and Pharisees, hypocrites! for ye pay tithe of mint, and anise, and cumin, and have omitted the weightier matters of the law, judgment, mercy, and faith; these ought ye to have done, and not to leave the other undone. Ye blind guides! which strain at a gnat, and swallow a camel. Woe unto you, scribes and Pharisees, hypocrites! for ye make clean the outside of the cup and of the platter; but within, they are full of extortion and excess.—Woe unto you, scribes and Pharisees, hypocrites! for ye are like unto whited sepulchres, which indeed appear beautiful outward, but are within full of dead men's bones, and of all uncleanness. Even so ye also outwardly

---

1 John Greenleaf Whittier, "Clerical Oppressors," *Anti-Slavery Poems.*

appear righteous unto men, but within ye are full of hypocrisy and iniquity."[1]

Dark and terrible as is this picture, I hold it to be strictly true of the overwhelming mass of professed Christians in America. They strain at a gnat, and swallow a camel. Could any thing be more true of our churches? They would be shocked at the proposition of fellowshipping a sheep-stealer; and at the same time they hug to their communion a man-stealer, and brand me with being an infidel, if I find fault with them for it. They attend with Pharisaical strictness to the outward forms of religion, and at the same time neglect the weightier matters of the law, judgment, mercy, and faith. They are always ready to sacrifice, but seldom to show mercy. They are they who are represented as professing to love God whom they have not seen, whilst they hate their brother whom they have seen. They love the heathen on the other side of the globe. They can pray for him, pay money to have the Bible put into his hand, and missionaries to instruct him; while they despise and totally neglect the heathen at their own doors.

Such is, very briefly, my view of the religion of this land; and to avoid any misunderstanding, growing out of the use of general terms, I mean by the religion of this land, that which is revealed in the words, deeds, and actions, of those bodies, north and south, calling themselves Christian churches, and yet in union with slaveholders. It is against religion, as presented by these bodies, that I have felt it my duty to testify.

I conclude these remarks by copying the following portrait of the religion of the south, (which is, by communion and fellowship, the religion of the north,) which I soberly affirm is "true to the life," and without caricature or the slightest exaggeration. It is said to have been drawn, several years before the present antislavery agitation began, by a northern Methodist preacher, who, while residing at the south, had an opportunity to see slaveholding morals, manners, and piety, with his own eyes. "Shall I not visit for these things? saith the Lord. Shall not my soul be avenged on such a nation as this?"[2]

---

1 Matthew 23:4–28.
2 Jeremiah 5:9, 29. The identity of the preacher is unknown.

"A PARODY

"Come, saints and sinners, hear me tell
How pious priests whip Jack and Nell,
And women buy and children sell,
And preach all sinners down to hell,
    And sing of heavenly union.

"They'll bleat and baa, dona like goats,
Gorge down black sheep, and strain at motes,
    Array their backs in fine black coats,
Then seize their negroes by their throats,
    And choke, for heavenly union.

"They'll church you if you sip a dram,
And damn you if you steal a lamb;
Yet rob old Tony, Doll, and Sam,
Of human rights, and bread and ham;
    Kidnapper's heavenly union.

"They'll loudly talk of Christ's reward,
And bind his image with a cord,
And scold, and swing the lash abhorred,
And sell their brother in the Lord
    To handcuffed heavenly union.

"They'll read and sing a sacred song,
And make a prayer both loud and long,
And teach the right and do the wrong,
Hailing the brother, sister throng,
    With words of heavenly union.

"We wonder how such saints can sing,
Or praise the Lord upon the wing,
Who roar, and scold, and whip, and sting,
And to their slaves and mammon cling,
    In guilty conscience union.

"They'll raise tobacco, corn, and rye,
And drive, and thieve, and cheat, and lie,
And lay up treasures in the sky,
By making switch and cowskin fly,
    In hope of heavenly union.

"They'll crack old Tony on the skull,
And preach and roar like Bashan bull,
Or braying ass, of mischief full,
Then seize old Jacob by the wool,
    And pull for heavenly union.

"A roaring, ranting, sleek man-thief,
Who lived on mutton, veal, and beef,
Yet never would afford relief
To needy, sable sons of grief,
    Was big with heavenly union.

"'Love not the world,' the preacher said,
And winked his eye, and shook his head;
He seized on Tom, and Dick, and Ned,
Cut short their meat, and clothes, and bread,
    Yet still loved heavenly union.

"Another preacher whining spoke
Of One whose heart for sinners broke:
He tied old Nanny to an oak,
And drew the blood at every stroke,
    And prayed for heavenly union.

"Two others oped their iron jaws,
And waved their children-stealing paws;
There sat their children in gewgaws;
By stinting negroes' backs and maws,
    They kept up heavenly union.

"All good from Jack another takes,
And entertains their flirts and rakes,
Who dress as sleek as glossy snakes,
And cram their mouths with sweetened cakes;
    And this goes down for union."

Sincerely and earnestly hoping that this little book may do something toward throwing light on the American slave system, and hastening the glad day of deliverance to the millions of my brethren in bonds—faithfully relying upon the power of truth, love, and justice, for success in my humble efforts—and solemnly pledging my self anew to the sacred cause,—I subscribe myself,
    FREDERICK DOUGLASS.
LYNN, Mass., April 28, 1845.

Appendix A: European Editions

1. Title Page and Frontispiece Portrait, *Narrative of the Life of Frederick Douglass, an American Slave* (Dublin: Webb and Chapman, 1845)

[A major bone of contention for Frederick Douglass across both Irish editions of his *Narrative* was the frontispiece portrait in which he chose to look his audiences "full in the face." In stark contrast to the Boston edition, which, as Maria Weston Chapman insisted, is "illustrated by a remarkably good engraving of the author," Douglass's first Irish edition included a substitute portrait that was not based on the US frontispiece but on a different engraving, very likely from a no longer extant daguerreotype that was taken of Douglass while he was in the UK. Much to Douglass's dissatisfaction, this engraving was subsequently reproduced by white British abolitionist Wilson Armistead (1819–68) in his historical volume *A Tribute for the Negro*, published in 1848. Frustrated, Douglass openly rejected this new likeness on the grounds that the engraver had chosen to represent him with "a much more kindly and amiable expression, than is generally thought to characterize the face of the fugitive slave."[1] In the run-up to the publication of this new edition, Douglass had tried everything to prevent the inclusion of this portrait. In January 1846, he wrote a letter to Richard Webb, his Irish publisher, in which he admitted to his direct communication with the artist as he sought to exert control over his likeness: "I gave direction to the engraver to make the print of the portrait shorter" (Appendix B3, p. 192). The following month, he voiced his ongoing disapproval to Webb in a postscript to another letter: "I have seen the new portrait. It has its faults—but I'll try no more—it must answer" (Appendix B4, p. 193).

Douglass was unable to leave matters alone, however. He held nothing back regarding his wholehearted rejection of the engraving by informing Webb a few months later, "You asked my opinion of the portrait. I gave it, and still adhere to it. That the picture don't suit is no fault of yours—or loss of yours.—I am displeased with it not because I wish to be, but because I can[']t help it. I am cirtain [sic] the engraving is not as good, as the original portrait. I don[']t like it, and I have said so without heat or thunder" (Appendix B7, p. 196). For Douglass, the newly commissioned portrait failed to capture the angst and

---

1   The leading scholars on the competing Irish editions and different engravings are Fionnghuala Sweeney and Alasdair Pettinger.

Frederick Douglass

Figure 8: Frontispiece, *Narrative of the Life of Frederick Douglass* (Dublin: Webb and Chapman, 1845).

anger characterizing the "face of the fugitive slave" by offensively trading in his benevolently smiling physiognomy and an ornately dressed, dandified figure. According to this representation of Douglass's jaunty and jovial facial expression, he was burdened neither with his own memory of his enslavement nor with the enslavement of his family members, for whom there was no liberation except in death. For the second Irish and third English editions, the publishers seem-

NARRATIVE OF THE LIFE

OF

FREDERICK DOUGLASS,

AN

AMERICAN SLAVE.

WRITTEN BY HIMSELF

What, ho!—our countrymen in chains!
The whip on *woman's* shrinking flesh!
Our soil still reddening with the stains,
Caught from her scourging, warm and fresh!
What! mothers from their children riven!
What! God's own image bought and sold!
Americans to market driven,
And barter'd, as the brute, for gold!—*Whittier*

DUBLIN:

WEBB AND CHAPMAN, GT. BRUNSWICK-STREET.

1845.

Figure 9: Title Page, *Narrative of the Life of Frederick Douglass* (Dublin: Webb and Chapman, 1845).

ingly heeded Douglass's criticism by returning to the Boston portrait; this confirmed that Douglass's opinion counted and that he held authorial sway over the publication of his *Narrative*.

Douglass was clearly not alone in his rejection of these distorted representations of his physiognomy. A few years later, on 17 March 1848, Charles Dickens (1812–70) wrote to his friend and actor W.C. Macready (1793–1873) announcing "[h]ere is Frederick Douglass."

He enclosed a copy of Douglass's *Narrative* with his letter only to confide that he considered the accompanying likeness so offensive that he removed it: "There was such a hideous and abominable portrait of him in the book, that I have torn it out, fearing it might set you, by anticipation, against the narrative" (qtd. in Storey and Fielding 198).][1]

2. Frederick Douglass, "Preface," *Narrative of the Life of Frederick Douglass, an American Slave* (Dublin: Webb and Chapman, 1845)

[Douglass wrote this Preface for publication in the first Dublin edition of his *Narrative*. In his second edition, he lengthened this Preface and added an "Appendix" in which he printed white US proslavery apologist A.C.C. Thompson's charge that he was not the author of his *Narrative*, along with his reply. He also excerpted "Critical Notices" of his *Narrative* that he had taken from the mainstream press and included an appeal, "To the Friends of the Slave," on behalf of the American Anti-Slavery Society.]

In May last, the present Narrative was published in Boston, Massachusetts, and when I sailed for England in September, about 4,500 copies had been sold. I have lately heard that a fifth edition has been called for. This rapid sale may be accounted for by the fact of my being a fugitive slave, and from the circumstance that for the last four years I have been engaged in travelling as a lecturing agent of the American Anti-slavery Society, by which means I became extensively known in the United States.

My visit to Great Britain has a threefold object. I wished to be out of the way during the excitement consequent on the publication of my book; lest the information I had there given as to my identity and place of abode, should induce my owner to take measures for restoration to his "patriarchal care." For it may not be generally known in Europe, that a slave who escapes from his master is liable, by the Constitution of the United States, to be dragged back into bondage, no matter in what part of the vast extent of the United States and their territories he may have taken refuge.

My next inducement was a desire to increase my stock of information, and my opportunities of self-improvement, by a visit to the land of my paternal ancestors.

My third and chief object was, by the public exposition of the contaminating and degrading influence of Slavery upon the slaveholder

---

1 I am indebted to Julia Sun-Joo Lee for her recovery of this letter. (See Lee, *The American Slave Narrative.*)

and his abettors, as well as the slave, to excite such an intelligent interest on the subject of American Slavery, as may react upon my own country, and may tend to shame her out of her adhesion to a system as abhorrent to Christianity and to her republican institution.

My last object is, I am happy to say, in a fair way of being accomplished. I have had public meetings in Dublin, Wexford, Waterford, Cork, Youghal, Limerick, Belfast, Glasgow, Aberdeen, Perth, and Dundee, within the five months which have elapsed since I landed in England. An edition of 2000 copies of my Narrative has been exhausted, and I am in great hopes that before my visit to Great Britain shall be completed, thousands and tens of thousands of the intelligent and philanthropic will be induced to co-operate with the noble band of American abolitionists, for the overthrow of the meanest, hugest, and most dastardly system of iniquity that ever disgraced any country laying claim to the benefits of religion and civilization.

I beg to refer my reader to the Preface to the First edition, and the Letter which follows it; to some notices of my Narrative from various sources, which will be found at the end of the book; and to the following notice of a public meeting held the evening previous to my departure from home, in the town of Lynn, Massachusetts, where I have resided for the last two years:

"Last Friday evening a meeting was held in Lyceum Hall, for the purpose of exchanging farewells with Frederick Douglass and James N. Buffum,[1] prior to their departure, on the ensuing day, for the Old World. The spacious hall was crowded to its utmost capacity—hundreds of men and women being obliged to stand all the evening. This was a most gratifying fact, and spoke volumes for the onward progress of the anti-slavery movement—since but six or seven years back, the people instead of meeting with two such anti-slavery men for the interchange of kindly feelings, would have been more likely to meet them for the purpose of inflicting some summary punishment. Hundreds of persons enjoyed on this occasion the first good opportunity they have had to judge of Frederick Douglass's ability as a speaker and a reasoner; and unless I am much mistaken, their judgment was such as not only to increase their respect for him, but for his race, and the great movement now on foot to release it from thraldom. He spoke twice, and both times with great power. His second effort sparkled with wit from beginning to end.

"The following resolutions were adopted, nem. con.[2]

---

1 James N. Buffum (1807–87) was a white US abolitionist who toured with Douglass during his antislavery campaign in Britain and Ireland and who later became the mayor of Lynn, Massachusetts, from 1869 to 70.
2 I.e., with no one contradicting.

"RESOLVED—As the sense of this great gathering of the inhabitants of Lynn and vicinity, that we extend to our esteemed fellow-citizen Frederick Douglass and James N. Buffum, whose proposed departure for England has brought this multitude together, our heartiest good wishes for a successful issue of their journey.

"RESOLVED—That we are especially desirous that Frederick Douglass, who came to this town a fugitive from slavery, should bear with him to the shores of the Old World, our unanimous testimony to the fidelity with which he has sustained the various relations of life, and to the deep respect with which he is now regarded by every friend of liberty throughout our borders."

3. **Title Page and Frontispiece Portrait,** *Narrative of the Life of Frederick Douglass, an American Slave*, **2nd [Irish] ed. (Dublin: Webb and Chapman, 1846)**

Figure 10: Frontispiece, *Narrative of the Life of Frederick Douglass* (Dublin: Webb and Chapman, 1846).

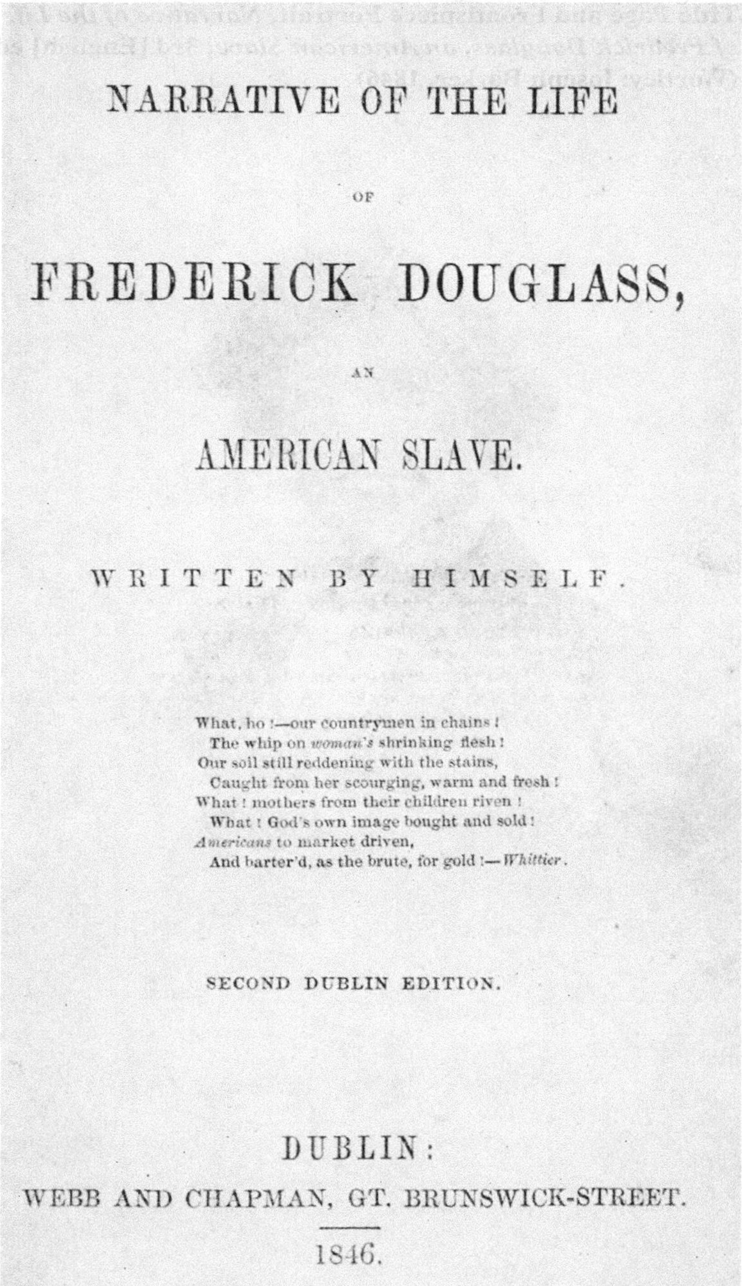

NARRATIVE OF THE LIFE

OF

FREDERICK DOUGLASS,

AN

AMERICAN SLAVE.

WRITTEN BY HIMSELF.

What, ho!—our countrymen in chains!
The whip on *woman's* shrinking flesh!
Our soil still reddening with the stains,
Caught from her scourging, warm and fresh!
What! mothers from their children riven!
What! God's own image bought and sold!
Americans to market driven,
And barter'd, as the brute, for gold!—*Whittier*.

SECOND DUBLIN EDITION.

DUBLIN:

WEBB AND CHAPMAN, GT. BRUNSWICK-STREET.

1846.

Figure 11: Title Page, *Narrative of the Life of Frederick Douglass* (Dublin: Webb and Chapman, 1846).

4. Title Page and Frontispiece Portrait, *Narrative of the Life of Fredrick Douglass, an American Slave*, 3rd [English] ed. (Wortley: Joseph Barker, 1846)

Figure 12: Frontispiece, *Narrative of the Life of Frederick Douglass* (Wortley, Leeds: Joseph Barker, 1846).

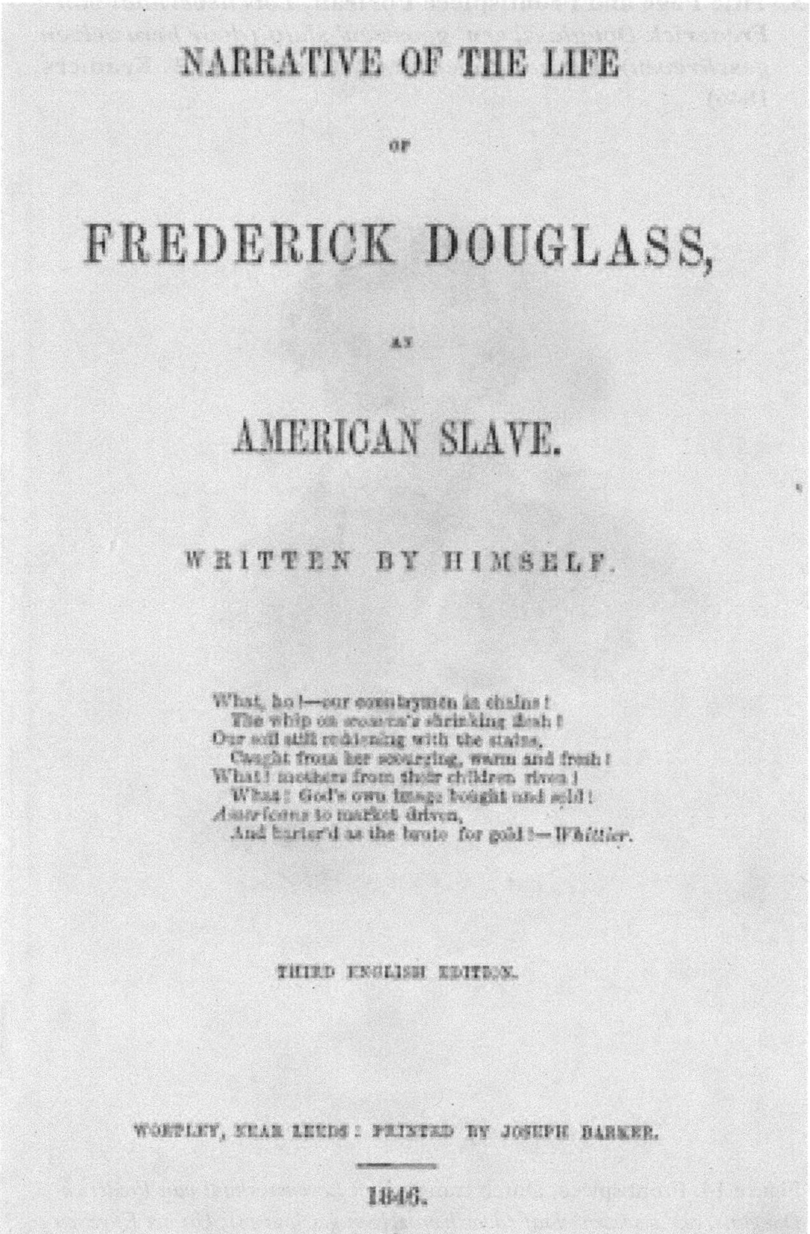

NARRATIVE OF THE LIFE

OF

FREDERICK DOUGLASS,

AN

AMERICAN SLAVE.

WRITTEN BY HIMSELF.

What, ho!—our countrymen in chains!
The whip on woman's shrinking flesh!
Our soil still reddening with the stains,
Caught from her scourging, warm and fresh!
What! mothers from their children riven!
What! God's own image bought and sold!
Americans to market driven,
And barter'd as the brute for gold!—*Whittier.*

THIRD ENGLISH EDITION.

WORTLEY, NEAR LEEDS: PRINTED BY JOSEPH BARKER.

1846.

Figure 13: Title Page, *Narrative of the Life of Frederick Douglass* (Wortley, Leeds: Joseph Barker, 1846).

5. Title Page and Frontispiece Portrait, *Levensverhaal van Frederick Douglass, een' gewezen' slaaf (door hem zelven geschreven); Uit het Engelsch* **(Rotterdam: H.A. Kramers, 1846)**

Figure 14: Frontispiece, Dutch translation: *Levensverhaal van Frederick Douglass, een' gewezen' slaaf (door hem zelven geschreven)*; *Uit het Engelsch* (Rotterdam: H.A. Kramers, 1846).

LEVENSVERHAAL

VAN

FREDERIK DOUGLASS,

EEN' GEWEZEN' SLAAF.

(DOOR HEM ZELVEN GESCHREVEN.)

UIT HET ENGELSCH.

ROTTERDAM,

H. A. KRAMERS.

1846.

Figure 15: Title Page, Dutch translation: *Levensverhaal van Frederick
Douglass, een' gewezen' slaaf (door hem zelven geschreven)*; *Uit het Engelsch*
(Rotterdam: H.A. Kramers, 1846).

6. Title page, *Vie de Frédéric Douglass, esclave américain, écrite par lui-même, traduite de l'anglais par S.-K. Parkes* (Paris: Pagnerre, 1848)

VIE

DE

FRÉDÉRIC DOUGLASS

ESCLAVE AMÉRICAIN,

ÉCRITE PAR LUI-MÊME,

TRADUITE DE L'ANGLAIS

PAR

S.-K. PARKES.

PARIS.

PAGNERRE, ÉDITEUR,

14 bis, rue de Seine.

1848

Figure 16: Title Page, French translation: *Vie de Frédéric Douglass, esclave américain, écrite par lui-même, traduite de l'anglaise, par S.-K. Parkes* (Paris: Pagnerre, 1848).

[S.-K. Parkes's French edition was published in Paris by Pagnerre. Parkes began her edition, which was accompanied by no frontispiece likeness, by writing a "Preface by the Translator" in which she summarized the publication history of Douglass's *Narrative*. Parkes is an author about whom it has been all but impossible to recover any biographical information, with the result that research into both her biography and her edition remains ongoing. In her Preface, Parkes informs her French readers of the work's bestselling status by explaining that the *Narrative* had gone through as many as five US editions, two Dublin editions, and a third in Leeds, with a total print run of 5,000 copies (6). She missed no opportunity to endorse the redemptive role of white over Black abolitionists by eulogizing Garrison's moral character following his initial meeting with Douglass in Nantucket in 1841: "Et pourtant cet homme remarquable n'était qu'un esclave, et un esclave fugitif, qui tremblait pour sa sûreté, et qui osait à peine croire qu'il existât sur le sol de l'Amérique un seul blanc qui voulût courir des risques en le traitant en ami, pour l'amour de Dieu et au nom de l'humanité" ("And yet this remarkable man was only a slave, and a fugitive slave, who feared for his safety and who hardly dared to believe that a single white man existed on American soil who would run the risk of treating him as a friend, for the love of God and in the name of humanity" [6–7]).[1] No passive adherent to white abolitionist principles, however, Parkes made the decision to quote from but not to reproduce Garrison's and Phillips's prefatory materials while also choosing to refer to Douglass's second Dublin edition, in which he reprinted Thompson's invective alongside his own response. In asking the question regarding whose testimony is to be trusted, Douglass's or his white master's, she turns to the evidence of white atrocity provided by his own body: "Les marques que le fouet a laissées sur le dos de Frédéric Douglass prouvent qu'll n'a pas toujours eu à se louer de la bonté de ses maîtres" ("The marks left by the whip on Frederick Douglass's back prove that he has not always benefited from the good will of his masters" [11]).

Parkes concludes the preface to her French translation by celebrating Douglass's oratorical prowess in a farewell speech he delivered in Bristol on 1 April 1847: "en présence d'un auditoire fort nombreux, qui écouta avec plaisir, avec intérêt et souvent avec admiration, les paroles tour à tour énergiques et touchantes de cet *esclave* éloquent, ou mieux dire de cet orateur extraordinaire" ("in the presence of a very large audience who listened with pleasure, with interest and often with admiration to this eloquent slave, or more accurately this excellent orator, whose words were energetic and touching by turns" [13]). For Parkes,

1 My translation, as expertly edited by specialist Claire Freeman.

Douglass's unparalleled status as an exemplary orator, author, and activist took precedence over any authenticating materials produced by his white patrons.

In the *Manchester Times* of 20 November 1847, a "Letter from Paris" written by a reporter identified solely as "Lacigogne" confirms that "[a] translation into French of the Life of Frederick Douglass has been undertaken with enthusiasm, and completed with much excellence, by Miss Parkes, of Bristol."[1] Lacigogne praises Pagnerre as the "distinguished publisher and agitator in the reform movement" and offers further avenues for research by noting that the "literary part of the publishing has been kindly undertaken by Countess d'Agout…. It will be, doubtless, agreeable to the many friends of Douglass and of the abolition cause in England to know of this; and it is to be hoped that the work may have a good effect on the cause in France."]

---

1   Hannah-Rose Murray kindly called this article to my attention.

Appendix B: Douglass's Correspondence, 1845–46

1. To Richard D. Webb, Belfast, 6 December 1845 (Anti-Slavery Collection, Boston Public Library)

[Irish born Richard David Webb (1805–72) was a leading figure in the Hibernian Antislavery Association. A leading publisher and editor, he worked closely with Frederick Douglass to produce the Irish editions of his *Narrative*.]

Belfast, Victoria Hotel, 6th December 1845

My Dear Friend, you have already been informed of our success in getting the cause before the people in this place. From all I can see now, I think it will be of the utmost importance that I remain here a much longer time than that allotted in the first instance. The field here is ripe for the harvest, this is the very hot bed of presbyterianism and free churchism,[1] a blow can be struck here more effectually than in any other part of Ireland. One nail drove in a sure place is better than a dozen driven at random, a bird in [the] hand is worth two in the bush. It is better to have a few true friends than a great many acquaintances. To be known thoroughly by a few is better than being known slightly by many. Well then, the conclusion I draw from this—though it may seem a most lame and impotent one—is that I had much better remain here—and go from here to Scotland than to go to Birmingham on the sixteenth Dec. Will you not my Dear friend do what you may to have me released[?] I think you will have little difficulty in doing so—if any think [sic] may be heard from the cold letters from Mr. Cadbury[2] which talk of some one[']s paying my expenses to the meeting &c &c. You can manage it I know if you think best—so here I have the matter. Well well my Books went last night at one blow. I want more I want more, I have many things to hope and—nothing to fear the papers of this morning took a favorable notice of my meeting last night, and a deep interest seems to be excited. I have written to

---

1 The Free Church of Scotland was founded in 1843 by members of the congregation who sought spiritual autonomy from the Church of Scotland. Presbyterianism refers to religious practices rooted in Protestantism.
2 Birmingham-born John Cadbury (1801–89) was a Quaker philanthropist who founded the world-renowned Cadbury chocolate factory in Bournville, England.

Shortt[1] telling him of my success in getting the methodists['] meeting house—in the face of letters prejudicial to me both from Cork and Dublin. Shortt did not like my remarks at the Exchange the other Evening. He has written me a long letter giving me his views of of [sic] the subject there ~~disgust~~[2] discussed. So you see I am not without counsel.

I found the blanket Thomas gave me of great service to me—many thanks to him for it. I had a call from Mrs. Webb of this town wishing to engage me for two days at her house. She is a very good proper looking person. I am engaged for one day only. Well you will want to know how I get on at the Hotel—comfor[t]able [sic]. The friends have placed me here they say to make me accessable [sic] to every one that wishes to see me. They have gained their purpose thus far "still they come," I can thus far truly say Everyone that hears me seems to think he has a special claim on my time to listen to his opinion of me. To tell me how much he condemned and how much he approved—Very well, let them come, I am ready for them though it is not the most agreeable

in great haste excuse the writing, very truly yours
F Douglass

2. To Richard D. Webb, Belfast, 24 December 1845 (Anti-Slavery Collection, Boston Public Library)

Belfast 24 Dec. 1845

My Dear Friend, The Books came agreeable to your direction—the getting letters from such persons as you name is a wise suggestion and I have already adopted measures to obtain them, Dr. Drew of this place—an episcopalian minister has read the narrative and speaks of it in the highest terms of approval—a letter may be obtained from him I know. There is also a presbyterian minister here the Rev Mr Nelson who I know would be happy to aid me with a letter. There will [be] no difficulty in getting letters if they are needed. I suppose they might be used in a part of the remaining 1,000 if sent forthwith, could they?

Another fine meeting here last night crowded to over flowing—in the independent chapel—I hold another on friday [sic] next—the Books go off grandly[.] A very kind quaker lady a Mrs. Wakefield I

---

1 According to McKivigan, Douglass is referring here to William Shortt, a British antislavery campaigner.
2 All strikeouts included here and elsewhere in this and other appendices are in the original manuscript.

believe her name is has taken the sale of them in hand They must go in such hands[.] Let us have the picture as soon as you can[.] I wrote yesterday to your Friend at Bristol. He is evidently of the right stamp. I got a letter last night from Friend Buffum,[1] he is now in London and proposes to join me if I wish him to do so. I shall write him to day and request him to meet me in Glasgow as early as the fifth of January if it will suit his convenience to come. I must see more of Joseph Sturge[2] before I can write more of him.

I wrote yesterday to Shortt counselling him to stand fast. My love to all the family—

Truly yours

F. Douglass

---

1 See p. 177, n. 1.
2 Joseph Sturge (1793–1859) was a British Quaker, radical abolitionist, and philanthropist. He was the organizer of the British and Foreign Anti-Slavery Society.

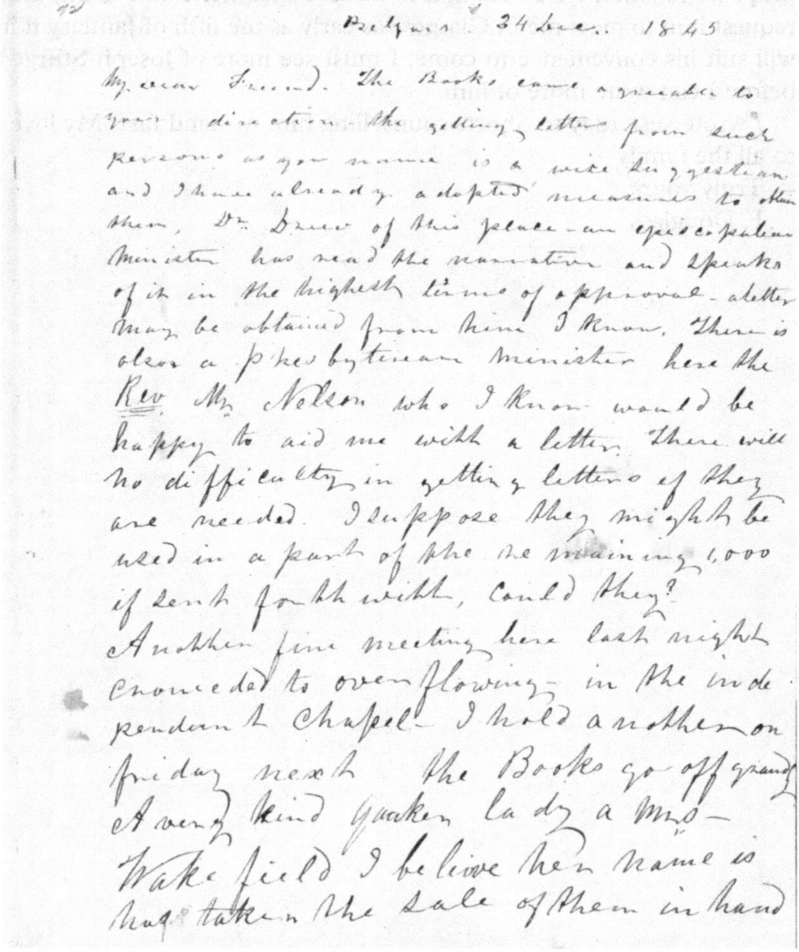

Figures 17a and 17b: Frederick Douglass to Richard D. Webb, Belfast, 24 December 1845 (Boston Anti-Slavery Collection). Courtesy of the Trustees of the Boston Public Library/Rare Books MS A.I.2.15, p. 90.

they must go in such hands let us
have the pictures as soon as you can
I wrote yesterday to your friend at
Bristol. He is ander by of the night
mail p. — I got a letter last night from
friend Buffum, he is now in London
and proposes to join me if I wish him
to do so. I shall write him to day and
request him to meet me in Glasgow
as early as the fifth of January
if it will suit his convenience to
come, I must see more of Joseph Sturge
before I can write more of him,
I wrote yesterday to Shorte counselling
him to stand fast. My love to all
the family. Truly yours

J Douglass

3. To Richard D. Webb, Perth, Scotland, 20 January 1846 (Anti-Slavery Collection, Boston Public Library)

Perth. jan [sic] 20th 1846

My dear Friend—I was just about leaving Glasgow for this place on the arrival of your last or I would have answered it immediately. If it be possible to make the alteration which you suggested about the length of the book—and to get it out in the time I mention in the last note—you will do so by al[l] means. I think it will look much better a little shorter [—] besides I gave direction to the engraver to make the print of the portrait shorter supposing you were prepared to make the alteration as you said. If you cannot get the edition off in time and make the alteration, I know no better way than to get it out in the old form. I met H.C. Wright[1] here last night he was in good spirit[s]—but was looking rather thin,—of course was glad to see us as we were him. A letter will reach me by directing to Wm. Smeale [sic][2] Glasgow as I shall return to that place in the course [of] eight or ten days.

I am sor[r]y you could not send me the three hundred copies for which I sent last week. When the next edition is published, I wish you to have it bound up at once, so that I may not have to wait, as I have had to do for the last edition.

I held two meetings in Glasgow—an account of which you will have from Wm. Smeale. It is a great loss to me to be without my narrative as I am dependent on it for all my support in this Country.

My warm regards to Mrs. Webb
Yours truly
Frederick Douglass

4. To Richard D. Webb, Dundee, Scotland, 10 February 1846 (Anti-Slavery Collection, Boston Public Library)

[In this letter, Douglass refers to his involvement in the "Send Back the Money" campaign, in which he joined radical reformers in petitioning the Free Church of Scotland to return the blood-stained money donated to their coffers by white southern US slaveholders.]

---

1 Henry Clarke Wright (1797–1870) was a white US radical and reformer and supporter of abolitionism and women's rights.
2 William Smeal (1792–1877) was a Scottish-born Quaker and antislavery radical.

Dundee 10th Feb. 1846

Dear Friend, We held a very good meeting here last night, crow[d]ed to overflowing with a people whose influence cannot but be felt by the free Church—Our faithful dealing with this church has at length had the effect to compel them to a defense of their conduct. They have until a few days since affected to dispise [sic] our effort[s], deeming this the best mode of silencing and defeating our exposure. They now see we are not to be put down by such cunning. Their Newspaper— the Dundee "Warden" has attempted to ward off our blows by attacking us personally, denouncing us as strangers unknown to respectable people in this country—but unfortunately for purpose they say in the next place we are in the pay of the establishment—sent for and hired by them. Thus they give us a good reputation by associating us with persons against whose moral characters, they dare not utter a single word. The agitation goes nobly on—all this region is in a ferment. The very boys in the streets are singing out "Send back that money.["] I am informed this morning by the Dundee "Courier" that the St. Perter's [sic] session—have unanimously recommended the sending back the money. I meet many free church people, who are anxcious [sic] to have the money sent back. I am cirtain [sic] that the people are right on this point—and if the money is not sent back it will be the fault of their leaders. We shall continue with unabated zeal to sound the alarm—the people shall be informed. James [Buffum] and myself leave here at one O'Clock to Day for Arbro[a]th where we hold a meeting this Evening[.] There to[o] the people are wide awake. This battling is rather unfavorable to the sale of my book—but the cause first every thing else afterwards.

My kind regards to Mrs. W and all inquiring Friends,

Yours truly

Frederick Douglass

P.s. I have seen the new portrait. It has its faults—but I'll try no more—it must answer. You will probably get it as soon as you get this. You will confer a favor—by sending a copy of the book containing it— as soon as bound—to our mutual Friends Misses Jennings[1]—Cork.

---

1 Isabel Jennings was the secretary of the Cork Ladies Antislavery Society in Ireland. Her sisters, Charlotte, Helen, and Jane, were also staunch abolitionist supporters.

5. To Maria Weston Chapman, Kilmarnock, Scotland, 29 March 1846 (Anti-Slavery Collection, Boston Public Library)

[Maria Weston Chapman (1806–85) was a white US abolitionist and secretary of the American Anti-Slavery Society.]

(Private).   F. Douglass.
Mrs. M W Chapman   Kilmarnock
                                                Scotland
                                                29th March 1846

My Dear Madam,

I take up my pen to thank you for the "liberty bell" and the kind note which you were pleased to send me by the Cambria. I have not yet found time to read the "Liberty bell" but hope to do so soon. My time is greatly taken up with immediate engagements growing necessarily out of my present contact with friends here. I find that in order to make my visit of service to our sacred cause at home, I must as far as possible concentrate my strength upon those circles in whose midst I find myself placed. I am trying to preach and practice a genuine antislavery life—turning neither to the right or left and I think not without success. I think you may safely calculate on seeing some proof of this at your next Bazaar. At the suggestion of Mr R.D. Webb I have inserted an appeal in behalf of the Bazaar in my narrative, so that wherever the narrative goes—there also goes an appeal in behalf of the Old organized Antislavery Bazaar. One of the first objects in my lectures—has been to make that Bazaar prominent and increase its [sic] by increasing its means—I have done so from no sordid motive, but because I believe it to be a powerful instrument in affording means to carry on our important antislavery Machinery[.] I say this the more freely because, though I consider my self as forming a humble part of that machinery I have never received any pecuniary aid directly from it. I have even managed to get on and keep in the field with very little means—lived in a small house paid a small rent, indulged in no luxuries[,] glad to get the common necessaries of life and have followed on with a glad heart and willing mind in the thin but brave ranks of our noble pioneer William Lloyd Garrison. Just before leaving the United States for this country—my warm and excellent friend J.N. Buffum—aware of my poverty, stepped forward with his characteristic liberality and kindly offered to collect a sufficient sum to pay my passage to this land. He tried and succeeded in getting 68 Dollars just 2 Dollars short of my expences [sic] in the steerage. I brought with me three hundred, and fifty dollars, money which I had saved from the sale of my narrative, for means to sustain me while here I have relied and still rely mainly upon the sale of my narrative. And thus far I have had [no] reason to complain, having already disposed of 2-000 copies. I have mentioned these facts and made these remarks because I have felt som[e] what [ag]greaved to see by a letter from you to Mr R.D. Webb of Dublin that you betray a want of confidence in me as a man, and an abolitionist, utterly inconsistent with all the facts in the history of my connection with the Antislavery enterprize [sic]. In that letter you were pointing out to Mr. Webb the necessity of his keeping a watch over myself and friend Mr Buffum – but as Mr Buffum was rich and I poor while there was little danger of but what Mr Buffum would stand firm, I might be bought up by the London committee. Now Dear Madam, you do me great injustice by such comparisons they are direct insinuations and when whispered in the ear of a stranger to whom I look up as a friend they are very embarrassing. Up to the time of hearing Mr. Webb read that letter I supposed I shared your confidence in common with that of the other members of the committee at Boston; I am disappointed. I can assure you Dear Madam that you have mistaken me altogether if you suppose that either the love of money or the hate of poverty will drive me from the ranks of the old organized antislavery society. But had I no more confidence in them, than you seem to have in me I would not take a second breath before leaving them. I have withstood the allurements of New organization liberty party—and no organization at home. Why should I not withstand the London committee, you have trusted me or seem to do so, at home, why distrust me or seem to do so abroad. Of one thing I am certain, and that is I never gave you any just cause to distrust me, and if I am to be watched over for evil rather than for good by my professed friends I can say with propriety, save me from my friends, and I will take care of my enemies. Had you[,] kind friend[,] previous to my leaving America given me face to face that advice and friendly counsel which your long experience, and superior, wisdom has richly enabled you to do, or written to me a kind letter as did my friend Mr Phillips warning me against the London committee, my feelings toward you as to him would be those of ardent gratitude. If you wish to drive me from the Antislavery society, put me under overseer ship and the work is done. Set some one to watch over me for evel [sic] and let them be so simple minded as to inform me of their office, and the last blow is struck. I have said what I now have because I wish you to know just how I feel toward you. I wish to be candid with my friend. It would have been quite easy to have passed the matter over had you not sent me the "liberty bell["], and made it my duty to write to you. When I parted from you at the Antislavery office on the morning of the 16 August

1845, I felt on leaving that you expected a faithful discharge of my duties abroad. I went forth feeling my self armed with the confidence reposed in me by yourself and the Board generally—resolved to do my duty. And although not sustained as I supposed myself to be, I can thus far challenge the strictest scrutiny into all my movements. I have neither compromise myself nor the character of my friends. But enough.

The cause goes nobly on. Our efforts—that is the efforts of friends Wright and Buffum and my own have been mainly directly toward exposing the conduct of the free church of Scotland in holding fellowship with slave holders and taking slave money to build free churches. The Antislavery Committee at Glasgow have succeeded in getting George Thompson[1] to join us in an effort to get the free church to send back the money.

Very respectfully

yours

Frederick Douglass

P.S. Will you do me the kindness to send the enclosed note to H.W. Williams, the former agent of the Antislavery office.

Yours &c. &c.

6. To Richard D. Webb, Glasgow, 16 April [?] 1846 (Antislavery Collection, Boston Public Library)

Glasgow, April 16 [?] 1846[2]

My Dear Friend—I have received the Books—and your letter of 10th ultimo.[3] I have addopted [sic] your advice as to how I might correct and amend the narrative. You asked my opinion of the portrait. I gave it, and still adhere to it,—though I hope not without due deference to yourself and those who think with you. That the picture don-t suit is no fault of yours—or loss of yours,—I am displeased with it not because I wish to be, but because I can[']t help. I am cirtain [sic] the engraving is not as good as the original portrait. I don[']t like it, and I have said so without heat or thunder. Pardon me if I venture to say you have trifled with me in regard to getting letters from clergymen. You were the first to suggest and advise it,—and now that I have taken the advice you are the first to condemn and oppose it. You ought to have thought of your predjudice [sic] against priests sooner. If clergymen

---

1 George Thompson (1804–78) was an English-born abolitionist and equal rights campaigner.

2 This date is written in different handwriting and clearly not Douglass's own.

3 I.e., 10 March.

read my narrative and approve of it, My predjudice [sic] against their office would be but a poor reason for rejecting the benefit of such approval—The enclosed is from Mr Nelson the Presbyterian Minister. I wish both it, and that of Dr. Drew, to be inserted in the second edition. To leave them out because they are ministers would be to show oneself as much and more sectarian than themselves. It would be vertually [sic] forbidding their casting out devils because they follow not us. The spirit of bigotry and sectarianism may exist, and be as deeply rooted in those who condemn sects as those who adhere to them, but I have no time to discuss the question nor is it necessary. Be so kind as to send me at once, three hundred copies of the Narrative to the care of Wm Smeale 161 Gallowgate. They will come safest by sending them in a strong box.

Let me have the second edition as soon as Possible, Making it shorter and thicker agreeable to your suggestion, in your former letter. Get as good, and if you can get better paper than that used in the first edition.

My first meeting here will be held tomorrow Eve. in the City Hall, a very large building. You shall here [sic] from me again soon. Please make my regards to Mrs. Webb and the children,

As ever, F. Douglass

7. To William Lloyd Garrison, Glasgow, 16 April 1846
(*Liberator*, 15 May 1846)

LETTER FROM FREDERICK DOUGLASS
GLASGOW, April 16, 1846

WM. LLOYD GARRISON:
MY DEAR FRIEND—I have given up the field of public letter-writing to my friend Buffum, who will tell you how we are getting on; but I cannot refrain from sending you a line, as a mere private correspondent. My health is good, my spirit is bright and I am enjoying myself as well as can be expected when separated from home by three thousand miles of deep blue ocean. I long to be at home—home sweet, sweet home! Be it ever so humble, "there is no place like home."[1] Nor is it merely to enjoy the pleasure of family and friends, that is wish to be at home: it is to be in the field, at work, preaching to the best of my ability salvation from slavery, in a nation fast hastening to destruction. I know it will be hard to endure the kicks and cuffs of the pro-slavery

---

1 Here Douglass is quoting from the song "Home, Sweet Home!," written by white US actor John Howard Payne (1791–1852) and included in his opera *Clari, or the Maid of Milan* (1823).

multitude, to which I shall be subjected; but there is glory in the battle, as well as in the victory.

I have been frequently counselled to leave America altogether, and make Britain my home. But this I cannot do, unless it shall be absolutely necessary for my personal freedom. I doubt not that my master is in a state of mind quite favorable to attempt at re-capture. Not that he wishes to make money by selling me, or by holding me himself, but to feed his revenge. I know he feels keenly my exposures, and nothing would afford him more pleasure than to have me in his power. He has suffered severe goadings, or he would not have broken the silence of seven years, to exculpate himself from the charges I have brought against him, by telling a positive lie. He says he can put his hand upon the Bible, and, with a clear conscience, swear he never struck me, or told anyone else to do so! The same conscientious man could put his hand into my purse and rob me of my hard earnings; and, with a clear conscience, swear he had a right not only to my earnings, but to my body, soul and spirit! We may, in this case, reverse the old adage—"He that will lie, will steal"—and make it, "He that will steal, will lie"—especially when, by lying, he may hope to throw a veil over his stealing. This positive denial, on his part, rather staggered me at the first. I had no idea the gentleman would tell a right down untruth. He has certainly forgotten when a lamp was lost for the carriage, without my knowledge, that he came to the stable with the cart-whip, and with its heavy lash beat me over the head and shoulders, to make me tell how it was lost, until his brother Edward, who was at St. Michaels on a visit at the time, came forward and besought him to desist; and that he best me until he wearied himself. My memory, in such matters is better than his. One would think, from his readiness to swear that he never struck me, that he held it to be wrong to do so. He does not deny that he used to tie up a cousin of mine, and lash her, and in justification of his bloody conduct quote, "He that knoweth his master's will, and doeth it not, shall be beaten with many stripes."[1] He finds fault with me for not mentioning his promise to set me free at 25. I did not tell many things which I might have told. Had I told of that promise, I should have also told that he had never set one of his slaves free; and I had no reason to believe he would treat me with any more justice and humanity, than any other one of his slaves. But enough.

Scotland is in a blaze of anti-slavery agitation—The Free Church and Slavery are the all-engrossing topics. It is the same old question of Christian union with slaveholders—old with us, but new with most people here. The discussion is followed by the same result as in

---

1 Luke 12:47.

America, when it was first mooted in the New-England Convention. There is such a sameness in the arguments, pro and con, that if you could be landed on this side of the Atlantic, without your knowledge, you would scarcely distinguish between our meetings here, and our meetings at home. The Free Church is in a terrible stew. Its leaders thought to get the slaveholders' money and bring it home, and escape censure. They had no idea that they would be followed and exposed. Its members are leaving like rats escaping from a sinking ship. There is a strong determination to have the slave money sent back, and the union broke up. In this feeling all religious denominations participate. Let slavery be beamed in on every side by the moral and religious sentiments of mankind, and its death is certain.

I am always yours,

FREDERICK DOUGLASS.[1]

8. To Richard D. Webb, Glasgow, 25 April 1846 (Anti-Slavery Collection, Boston Public Library)

[April 2~~6~~ 5 1846][2]

Dear Friend, I have just received your kind note containing a detailed account of my indebtedness to you, and I hasten to transmit the sum necessary to its payment. My object in asking who you had left books with was to enable me to collect payment for them in such places as it might be convenient for me to do so. I did not expect you to tell me nor did I want to know to whom you had sold books for which you had received the money. It seems you have on hand just 506 bound copies. These I hope you will keep unless you can get the cash for them, for I think from what friend Thompson told me that I may easily dispose of them when I get into England. The fighting armour is by no means the most favorable one for a Book Seller. I have had this armour on ever since I came into Scotland.

This has been a proud week for our cause in Glasgow. We have had one Antislavery meeting, one Anti War and two Lectures by Mr Thompson on India. We go to night to Paisley a tremendous gathering is expected—Send back the money is still our watch word. I would

---

1 There were some difficulties in reading a few sentences in this manuscript due to the inferior condition of the original newspaper pages. As a result, I am indebted to the editors of *The Frederick Douglass Papers: Series One, Volume 1, 1841–46* for clarification regarding one or two of Douglass's phrases and his uses of vocabulary as provided by their transcription.

2 This date is written in another hand and amended from 26 to read 25 in light of Douglass's own dated postscript.

write you a long letter but my sight fails me[.] I have had a difficulty
with my right eye which has troubled me very much.

A speedy return of health to Dear Ricky[1]—in haste yours truly
F Douglass

26th April 1846

P.S. I find since writing this that I can't get a Draft before
Monday, I will try then.

I[n] haste yours

F.D.

---

1   Richard Webb Jr. was the son of Richard and Helen Webb.

Appendix C: Douglass's Speeches and Writings

1. "I Have Come to Tell You Something about Slavery: An Address Delivered in Lynn Massachusetts in October 1841," *Pennsylvania Freeman*, 20 October 1841

[This account is one of the earliest written reports of Douglass's oratorical performances to appear prior to the publication of his *Narrative* four years later. The reporter who identifies her- or himself solely by the initials E.M.D. provides us with an annotated transcription in which she or he juxtapose Douglass's voice with her or his own. Here and across all published transcripts of Douglass's speeches, we are faced with significant difficulties surrounding the accuracy and reliability of the transcriber. This is a serious problem confronting researchers of Douglass's speeches in the early years of his career as a public speaker, when he had comparatively little control over their transcription, publication, or dissemination. As a general rule, all accounts of Douglass's antebellum speeches must be examined with extreme caution. As will be seen here—and across all the speeches included in this appendix—the vast majority of reporters failed to spell Douglass's name correctly, typically losing either the "k" of his first name and/or the second "s" of his last.]

FREDERIC [SIC] DOUGLASS

A short time since, when on a visit to Lynn, (Mass.) I had the pleasure of hearing an address from Frederic [sic] Douglass, the runaway slave. It was delivered with energy, and evidently from one unaccustomed to make speeches, yet it came so spontaneously that it thrilled through every one present, and compelled them to feel for the wrongs he had endured. He has been about three years out of slavery. He is a man of intelligent mind, and expresses himself well. The following is the substance, and in some parts the language of his address.

"I feel greatly embarrassed when I attempt to address an audience of white people. I am not used to speak to them, and it makes me tremble when I do, because I have always looked up to them with fear. My friends, I have come to tell you something about slavery—what *I know* of it, as I have *felt* it, when I came North, I was astonished to find that the abolitionists knew so much about it, that they were acquainted with its deadly effects as well as if they had lived in its midst. But though they can give you its history—though they can depict its horrors, they cannot speak as I can from *experience*; they cannot refer you to a back covered with scars, as I can; for I have felt these wounds, I have suffered under the lash without the power of resisting. Yes, my blood has sprung out as the lash embedded itself in my flesh. And yet my master has the reputation of being a pious man and a good Christian. He was a class leader in the Methodist church. I have seen this pious class leader cross and tie the hands of one of his young female slaves, and lash her on the bear [sic] and justify the dead by the quotation from the Bible, 'he who knoweth his master's will and doeth it now, shall be beaten with many stripes.'

"Our masters do not hesitate to prove from the Bible that slavery is right, and ministers of the Gospel tell us that we were born to be slaves:—to look at our hard hands, and see how wisely Providence has adapted them to do the labor; and then tell us, holding up their delicate white hands, that theirs are not fit to work. Some of us know very well that we have not time to cease from labor, or ours would get soft too; but I have heard the superstitious ones exclaim—and ignorant people are always superstitious—that 'if ever a man told the truth, that one did.'

"A large portion of the slaves *know* that they have a right to their liberty.—It is often talked about and read of, for some of us know how to read, although all our knowledge is gained in secret.

"I well remember getting possession of a speech by John Quincy Adams,[1] made in Congress about slavery and freedom, and reading it to my fellow slaves. Oh! what joy and gladness it produced to know that so great, so good a man was pleading for us, and further, to know that there was a large and growing class of people in the north called abolitionists, who were moving for our freedom. This is known all through the south, and cherished with gratitude. It has increased the slaves' hope for liberty. Without it his head would faint within him; his patience would be exhausted. On the agitation of this subject he has built his highest hopes. My friends let it not be quieted, for upon you the slaves look for help. There will be no outbreaks, no insurrections, whilst you continue this excitement: let it cease, and the crimes that would follow cannot be told.

"Emancipation, my friends, is that cure for slavery and its evils. It alone will give to the south peace and quietness. It will blot out the insults we have borne, will heal the wounds we have endured, and are even now groaning under, will pacify the resentment which would kindle to a blaze were it not for your exertions, and, though it may never unite the many kindred and dear friends which slavery has torn asunder, it will be received with gratitude and a forgiving spirit. Ah! how the slave yearns for it, that he may be secure from the lash, that

---

1 John Quincy Adams (1767–1848) was a statesman and the sixth president.

he may enjoy his family, and no more be tortured with the worst feature of slavery, the separation of friends and families. The whip we can bear without a murmur, compared to the idea of *separation*. Oh, my friends, you cannot feel the slave's misery, when he is separated from his kindred. The agony of the mother when parting from her children cannot be told. There is nothing we so much dread as to be sold farther south. My friends, we are not taught from books; there is a law against teaching us, although I have heard some folks say we could not learn if we had a chance. The northern people say so, but they south do not believe it, or they would not have laws with heavy penalties to prevent it. The northern people think that if slavery were abolished, we would all come north. They may be more afraid of the free colored people and the runaway slaves going south. We would all seek our homes and our friends, but, more than all, to escape from northern prejudice, would we go to the south. Prejudice against color is stronger north than south; it hangs around my neck like a heavy weight. It presses me out from among my fellow men, and, although I have met it at every step the three years I have been out of southern slavery, I have been able, in spite of its influence, 'to take good care of myself.'"

Let us give heed to the advice of this unlettered champion of freedom. Dare we pass by his warnings in silence and apathy? He represents the dumb, the millions from whom we but occasionally hear, and most frequently through their oppressors. What an anti-slavery feeling would at once grow up, if the slaves of the south could have a printing press of their own, with ability through it to spread before the people their wrongs. Yes, a tenth of their daily sufferings would kindle such an excitement as we have not yet seen. Then are not *we very* "guilty concerning our brother," *we* who *know* his wrongs, and profess to feel for him "as though bound with him." My heart sickens at the apathy among *the professed friends of the slave*. If our responsibilities are such as he has described, and I faithfully believe they are, why are we so inactive.

E.M.D.

2. **"Speech of Frederic [sic] Douglass, a Fugitive Slave,"** *National Anti-Slavery Standard*, 23 December 1841: 114

SPEECH OF FREDERICK DOULAS [SIC], A FUGITIVE SLAVE.
Delivered at the meeting of the Plymouth County Anti-Slavery Society.

Mr. Douglas [sic] then rose, and gave an account of the effects of this prejudice, as he had experienced them in his own person. He alluded to his being dragged out of the cars lately, on the Eastern railroad, after paying full fare, where the dogs of his fellow passengers were suffered to remain. He told of the obstacles which his complexion threw in the way of his obtaining employment at his trade, (a caulker.) At the South, he said there was none of this prejudice; there he worked at his trade, and earned for his master $900 a week; money, which that master had no more right to, said he, "than any of you, my hearers, have to your neighbor's earnings." There he used to ride by the side of his mistress, at her own request—there white children are often nursed by colored women—and there they have no "Jim Crow pews" up aloft in their churches.

"At the South," he continued, "I was a member of the Methodist church. When I came north, I thought one Sunday I would attend communion, at one of the churches of my denomination, in the town where I was staying. The white people gathered round the altar, the blacks clustered by the door. After the good minister had served out the bread and wine to one portion of those near him, he said, 'These may withdraw and others came forward;' thus he proceeded till all the white members had been served. Then he drew a long breath, and looking out towards the doors, exclaimed, 'Come up, colored friends, come up! for you know, God is no respecter of persons.'—I haven't been there to see the sacrament taken since.

"At New Bedford, where I live, there was a great revival of religion not long ago—many were converted, and 'received,' as they said, 'into the kingdom of heaven.' But it seems, the kingdom of heaven is like a net; at least so it was according to the practice of these pious Christians; and when the net was drawn ashore, they had to set down and cull out the fish. Well, it happened now that some of the fish had rather black scales; so these were sorted out and packed by themselves. But among those who experienced religion at this time was a colored girl; she was baptised in the same water with the rest; so she thought she might sit at the Lord's table, and partake of the same sacramental elements with the others. The deacon handed round the cup, and when he came to the black girl, he could not pass her, for there was the minister looking right at him, and as he was a kind of an abolitionist, the deacon was rather afraid of giving him offense; so he handed the girl the cup, and she tasted. Now it so happened that next to her sat a young lady who had been converted at the same time, baptised in the same water, and put her trust in the same blessed Saviour; yet when the cup, containing the precious blood which had been shed for all, came to her, she rose in disdain, and walked out of the church. Such was the religion she had experienced!

"Another young lady fell into a trance. When she awoke, she declared she had been to heaven. Her friends were all anxious to know what and whom she had seen there; so she told the whole story. But there was one good old lady whose curiosity went beyond that of all the others—and she inquired of the girl that had the vision, if she saw any black folks in heaven? After some hesitation, the reply was, 'Oh! I didn't go into the kitchen!'

"Thus you see, my hearers, this prejudice goes even into the Church of God. And there are those who carry it so far that it is disagreeable to them even to think of going to heaven, if colored people are going there too! And whence comes it? The grand cause is slavery; but there are others less prominent; one of them is the way in which children in this part of the country are instructed to regard the blacks."—"Yes!" exclaimed an old gentleman, interrupting him—"When they behave wrong, they are told, "black man come catch you!"

"Yet people in general," continued Douglas [sic], "will say they like colored men as well as any other, *but in their proper place*. Who is to decide what is their proper place? They assign us that place; they don't let us do it for ourselves nor will they allow us a voice in the decision. They will not allow that we have a head to think, and a heart to feel, and a soul to aspire. They treat us not as men, but as dogs—they cry 'Stu-boy!' and expect us to run and do their bidding. That's the way we are liked. You degrade us, and then ask why we are degraded—you shut our mouths, and then ask why we don't speak—you close your colleges and seminaries against us, and then ask why we don't know more.

"But all this prejudice sinks into insignificance in my mind, when compared with the enormous iniquity of the system which is its cause—the system that sold my four sisters and my brother into bondage—and which calls on its priests to defend it even from the Bible! The slaveholding ministers preach up the divine right of slaveholders to property in their fellow-men. The southern preachers say to the poor slave, 'Oh! if you wish to be happy in time, happy in eternity, you must be obedient to your masters; their interest is yours. God made one portion of men to do the working, and another to do the thinking; how good God is! Now, you have no trouble or anxiety; but, ah! you can't imagine how perplexing it is to your masters and mistresses to have so much thinking to do in your behalf! You cannot appreciate your blessings; you know now how happy a thing it is for you, that you were born of that portion of the human family which has the working, instead of the thinking to do! Oh! how grateful and obedient you ought to be to your masters! How beautiful are the arrangements of Providence! Look at your hard, horny hands—see how nicely they are adapted to the labor you have to perform! Look at our delicate fingers, so exactly fitted for our station, and see how manifest it is that God designed us to be his thinkers, and you the workers—oh! the wisdom of God!'—I used to attend a Methodist church in which my master was a class-leader; he would talk most sanctimoniously about the dear Redeemer, who was sent 'to preach deliverance to the captives, and set at liberty them that are bruised'—he could pray at morning, pray at noon, and pray at night; yet he could lash up my poor cousin by his two thumbs, and inflict stripes and blows upon his bare back, till the blood streamed to the ground! all the time quoting scripture for his authority, and appealing to that passage of the Holy Bible which says, 'He that knoweth his master's will, and doeth it not, shall be beaten with many stripes!' Such was the amount of this good Methodist's piety!".

3. "I Stand Here a Slave: An Address Delivered in Boston, Massachusetts, on 28 January 1842," *Liberator*, 4 and 18 February 1842

[Douglass delivered this speech at a "Great Meeting" held in support of the "Abolition of Slavery in the District of Columbia" at Faneuil Hall, Boston, on 28 January 1842. According to a reporter working for the *Liberator*, there were 5,000 people in attendance. The editors of the first seminal volume of the inspirational *Frederick Douglass Papers: Series One: Speeches, Debates and Interviews 1841–46* collection have titled this speech "The Southern Style of Preaching to Slaves: An Address Delivered in Boston, Massachusetts, on 28 January 1842." Working with Douglass's original phrasing, I have selected the title "I Stand Here a Slave."]

MR. DOUGLAS [SIC], a man of color, here came forward.
MR GARRISON. It is recorded in holy writ, that a beast once spoke. A greater miracle is here to-night. A chattel becomes a man. [Applause.]
MR. DOUGLAS. I rejoice to be permitted, as well as to be able to speak upon this subject in Faneuil Hall. I will not detain you long, for I stand here a slave. [No! no! from the meeting.] A slave at least in the eye of the Constitution. [No! no! *with emphasis from the meeting.*] It is a slave by the laws of the South, who now addresses you. [That's it! *from the meeting.*] My back is scarred by the lash—that I could show you. I would I could make visible the wounds of this system upon my soul. I merely rose to return you thanks for this cheering sight, representing as I do the two and a half millions remaining in that bondage from which I have escaped. I thank God that I have the opportunity to do it. Those bondmen, whose cause you are called to espouse, are

entirely deprived of the privilege of speaking for themselves. They are goods and chattels, not men. They are denied the privileges of the Christian—they are denied the rights of the citizen. They are refused the claims of the many. They are not allowed the rights of the husband and the father. They may not name the name of Liberty. It is to save them from all this, that you are called. Do it!—and they who are ready to perish shall bless you! Do it!—and all good men will cheer you onward! Do it!—and God will reward you for the deed; and your own consciences will testify that you have been true to the demands of the religion of Christ. [Applause.]

But what a mockery of his religion is preached at the South! I have been called upon to describe the style in which it is set forth. And I find our ministers there learn to do it at the northern colleges! I used to know they went away somewhere, I did not know where, and came back ministers: and this is the way they would preach. They would take a text—say this:—"Do unto others as you would have other do unto you." And this is the way they would apply it. They would explain it to mean, "slaveholders, do unto *slaveholders* what you would have them do unto you;"—and then, looking impudently up to the slaves' gallery, (for they have a place set apart for us, though it is said they have no prejudice,) just as is done here in the northern church: looking high up to the poor colored drivers and the rest, and spreading his hands gracefully abroad, he says, (mimicking,) "And you too, my friends, have souls of infinite value—souls that will live through endless happiness or misery in eternity. Oh, *labor diligently* to make your calling and election sure. Oh, receive into your souls these words of the holy apostle—'Servants, be obedient unto your masters. [Shouts of laughter and applause.] Oh, consider the wonderful goodness of God! Look at your hard, horny hands, your strong muscular frames, and see how mercifully he has adapted you to the duties you are to fulfill! [continued laughter and applause]—while to your masters, who have slender frames and long delicate fingers, he has given brilliant intellects, that they may do the *thinking*, while you do the *working*.' [shouts of applause.] It has been said here at the North, that the slaves has the gospel preached to them. But you will see what sort of gospel it is:—a gospel which, more than chains, or whips, or thumbscrews, gives perpetuity to this horrible system.

4. **"The Antislavery Movement: The Slave's Only Earthly Hope: An Address Delivered in New York, New York, on 9 May 1843," *National Anti-Slavery Standard*, 18 May 1843**

[Douglass delivered this speech at the meeting of the Tenth Anniversary of the American Antislavery Society held at Apollo Hall, New

York City, on 9 May 1843. While the reporter, in typical fashion, included no title in the original transcription, scholars have arrived at this title because it is a direct quotation of the resolution that Douglass took as the premise for his speech.]

Frederick Douglass, was next introduced to the meeting. He said: "I have myself been a slave, and I do not expect to awaken such an interest in the minds of this intelligent assembly, as those have done who spoke before me. For I have never had the advantage of a single day's schooling, in all my life; and such have been my habits of life, as to instill into my heart a disposition I never can quite shake off, to cower before white men. But one thing I can do: I can represent here the slave,—the human chattel, the despised and oppressed, for whom you, my friends, are laboring in a good and holy cause. As such a representative, I do not fear that I shall not be welcome to all true-hearted abolitionists. [Applause.]

"I offer you, Mr. President," continued Douglas, "the following resolution, and desire to say a few words in it[s] support:

"2. Resolved, That the anti-slavery movement is the only earthly hope of the American slave?

"There is a truth, sir, asserted in this resolution that is almost every where, and by almost every body, denied. Instead of being regarded as a powerful aid to abolition, it is far too generally viewed as retarding that event. But this is a grievous error. I know, for I speak from experience. It has been imagined that the slaves of the South are not aware of the movements made on their behalf, and in behalf of human freedom, every where, throughout the northern and western States. This is not true. They do know it. They knew it from the moment that the spark was first kindled in the land. They knew it as soon as you knew it, sir, in your own New England. Did not petitions by thousands, immediately go forth for the abolition of slavery in the District of Columbia, and in the territories, and for the overthrow of the internal slave trade? Heard we not that? And in the curses of our masters against the abolitionists, did we not feel instinctively that these same abolitionists were our friends? And in every form of opposition to the great cause, did we not hear it?

"Prior to this movement, sir, the slave in chains had no hope of deliverance—no hope of any peace or happiness within this vale of tears. Darkness and despair rested gloomily upon his prospect, and not a ray of light was thrown across. But when he heard of this movement, hope sprang up in my mind, and in the minds of many more. I knew, I felt, that truth was above error, that right was above wrong, that principle was superior to policy; and under the peaceful and beneficent operation of abolitionism, I felt that I should one day be free. [Loud and protracted applause.]

"The speakers went on to say that there was no hope for the slave in Church, or State, or in the working of society, framed as it now is; nothing whatever in any of the institutions of the day. But in the American Anti-Slavery Society, the slave sees an exposition of his true position in the scale of being. He finds that he is, indeed, a Man,—admitted, recognized as such, as he is by them, and he goes on, calmly and quietly, hoping in his chains that the day may come, when by their aid, he shall be relieved from his thraldom! [Applause.] For this society, sir, is above either Church or State; it is moving both, daily, more and more. What do we see? Massachusetts has closed her gaols, and her court-rooms, against the slave-hunters, and has bidden them to look for no aid at the hands of her people, in this unholy work. Thus is the great work going on!

"And, sir, the slave sees that God has raised up a mighty work in his behalf, among the people of the North, when he observes the reluctance with which the slave owner now makes his tours to the North. The slave is now not taken as a part of the retinue of his master, on the boot of the stage, as before. He soon finds his 'property' among the missing, if he does: and then he comes back, and curses the abolitionists of the North; and, in answer to the question, where is Sam, or Dick, or Bill? slaves who have remained behind, hear him say, the infernal abolitionists have got hold of him, they begin to feel that they have friends, and that the time will come, when the exertions of such will be used for their deliberation, as well as that of their brethren. This it is which teaches the poor slave where his hope is,—that it is in the 'anti-slavery society,'—and in the growing feeling at the North, is favor of the oppressed, and against oppression." [Vociferous applause.]

And Mr. Douglas wound up this extraordinary speech, with a family exhortation to abolitionists to go on, in the confidence of a good cause, to the breaking of bonds, the unloosing [sic] of shackles, and the liberation of the enchained, the enthralled, and the oppressed. He sat down amidst very warm and enthusiastic applause.

Abby Kelley[1] then came forward, and was greeted with warm and long-continued applause. She said that she rose to second the resolution which had been offered by Frederic Douglas [sic]; that he had been a slave; that he was now free, and could speak for himself; but that his mother and sister were still in the hands of the outragers; and that it was therefore fit that she, a woman, should stand there by his side, and bear her testimony in favor of the cause, which had made him, and which, under God, would make them free! She mourned

---

1 Abby Kelley (1811–77) was a white US reformer, radical, and abolitionist.

over the past, that yet, by the laws of New-York, and other States, he was even now a slave; and she exulted over the reflection that there was a growing feeling among the people, which would not rest until that opinion was uprooted. Now, all parties, all social organizations, whether civil or ecclesiastical, were but the coadjutors of slavery; no matter what the denomination—Presbyterian, Baptist, Methodist, what not! The slave has no hope in them, or in any of the philanthropic movements of the day. She begged all not to be discouraged; she warned them that the time was nigh when their enemies would fall on each other, and destroy each other. They were a Spartan band, and had only need to keep together, firmly, to accomplish this great object. She invoked abolitionists to listen to the teachings they had just heard from the lips of Douglas [sic]. The slave knows, and feels, and appreciates the position of the slave, better than any one else can do; and it was the duty of all true-hearted abolitionists to go forward bravely, and untiringly, and sustain them in their efforts for freedom. (Applause.).

5. "Your Religion Justifies Our Tyrants, and You Are Yourselves Our Enslavers," *Herald of Freedom* [Concord, New Haven], 16 February 1844

[This account of Douglass's speech as reported by Nathaniel P. Rogers (1794–1846), a white US abolitionist and editor, appeared in *Herald of Freedom* with no title. The editors of the first volume of the *Frederick Douglass Papers: Series One: Speeches, Debates and Interviews 1841–46* collection title this speech "Southern Slavery and Northern Religion." I arrive at this new title, "Your Religion Justifies Our Tyrants, and You Are Yourselves Our Enslavers," by borrowing directly from Douglass's own opening words.[1]]

Frederick Douglass lectured here Sunday evening, to a crowded Court House. He was here during all Sunday, and spoke at our Sunday meetings, and it was known generally to the people here, and there was great curiosity to see him, and hear his eloquence. But no meeting house was offered to him,—or to the people, rather, who wished to hear him—and would have [been] profoundly interested in the grandeur of his speech. He had to speak, and the audience had to hear, in an inconvenient, uncomfortable room. The sects know here,

---

1 Due to the illegibility of a paragraph of this speech in the microfilmed copy of the newspaper to which I had access, I am indebted to John Blassingame and the other editors of the *Frederick Douglass Papers: Series One: Speeches, Debates and Interviews 1841–46* for the light they shed on otherwise indecipherable content.

that Anti-Slavery will never again ask them for a meeting house. We will furnish them orators of the first cast, and they are in famishing want of good speaking—but they must come to the cold and noisy Court Room and dirty Town Hall, to hear, so long as they shut up their clean and comfortable synagogues against us. We have asked for them long enough. It would be dishonorable begging, to ask again. If the meeting house is *capable* of being opened to the truth, they had better offer them to us. I believe it is not capable of it—and therefore that they will never open them to anti-slavery. I would here suggest that there ought to be a Lyceum Hall erected in this place, where TRUTH could be spoken. What a commentary on the character of the numerous Temples here. I tell the people the Truth *can never be admitted into an Idol Temple.*

Douglass spoke excellently Sunday afternoon, and to a pretty numerous audience—many of them not accustomed to attend our meetings.—He was advertised as a "fugitive *from* slavery." He said he was not a fugitive *from* slavery—but a fugitive *slave*. He was a fugitive, he said, not *from* slavery—but *in* slavery. To get from it—he must go beyond the limits of the American Union. He asked them why it was that he—such as they saw him before them, must wander about in their midst, a *fugitive* and a *slave*. He *demanded* the reason. It is because of your Religion, he sternly replied, which sanctifies the system under which I suffer, and dooms me to it, and the millions of my brethren now in bondage. Your religion justifies our tyrants, and you are yourselves our enslavers. I see my enslavers here in Concord, and before my eyes—if any are here who countenance the church and the religion of your country. Other influences helped sustain the system of slavery, he said, but this is its sanctioner and main support.

In the evening Douglass made a masterly and most impressive speech. The house was crowded, and with the best of our people—no clergy—and but few of the bigots, who are past hearing. He began by a calm, deliberate and very simple narrative of his life. He did not detail personal sufferings—though he said he might—if inclined to. His fate had been mild compared to that of slaves generally. He, to be sure, had to go naked, pretty much during the earlier years of childhood, and feed at a trough like a pig, under the care of his old grandmother, who, past her labor, was turned out, charged to dig her own subsistence, and that of a few little ones, out of a patch of ground allotted her. These little ones were separated from their mothers, that they might early be without ties of kindred. He did not remember his mother, I think he said, and never knew who was his father. He never knew in his first six years anything about a bed—any more than the pigs did. He remembered stealing an old salt bag, into which he used to creep, and sleep, on the earth floor of the negro hut, at his old grandmother's. She, by the way, had reared twelve children of her own, for the market—all sold and gone from her—and she now blind and alone, if she is alive, and none left with her to bring her a cup of cold water. His own back he said was scarred with the whip—but still he had been a favored slave. He was sent to a slave-breaker, when some 16 or 17 years old—his master not being able to manage him. An attempt at breaking him once brought on a struggle between him and the Jockey. The result of it was such that the Jockey did not care to repeat it, while his care for his reputation, as a successful breaker, kept him from getting help to manage a slave boy—and Frederick escaped farther whipping from him afterwards.—After narrating his early life briefly—his *schooling*—the beginning of the wife of his master's relative to teach him letters, and the stern forbidding of it, by her husband—which Frederick overheard—how he caught a little teaching here and there from the children in the streets—a fact, he said, which accounted to him for his extraordinary attachment to children—after getting through this, in a somewhat suppressed and hesitating way—interesting all the while for its facts, but dullish in manner—and giving I suspect, no token to the audience of what was coming—though I discerned, at times, symptoms of a brewing storm—he closed his slave narrative, and gradually let out the outraged humanity that was laboring in him, in indignant and terrible speech. It was not what you could describe as oratory or eloquence. It was sterner—darker—deeper than these. It was the volcanic outbreak of human nature long pent up in slavery and at last bursting its imprisonment. It was the storm of insurrection—and I could not but think, as he stalked to and fro on the platform, roused up like the Numidian Lion[1]—how that terrible voice of his would ring through the pine glades of the South, in the day of her visitation—calling the insurgents to battle and striking terror to the hearts of the dismayed and despairing mastery. He reminded me of Toussaint[2] among the plantations of Haiti.—There was great oratory in his speech—but more of dignity and earnestness than what we call eloquence. He was not up as a speaker—performing. He was an insurgent slave taking hold on the right of speech, and charging on his tyrants the bondage of his race. One of our Editors ventured to cross his path by a rash remark. He better have run upon a Lion. It was fearful, but magnificent, to see

---

1   For an in-depth discussion of the competing symbolism surrounding this description of Douglass as the Numidian Lion, see Hairston 105.

2   Formerly enslaved and self-emancipated revolutionary Toussaint Louverture (1742–1803) was an orator, writer, philosopher, military general, political thinker, and the founder of Haiti as the first Black republic in the western hemisphere.

how magnanimously and lion-like the royal fellow tore him to pieces, and left his untouched fragments scattered around him.

6. "I Will Venture to Say a Word on Slavery: An Address Delivered in New York, New York on 6 May 1845," *National Anti-Slavery Standard*, 22 May 1845

[Douglass delivered this speech at the Twelfth Anniversary Meeting of the American Anti-Slavery Society held at the Tabernacle in New York and presided over by William Lloyd Garrison. The reporter included no title, with the result that the editors of the first volume of the *Frederick Douglass Papers: Series One: Speeches, Debates and Interviews 1841–46* collection titled the speech "My Slave Experience in Maryland." I have instead opted for the title "I Will Venture to Say a Word on Slavery," by borrowing directly from Douglass's own opening words. A variation of this speech was reported in the *Liberator* on 16 May 1845].

FREDERICK DOUGLAS [SIC] was next introduced to the audience, Mr. Garrison observing that he was one who, by the laws of the South, had been *chattel*, but who was now, by his own intrepid spirit and the laws of God, a *man*. He proceeded:—I do not know that I can say anything to the point. My habits and early life have done much to unfit me for public speaking, and I fear that your patience has already been wearied by the lengthened remarks of other speakers, more eloquent than I can possibly be, and better prepared to command the attention of the audience. And I can scarcely hope to get your attention even for a longer period than fifteen minutes. Before coming to this meeting, I had a sort of desire—I don't know but it was vanity—to stand before a New-York audience in the Tabernacle. But when I came in this morning, and looked at those massive pillars, and saw the vast throng which had assembled, I got a little frightened, and was afraid that I could not speak; but now that the audience is not so large and I have recovered from my fight, I will venture to say a word on Slavery. I ran away from the South seven years ago—passing through the city in no little hurry, I assure you—and lived about three years in New Bedford, Massachusetts, before I became publicly known to the anti-slavery people. Since then I have been engaged for three years in telling the people what I know of it. I have come to this meeting to throw in my mite, and since no fugitive slave has preceded me, I am encouraged to say a word about the sunny South. I thought, when the eloquent female who addressed this audience a while ago, was speaking of the horrors of Slavery, that many an honest man would doubt the truth of the picture which she drew; and I can unite with the gentleman from Kentucky in saying, that she came far short of describing them.[1] I can tell you what I have seen with my own eyes, felt on my own person, and know to have occurred in my own neighborhood. I am not from any of those States where the slaves are said to be in their most degraded condition; but from Maryland, where Slavery is said to exist in its mildest form; yet I can stand here and relate atrocities which would make your blood to boil at the statement of them. I lived on the plantation of Col. Lloyd, on the eastern shore of Maryland, and belonged to that gentleman's clerk. He owned, probably, not less than a thousand slaves. I mention the name of this man, and also of the persons who perpetrated the deeds which I am about to relate, running the risk of being hurled back into interminable bondage—for the sake of humanity, I will mention the names, and glory in running the risk. I have the gratification to know that if I fail by the utterance of truth in this matter, that if I shall be hurled back into bondage to satisfy the slaveholder—to be killed by inches—that every drop of blood which I shall shed, every groan which I shall utter, every pain which shall rack my frame, every sob in which I shall indulge, shall be the instrument, under God, of tearing down the bloody pillar of Slavery, and of hastening the day of deliverance for three millions of my brethren in bondage. I therefore tell the names of these bloody men, not because they are worse than other men would have been in their circumstances. No, they are bloody from necessity. Slavery makes it necessary for the slaveholder to commit all conceivable outrages upon the miserable slave. It is impossible to hold the slaves in bondage without this. We had on the plantation an overseer, by the name of Austin Gore, a man who was highly respected as an overseer—proud, ambitious, cruel, artful, obdurate. Nearly every slave stood in the utmost dread and horror of that man. His eye flashed confusion amongst them. He never spoke but to command, nor commanded but to be obeyed. He was lavish with the whip, sparing with his word. I have seen that man tie up men by the two hands, and for two hours, at intervals, ply the lash. I have seen women stretched up on the limbs of trees, and their bare backs made bloody with the lash. One slave refused to be whipped by him—I need not tell you that he was a man, though black his features, degraded his condition. He had committed some trifling offense—for they whip for trifling offences—the slave refused to be whipped, and ran—he did not stand to and fight his master as I did once, and might do again—though I hope I shall not have occasion to do so—he ran and stood in a creek, and refused to come out. At length his master told him he would shoot him if he did not come out. Three calls were to be given him. The first,

---

1 The figures referred to in this sentence are unknown.

second, and third, were given, at each of which the slave stood his ground. Gore, equally determined and firm, raised his musket, and in an instant poor Derby was no more. He sank beneath the waves, and naught but the crimsoned waters marked the spot. Then a general outcry might be heard amongst us. Mr. Lloyd asked Gore why he had resorted to such a cruel measure. He replied, coolly, that he had done it, from necessity; that the slave was setting a dangerous example, and that if he was permitted to be corrected and yet save his life, that the slaves would effectually rise and be free men, and their masters be slaves. His defence was satisfactory. He remained on the plantation, and his fame went abroad. He still lives in St. Michaels, Talbot County, Maryland, and is now, I presume, as much respected, as though his guilty soul had never been stained with his brother's blood. I might go on and mention other facts if time would permit. My own wife had a dear cousin who was terribly mangled in her sleep, while nursing the child of a Mrs. Hicks. Finding the girl asleep, Mrs. Hicks beat her to death with a billet of wood, and the woman has never been brought to justice. It is not a crime to kill a negro in Talbot county, Maryland, further than it is a deprivation of a man's property. I need to know of one who boasted that he had killed two slaves, and with an oath would say, "I'm the only benefactor in the country."

Now, my friends, pardon me for having detained you so long; but let me tell you with regard to the feelings of the slave. The people at the North say—"Why don't you rise? If we were thus treated we would rise and throw off the yoke. We would wade knee deep in blood before we would endure the bondage." You'd rise up! Who are these that are asking for manhood in the slave, and who say that he has it not, because he does not rise? The very men who are ready by the Constitution to bring the strength of the nation to put us down! You, the people of New-York, the people of Massachusetts, of New England, of the whole Northern States, have sworn under God that we shall be slaves or die! And shall we three millions be taunted with a want of the love of freedom, by the very men who stand upon us and stay, submit, or be crushed? We don't ask you to engage in any physical warfare against the slaveholder. We only ask that in Massachusetts, and the several non-slaveholding States in Massachusetts, and the several non-slaveholding States which maintains a union with the slaveholder— who stand with your heavy heels on the quivering heart-strings of the slave that you will stand off. Leave us to take care of our masters. But here you come up to our master and tell them that they ought to shoot us—to take away our wives and little ones—to sell our mothers into interminable bondage, and sever the tenderest ties. You say to us, if you dare to carry out the principles of our fathers, and we'll shoot you down. Others may tamely submit; not I. You may put the chains upon me and fetter me, but I am not a slave, for my master who puts the chains upon me, shall stand in as much dread of me as I do of him. I ask you in the name of my three millions of brethren at the South. We know that we are unable to cope with you in numbers; you are numerically stronger, politically stronger, than we are—but we ask you if you will rend asunder the heart and mangle the body of the slave? If so, you must do it at your own expense. While you continue in the Union, you are as bad as the slaveholder. If you have thus wronged the poor black man, by stripping him of his freedom, how are you going to give evidence of your repentance? Undo what you have done[.] Do you say that the slave ought not to be free?—These hands—are they not mine? This body—is it not mine? Again, I am your brother, white as you are. I'm your blood-kin. You don't get rid of me so easily. I mean to hold on to you. And in this land of liberty, I'm a slave. The twenty-six States that blaze forth on your flag, proclaim a compact to return me to bondage if I run away, and keep me in bondage if I submit. Wherever I go, under the aegis of liberty, there I'm a slave. If I go to Lexington or Bunker Hill, there I'm a slave, chained to perpetual servitude. I may go to your deepest valley, to your highest mountain, I'm still a slave, and the bloodhound may chase me down. Now I ask you if you are willing to have your country the hunting-ground of the slave. God says thou shall not oppress: the Constitution says oppress: which will you serve, God or man? The American Anti-Slavery Society says God, and I am thankful for it. In the name of my brethren, to you, Mr. President, and the noble band who cluster around you, to you, who are scourged on every hand by priest, people, politician, Church, and State, to you I bring a thankful heart, and in the name of three millions of slaves, I offer you their gratitude for your faithful advocacy in behalf of the slave.

7. "Frederick Douglass in behalf of George Latimer," *Liberator*, 18 November 1842

[Douglass published this public letter that he addressed to William Lloyd Garrison in support of fugitive slave George Latimer in the *Liberator*. In a bold departure, he relied on his pen rather than his voice due to his exposure to debilitating health problems that had temporarily prevented him from delivering a speech in support of Latimer's struggles for freedom. Latimer (1819–96) had been born into slavery in Norfolk, Virginia, and had escaped to freedom in the north with his wife, Rebecca, only to be subsequently arrested in Boston. Douglass was one of the many individuals involved in the campaign for his release. Following ongoing legal wrangles, the freedom of Latimer and his wife was eventually purchased from their slaveowner, James B. Gray.]

Frederick Douglass in behalf of Geo. Latimer.

LYNN, November 8th, 1842.

DEAR FRIEND GARRISON:

The date of this letter finds me quite unwell. I have for a week past been laboring, in company with bro. Charles Remond,[1] in New-Bedford, with special reference to the case of our outraged brother, George Latimer, and speaking almost day and night, in public and in private; and for the reward of our labor, I have the best evidence that a great good has been done. It is said by many residents that New-Bedford has never been so favorably aroused to her anti-slavery responsibility as at present. Our meetings were characterized by that deep and solemn feeling which the importance of the cause, when properly set forth, is always calculated to awaken. On Sunday, we held three meetings in the now town hall, at the usual meeting hours, morning, afternoon, and evening. In the morning, we had quite a large meeting, at the opening of which, I occupied about an hour, on the question as to whether a man is better than a sheep. Mr. Dean then made a few remarks, and after him, Mr. Clapp,[2] of Nantucket, arose and gave his testimony to the truth, as it is in anti-slavery. The meeting then adjourned, to meet again in the afternoon. I said that we held our meetings at the regular meeting hours. Truth requires me to make our afternoon meeting an exception to this remark. For long before the drawling, lazy church bells commenced sounding their deathly notes, mighty crowds were making their way to the town hall. They needed no bells to remind them, of their duty to bleeding humanity. They were not going to meeting to hear as to the best mode of performing water baptism; they were not going to meeting to have their prayers handsomely said for them, or to say them, merely, themselves; but to pray, not in word, but in deed and in truth; they were not going thither to be worshipped, but to worship, in spirit and in truth; they were not going to sacrifice, but to have mercy; they did not go there to find God; they had found him already. Such I think I may safely say of a large portion of the vast assembly that met in the afternoon. As I gazed upon them, my soul leaped for joy; and, but for the thought that the time might be better employed, I could have shouted aloud.—After a short space, allotted to secret or public prayer, bro. J.B. Sanderson[3] arose and requested the attention of the audience to the reading of a

---

1 Charles Remond (1810–73) was a free-born African American activist, abolitionist, reformer, writer, and orator.

2 These figures are unknown.

3 Born in New Bedford, Massachusetts, Jeremiah Burke Sanderson (1821–75) was an African American radical abolitionist, activist, author, civil rights leader, and close personal friend of the Douglass family.

few passages of scripture, selected by yourself in the editorial of last week. They did give their attention, and as he read the solemn and soul-stirring denunciations of Jehovah, by the mouth of his prophets and apostles, against oppressors, the deep stillness that pervaded that magnificent hall was a brilliant demonstration, that the audience felt that what was read was but the reiteration of words which had fallen from the great Judge of the universe. After reading, he proceeded to make some remarks on the general question of human rights. These, too, seemed to sink deep into the hearts of the gathered multitude. Not a word was lost; it was good seed, sown in good ground, by a careful hand; it must, it will bring forth fruit.

After him, rose bro. Remond, who addressed the meeting in his usual happy and deeply affecting style. When he had concluded his remarks, the meeting adjourned to meet again at an early hour in the evening. During the interval, our old friends and the slaves' friends, John Butler, Thomas Jones, Noah White, and others, were engaged in carrying benches from liberty hall to the town hall, that all who came might be accommodated with seats. They were determined to do something for humanity, though by so doing, they should be ranked with sabbath-breakers. Christianity prays for more of just such sabbath-breakers as these, and may God grant by an overwhelming revival of anti-slavery truth, to convert and send forth more just such.

The meeting met according to adjournment, at an early hour. The splendid hall was brilliantly lighted, and crowded with an earnest, listening audience, and notwithstanding the efforts of our friends before named to have them seated, a large number had to stand during the meeting, which lasted about three hours; where the standing part of the audience were, at the commencement of the meeting, there they were at the conclusion of it; no moving about with them; any place was good enough, so they could but hear. From the eminence which I occupied, I could see the entire audience; and from its appearance, I should conclude that prejudice against color was not there, at any rate, it was not to be seen by me; we were all on a level, every one took a seat just where they chose; there was neither men's side, nor women's side; white pew, nor black pew; but all seats were free, and all sides free. When the meeting was full gathered, I had something to say, and was followed by bro. Sanderson and Remond. When they had concluded their remarks, I again took the stand, and called the attention [of the] meeting to the case of bro. George Latimer, approved the finishing stroke of my present public speaking. On taking my seat, I was seized with violent pain in my breast, which continued till morning, and with occasional raising of blood; this past [sic] off in about two hours, after which, weakness of breast, a cough, and shortness of breath ensued, so that now such is the state of my lungs that I am unfit for public speaking, for the present. My condition goes harder with me, much harder than it would at ordinary times. These are certainly extraordinary times; times that demand the efforts of the humblest of our most humble advocates of our perishing dying fellow-countrymen. Those that can whisper freedom, should be doing even that, though they can only be heard from one side of their fire place to the other. It is a struggle of life and death with us just now. No sword that can be used, be it never so rusty, show lay idle in it[s] scabbard. Slavery, our enemy, has landed in our very midst and commenced its bloody work. Just look at it: here is George Latimer a man— a brother—a husband—a father, stamped with the likeness of eternal God, and redeemed by the blood of Jesus Christ, out-lawed, hunted down like a wild beast, and ferociously dragged through the streets of Boston, and incarcerated within the walls of Leverett-st. jail. And all this is done in Boston—liberty-loving, slavery-hating Boston—intellectual, moral, and religious Boston. And why was this—what crime had George Latimer committed? He had committed the crime of availing himself of his natural rights, in defence of which the founders of this very Boston enveloped her in midnight darkness, with the smoke proceeding from their thundering artillery. What a horrible state of things is here presented. Boston has become the hunting-ground of merciless men-hunters, and man-stealers. Henceforth we need not portray to the imagination of northern people, the flying slave making his way through thick and dark woods of the South, with white fanged blood-hounds yelping on his blood-stained track; but refer to the streets of Boston, made dark and dense by crowds of professed christians. Take a look at James B. Gray's new pack, turned loose on the track of poor Latimer. I see the blood-thirsty animals, smelling at every corner, part with each other, and meet again; they seem to be consulting as to the best mode of coming upon their victim. Now they look sad, discouraged—tired, they drag along, as if the[y] were ashamed of their business, and about to give up the chase; but presently they get a sight of their prey, their eyes brighten, they become more courageous, they approach their victim unlike the common hound. They come upon him softly, wagging their tails, pretending friendship, and do not pounce upon him, until they have secured him beyond possible escape. Such is the character of James B. Gray's new pack of two-legged blood-hounds that hunted down George Latimer, and dragged him away to the Leverett-street prison but a few days since. We need not point to the sugar fields of Louisiana, or to the rice swamps of Alabama, for the bloody deeds of this soul-crushing system, but to the city of the pilgrims. In future, we need not uncap the bloody cells of the horrible slave prisons of Norfolk, Richmond, Mobile, and New-Orleans, and depict the wretched and forlorn condition of their miserable inmates, whose groans rend the air, pierce heaven, and disturb the Almighty; listen no longer at the snappings of the bloody slave-drivers' lash. Withdraw your attention, for a moment, from the agonizing cries coming from hearts bursting with the keenest anguish at the South, gaze no longer upon the base, cold-blooded, heartless slave-dealer of the South, who lays his iron clutch upon the hearts of husband and wife, and, with one mighty effort, tears the bleeding ligaments apart which before constituted the twain one flesh. I say, turn your attention from all this cruelty abroad, look now at home—follow me to your courts of justice—mark him who sits upon the bench. He may, or he may not—God grant he may not—tear George Latimer from a beloved wife and tender infant. But let us take a walk to the prison in which George Latimer is confined, inquire for the turn-key; let him open the large iron-barred door that leads you to the inner prison. You need go no further. Hark! listen! hear the groans and cries of George Latimer, mingling with which may be heard the cry—my wife, my child—and all is still again.

A moment of reflection ensues—I am to be taken back to Norfolk—must be torn from a wife and tender babe, with the threat from Mr. Gray that I am to be murdered, though not in the ordinary way—not to have my head severed from my shoulders, not be hanged—not to have my heart pierced through with a dagger—not to have my brains blown out. No, no, all these are too good for me. No: I am to be killed by inches. I know not how; perhaps by cat-hauling until my back is torn all to pieces, my flesh is to be cut with the rugged lash, and I faint; warm brine must now be poured into my bleeding wounds, and through this process I must pass, until death shall end my sufferings. Good God! save me from a fate so horrible. Hark! hear him roll in his chains; "I can die, I had rather, than go back. O, my wife! O, my child!" You have heard enough. What man, what Christian can look upon this bloody state of things without his soul swelling big with indignation on the guilty perpetrators of it, and without resolving to cast in his influence with those who are collecting the elements which are to come down in ten-fold thunder, and dash this state of things into atoms?

Men husbands and fathers of Massachusetts—put yourselves in the place of George Latimer; feel his pain and anxiety of mind; give vent to the groans that are breaking through his fever-parched lips, from a heart emersed [sic] in the deepest agony and suffering; rattle his chains, let his prospect be yours, for the space of a few moments. Remember George Latimer in bonds as bound with him; keep in view the golden rule—"All things whatsoever ye would that men should do unto you, do ye even so to them." "In as much as ye did it unto the least of these my brethren ye have done it unto me."[1]

---

1 Matthew 7:12 and 25:40.

Now make up your minds to what your duty is to George Latimer, and when you have made your minds up, prepare to do it and take the consequences, and I have no fears of George Latimer going back. I can sympathize with George Latimer, having myself been cast into a miserable jail, on suspicion of my intending to do what he is said to have done, viz. appropriating my own body to my use.

My heart is full, and had I my voice, I should be doing all that I am capable of, for Latimer's redemption. I can do but little in any department; but if one department is more the place for me than another, that one is before the people.

I can't write to much advantage, having never had a day's schooling in my life, nor have I ever ventured to give publicity to any of my scribbling before; nor would I now, but for my peculiar circumstances.

Your grateful friend,

FREDERICK DOUGLASS

8. "No Union with Slaveholders: An Address Delivered in Boston, Massachusetts: 28 May 1844," *National Anti-Slavery Standard*, 25 July 1844

[Douglass delivered this speech during the Massachusetts Antislavery Society New England Convention held in Boston. Again, his speech was transcribed with no title, with the result that the editors of the first volume of the *Frederick Douglass Papers: Series One: Speeches, Debates and Interviews 1841–46* collection titled his speech "No Union with Slaveholders." I have retained this title here on the grounds that it is a direct quotation of Douglass's own words.]

Mr. DOUGLAS [sic].—I do not know, Sir, that I shall be able to throw any new light upon this subject. I am here more to bear my testimony, than to argue the question. I rejoice, however, to see so large a portion of the people here to discuss it, and may the discussion only cease when Slavery shall be no more.

I have heard many things said as to the utility of dissolving the Union. We are told by the opponents of that measure, that the Constitution depends on the people, and we are told also, on the same side, that it needs no alteration. I confess, that had it descended to me from the clouds, I might have questioned its merits, in consequence of what appears upon the face of it. But, knowing as I do its origin, and the characters of its framers, and seeing as I do, how it was written, as it were, in the blood of thousands and thousands of slaves, I think it not an Anti-slavery document. Even had it come to me from above, I do not think it could have stood the test of impartial examination. I should have been compelled when I came to the clause respecting the return of persons held to service of labor, to think that something else than freedom was meant, if not to acknowledge that Slavery stared me in the face. But without going into a minute examination of every clause, I should conceive its intent respecting Slavery to be proved by this fact, if there were no other; that the laws passed immediately after its adoption, and by the very men who framed and accepted it, were laws upholding Slavery. That shows that they knew they might maintain Slavery under it.

Mr. President, it is sufficient for me at least to prove its character, that I am a slave under the Constitution. Wherever the stars and stripes wave, I am a slave! It's cold—it's dead—it falls twice dead on my ear—all this talk about the Anti-slavery Constitution, and the glorious Union. There is not law enough, or strength enough in any State of the Union, to hinder me from being dragged away from being a slave—not even here in Massachusetts. If you resist what the men appointed to decide upon the meaning of the Constitution declare to be the law, you are a mobocrat—an insurrectionist.

But when I heard this sound of disunion with slaveholders, it fell like angelic melody on my heart. That's good for the slave, I said: that will free the slave! That's the reason that we have Slavery now—(and the slaveholder knows it, however gentleman here may fail to perceive it,)—that the North strengthens him with all her own strength. It is because this whole nation have sworn by the God who made them, that the slave should be a slave or die! (Stillness of strong sensation). The Slave knows this. He knows that you are pledged and bound to each other to crush him down. It is this blood Union that I wish should cease. I only ask you, that will no longer crush and slay us. Tell the slaveholder that if he will still hold slaves, it must be only his own responsibility; by his own unaided strength.

I am astonished at the existence of any desire on the part of pious and religious men, to be in union with slaveholders. What is their character? Are they so very pious and religious? Oh, yes! they're very pious; and the North knows how to suit them, when there's to be a nomination with a style of piety that will unite perfectly with their own. The South brings forward for your President, Henry Clay,[1] and the North stands ready with the vice-President—the Rev. Mr. Frelinghuysen! [Great and long-continued applause mingled with hissing.]

Mr. President, of course I did not mean any harm to Mr. Frelinghuysen; I was only illustrating the nature and the character of the Union, by this match that they have made between the piety of the North, and the Slavery of the South. I meant no harm to Henry Clay.

---

1 Henry Clay (1777–1852) was a Virginia-born white US senator, lawyer, and slaveholder.

They have married Henry to Frelinghuysen, (tremendous applause,) and it's a type of the National Union; but I am astonished that Freemen do not forbid the banns.[1] Why, what have they about them at the South, that you should endure this political Union? Why should you love such association with the whip, and with the pistol, and with the bowie-knife? There are your great men in Congress—look at them! Your Choate, and your Bates![2] Do they rise to say a word about your business that they're sent there to do—they're bullied down, and obliged to sit there and hear Massachusetts scoffed at and insulted! They had to sit and listen; and so are all the North bullied down by them. And you consent to be their kidnappers! their putters down of insurrections!

I admit, with friend White,[3] that they do not care about the Union, except as it supports Slavery. [Mr. Douglas here read the testimony of Mr. Arnold, of Tennessee, and of the Editor of the Maysville Intelligencer, to show the reliance of the Slaveholder upon the Union for the support of the system.[4]]

My friends have spoken of the decrease of our influence, which they think will be the consequence of dissolution. They seem to think that there is some geographical change to take place in consequence. They seem to think that the North is to go to the North pole, and the South to fly away out of sight to the South pole. They overlook the fact, that no such change can take place, and that a moral change is the only one to follow. But this moral change will be all-sufficient. Until it takes place, the slaveholder cannot be seen and known as he is by the people. Who cannot be seen and known as he is by the people? Who can fix the brand of murderer—thief—adulterer, on the brow of the man that you associate with, and salute as honorable? The Honorable Henry Clay! the Honorable John C. Calhoun![5] And those ministers who come to the North with the price of blood in their hands—how shall moral principle be diffused among the people on the subject of slavery, while they are hailed as Reverend! Withdraw from them the Sanction of the men who do not hold slaves, and how quickly would the character of Slavery been seen as it is. The people would then as

---

1 Banns refers to the public notice that is read out on three successive Sundays in a parish church announcing a forthcoming marriage and providing the congregation with an opportunity to voice their protest.

2 These figures cannot be identified.

3 William Abijah White (1818–56) was a white radical abolitionist and close friend of Frederick Douglass.

4 These figures cannot be identified.

5 John C. Calhoun (1782–1850) from South Carolina served as vice-president of the United States and was a political thinker, slaveholder, and writer of proslavery propaganda.

soon think of seeking a union with Algerine [sic] pirates themselves. We acknowledge, now, in words, that Slavery is a crime; but still, we have been so long in association with it, that we think a man may commit it, and yet be honorable.

I heard something said of British and American oppression. But, Sir, the hungry Englishman is a freeman; while the slave is not only hungry, but a slave. The Briton says to his victim, Work for me or you shall starve; and the American says to the slave, Work, or you shall be whipped. This was defined by Mr. Walker[1] to be the difference. But I know something of this matter at home, and I have found that we say, "whip!" and "starve!" too. The slave is entirely unmanned. The master is at once his conscience, his owner, body and spirit, his all. The master decides when and where, and with whom he shall go—when and where, and how, and by whom he shall be punished. None of these may be desired, as I am informed, by a nobleman of England, be he ever so noble. But here the master lays his foul clutch upon his throat—he makes his iron grasp felt in the soul. He says to the immortal spirit, thou shalt not aspire! he says to the immortal spirit, thou shalt not aspire! he says to the intellect, thou shalt not expand! to the body, thou shalt not go at large! Could he say all this were it not for the Union! I say, then, the Union does it. [Great applause.]

The Union may be illustrated in this way. I have ten men in a height of rope. Now, it is plain that one man can't hold ten, and I call to you, and you, and you, gentlemen, and beg your aid. But you say to me, Douglass, we've decided, objects to holding men in that way. We've conscientious scruples. We're not friendly to holding me. We will surround you, however, and take an interest in the matter as far as to hinder their getting away from you. Just so the circle of Northern opinion and political union unites with that of the South around the slave.

I take for my watch-word, "No Union with Slaveholders," not because I have any hatred to the Slaveholder. I love him as truly as I do the slave. But I do it because I see that there is, comparatively, no efficacy in all that you can say or do against his crime, as long as he can taunt you with your co-operation. True, he says, I run my fist in my slave's pocket, but you say you'll strike him down if he resists me; you are as bad as I am.

My friend White said, that Slavery existed before the Union, and not in consequence of the Union. Sir, I lived before I drew the present air I draw; but I live now, by the air I draw. Had Slavery been deprived of the benefit it formed the Union to obtain, it could not have lived. It would, long ere this, have ceased by public opinion or insurrection. But through the means of the Union, it has gone on, blunting our

1 This figure is unknown.

moral sense, till we have lost our moral discrimination. When a white man suffers we are full of sympathy. A nation was in tears at the bursting of the Paixhan gun.[1] But when a slave shrieks out in his agony—when McIntosh calls out of the flames to the whole assembled people around the stake—"shoot me! shoot me!"—who cares! he's a negro! he's a slave! what right had he to defend his wife or daughter against a white man! he shall die in a slow fire. This was in one of the slave States of our Union. Look now at the District of Columbia, the seat of our United Government. The Hon. Seth M. Gates[2] told me that he saw there a woman start out of a half-opened slave-prison gate; and before she had run far, three men who witnessed it, also started at a distance, started to head her off, before she should be able to cross the bridge, which would give her a chance of escape. True to their Virginia instincts, they succeeded in reaching the bridge immediately after her. A moment more, and she would have been in their grasp. But her resolution was taken. She leaped from the bridge into the river, and sunk to rise no more. She preferred death to the protection of the Union. The slaves flee as from a pestilence, away from the Union. It is this fearful union with slaveholders—the power and perpetuity of that system which we have met to abolish; and I ask the good people here to-night, to yield to its demands no longer.

I have been, Mr. President, all my life, in a situation to see and feel the practical bearings of the Union. I have had the sound of the lash to impel me on in my labors for its termination. Had I invoked the Union in any of my sufferings under it, I had done it in vain. Who is it that can do so, in case of need! Could Nat Turner[3] do so? (A nobler name is not to be found in the annals of revolutions!) It was not he who could appeal to this Union, formed to preserve Liberty.

But the Slaveholders—(he gave them enough to do, to watch their own cradles and their own hearths;) and they flew to the Union for

---

1 The Paixhan gun is a naval gun designed by French military general Henri-Joseph Paixhans (1783–1854).

2 Seth Merrill Gates (1800–77) was a white US politician and member of the House of Representatives.

3 Born into US slavery, Nathaniel Turner (1800–31) was a preacher, papermaker, and radical revolutionary. As a Black freedom-fighter, philosopher, thinker, and military general who understood slavery as a violation of all human rights, he led a rebellion in August 1831 in which he and his leaders executed white southern slaveholders in Southampton County, Virginia, as retribution for their crimes against Black humanity. On 11 November 1831 he was executed, and vast numbers of African American women, children, and men, enslaved and free, were murdered by white authorities in the reign of white supremacist terror that followed in the wake of his revolutionary campaign.

help, and obtained it. I have been informed that one hundred men from Maine, were immediately ordered to their assistance, commanded by a Colonel White, of Manchester, Massachusetts. Why could not Madison Washington[1] strike for Liberty on the soil of Virginia? The Union overawed him! he must wait till he is at the mercy of the waves, with less odds against him than a whole nation to brand him as mutineer and a murderer. Yes, Sir, Daniel Webster[2] demanded him as such, and not in the name of the South alone, but of this whole country. One such fact on the side of dissolution would show me that I ought to go for it.

I have not much intellect, but nobody need pretend to me that by being a party to the Union he is not pledged to keep down the slaves. Why are you pledged to what you agree to? and how ineffably mean do you look—how cowardly, standing with fourteen millions of "free and enlightened people!" to keep down two millions of ignorant suffering slaves in the dust! You see it plainly when a great lubber-headed fellow gets holds of a little one in the street. Just so the whole world sees your American Union for the holding of slaves. [Continued applause.]

9. "The Black Man Was No Less a Man because of His Color: An Address Delivered in Norristown, Pennsylvania: 12 August 1844," *Pennsylvania Freeman*, 22 August 1844

[Douglass delivered this speech at the Annual Meeting of the Anti-Slavery Society in Norristown, Pennsylvania, and it was previously unknown to scholars until it was discovered by pioneering researcher Gregory Lampe and reproduced in his seminal volume, *Frederick Douglass: Freedom's Voice, 1818–1845*. While Lampe chose to title this speech, which was printed without a title in the *Pennsylvania Freeman*, "The Progress of the Cause," I have borrowed from Douglass's own words to arrive at the following title, "The Black Man Was No Less a Man Because of His Color." However, this is an especially difficult challenge in this case because this is one of many of Douglass's speeches that was reported almost entirely in the third person. That said, there seems little doubt that the reporter's insertion of this declaration constitutes, if not Douglass's words exactly, then probably very close to them due to the characteristic fusion of political force, radical protest, and rhetorical power that was typical of his oratorical performances more generally.]

---

1   For further information regarding the revolutionary heroism of Black liberator Madison Washington, see the discussion in the Introduction (p. 14).
2   Daniel Webster (1782–1852) was a white US politician, lawyer, and senator.

Frederick Douglass said he was always ready to speak on slavery, and added, in reply to some one who desired to have his name and that of the preceding speaker announced, that he was afraid we cared too much to know *who* it is that speaks, instead of weighing well *what* was said. He was accustomed to meetings where it was not decided who should speak, but where any one might speak on any proposition, either in favor or against it, and bear his testimony by voting or in any other way. He did not find fault with the proceedings of the Society in declaring who should and who should not be members, but he did not feel so much at home in such meetings. This, however, should not prevent his speaking. He was there as an abolitionist, and as a slave, for whose redemption abolitionists were toiling, and he felt it to be a duty and a privilege to testify in behalf of anti-slavery, and to strive to warm the hearts of all who were laboring to promote the spread of its principles.

To him, there was no more deeply interesting time in the history of the anti-slavery cause than the present. We were receiving intelligence from all parts of the growth of the cause, and he had listened with deep interest to the soul-stirring report we had just heard read, and rejoiced in the evidences it presented of the progress of anti-slavery in this quarter. It has advanced rapidly in Massachusetts, and, in fact, throughout New England, but abolitionists here have as much reason to congratulate themselves, as we have there. Although he had been here but a short time, he had seen a great improvement since he was last among us, and he felt cheered and encouraged by it. Colored people in New England are much better treated than they were a short time since. It had been but two or three years since they were every where repulsed. They were treated with indignity in meeting houses, subjected to insult upon highways and by-ways, in the stage, the steamboat, and railroad car. Everywhere were they met by a prejudice which crushed them to the earth. This existed yet to some extent, but had very much dwindled away. On all the railroads in New England, except one of some thirty or forty miles, all distinctions on account of color were done away with. A great advance had been made. Two years since, a colored man who would have ventured into any other than the Jim Crow car would have been kicked and cuffed and dragged out, and it was useless for him to appeal to law for redress, for courts and railroads were both prejudiced. How was this change effected? By preaching the truth—by showing the absurdity of this prejudice—that the black man was no less a man because of his color.

On the first of August they had a heart-cheering demonstration of the progress which anti-slavery had made in New England. The celebration of West India Emancipation,[1] in Hingham, was one of the

---

1   The British West Indies Emancipation Act took effect from 1 August 1838

most brilliant and glorious gatherings of abolitionists which had ever taken place in this country—there were not less than seven thousand persons there, and the spirit which prevailed, as well as the number, was cheering. They evinced a feeling which cannot be conceived by those who were not present, and the abolitionists of New England were amply compensated by it for all the afflictions and trials they had endured since the commencement of the warfare. They there saw in miniature what they will see in full reality, and this was done, sir, by "scattering the living coals of truth"[1] upon the nation's naked heart. Abolitionists have used no other means than preaching the truth— they have been scoffed at and persecuted, but the result of their labors as seen that day—the number and spirit of that gathering will exert an influence which shall be felt not only in Boston but from one end of Massachusetts to the other. We should feel encouraged to go forward.

We are great sticklers for individualism in Massachusetts—we express our own thoughts in our own way—speak out our own ideas in independence, and that is what we want.

10. **"Slavery and the Annexation of Texas to the United States,"** *Liberator*, 12 December 1845

[Douglass delivered this speech at an antislavery meeting held in Independent Chapel, Cork, Ireland, and the report was first printed in the *Cork Examiner* and then copied in the pages of the *Liberator*. Before he gave his speech, a member of the Anti-Slavery Society of Cork expressed the organization's debt of gratitude to Douglass for his anti-slavery activism. They credited his antislavery efforts as the sole reason for their having "been stirred up to renewed and active life for the deliverance of the captive." The radical impact of transatlantic reform networks in galvanizing support for the abolitionist movement is indisputably in evidence here. While the editors of the first volume of the *Frederick Douglass Papers: Series One: Speeches, Debates and Interviews 1841-46* collection chose to title this speech "Slavery and Texas," I have adapted the title to reproduce Douglass's original phrasing. In this speech, which he delivered before a transatlantic audience, Douglass protested against the admission of Texas as a slaveholding state into the Union on 29 December 1845, in order to shore up his virulent protest against the ongoing expansion of the "patriarchal institution" across US territory.]

---

1 John Greenleaf Whittier, "Our Countrymen in Chains!" This poem was published as a broadside by the New York Anti-Slavery Office in 1837. A digitized copy is available online: http://www.loc.gov/pictures/item/2008661312/.

The votes of thanks and the reading of the Address were loudly applauded by the meeting.

Mr. Douglass arose, and was received with enthusiastic cheering. When it subsided, he said—The sentiments of gratitude expressed by the meeting are in perfect unison with my own. Never was I held under great obligations to the press, and to the proprietors of public buildings, than I have been since in Cork, and I express my sincere gratitude for it in behalf of the bondsmen. Particularly am I indebted to the press for their freedom in copying the few feeble words I have been able to say in this city, that they may return to my land, and sound terribly in the ears of the oppressors of my country-men. Mr. President, the address which has been read, I certainly was not expecting. I expected to go through the length and breadth of your country, preaching to those who are ready to hear the groans of the oppressed. I did not expect the high position that I enjoy during my stay in the city of Cork, and not only here, but in Dublin. The object which we have met to consider is the annexation of Texas to the United States. You have perhaps heard that in America, when an individual has absented himself unaccountably for any time, such a person is said to have gone to Texas, few knowing where it is. Texas is that part of Mexico, bounded on the North by the United States, on the South side by the Gulf of Mexico. The extent of this country is not correctly known. It is as large as France—a most prolific soil—climate most salubrious. The facilities for commercial and agricultural proceedings are unsurpassed any where. A Mr. Austin[1] obtained a grant of the Royal Government, to settle three hundred families in Texas with an understanding that such families should obey the laws then existing, and also, that they should be members of the Roman Catholic religion. He succeeded in introducing 30 families. His son took up the business, and introduced three hundred families. Before he succeeded, the revolution in Mexico[2] severed the Mexican provinces from the crown, and the contract was rendered void. He made application to the new government, and obtained a similar contract. Other men in the west made similar applications to the Mexican Government. Among the rest were Irishmen, and they were among the few who fulfilled their contracts.

---

1   Stephen F. Austin (1793–1836) is colloquially known as the "Father of Texas" on the grounds that he was responsible for convincing 300 families to come and settle in the region in 1825.

2   Douglass is referring to the founding of the Republic of Mexico, which was established as a federal constitution in 1824 following the nation having obtained its independence from Spain as a result of the War of Mexican Independence (1810–21).

The consequence of making the Catholic religion a necessary qualification to settle in Texas afforded opportunity for hypocrisy. A number of persons not of Catholic persuasion entered the territory, and made complaints. They succeeded in fomenting a revolt against the Mexican Government. Soon after, the Texans managed to lodge complaints of oppression against it. Under these pretences they declared for religious freedom, applied to the United States for sympathy for religious liberty. After getting the property under conditions of submission, they turn around for sympathy in a revolt in behalf of religious toleration. Mexico came forward nobly and abolished slavery in Texas. In open violation of this, slaves were introduced. Mexico, outraged at this violation of her laws, attempted to compel obedience—this resulted in the revolution. Texas applied to the United States for assistance. Here came the deed that ought to bring down on the United States the *united* execration of the world. She pretended to be in a friendly relation with Mexico. Her Congress looked on with indifference on the raising of troops to aid the slaveholding Texans in wresting from the Mexicans, Texas—Indeed, they encouraged it. Texians [sic] succeeded in holding at bay the Mexican Government. The United States with indecent haste recognized the independence of Texas. This was the preparatory step to the consummation of the annexation to the Union. The object was that of making Texas the market for the surplus slaves of the North American States.

The Middle States of the United States are slaveraising States. In 1837, you might meet in Virginia hundreds of slaves handcuffed and chained together, driving southward to be sold. The Southern States were formerly those where the slaves brought the highest price, but at present they are fully supplied with slaves; and there is a consequent reduction in the price of human flesh and bones. In 1836 slaves brought from 1000 to 1500 dollars; but a year ago, the price was reduced to 600 dollars.—The slaveholders saw the necessity of opening a new country where there would be a demand for slaves. American should be considered a band of plunderers for the worst purposes. Should they go to war with three millions of slaves in their bosom, only looking for the first favorable opportunity of lifting their arms in open rebellion? American statesmen are aware of this. The reasons they give for the annexation of Texas not only prove them to be rotten at heart, but a band of dastards. They say that Mexico is not able to go to war, therefore we can take their country. I dare the Americans to reach their arms to Canada. The conduct of America, in this particular, has not been sufficiently dwelt upon by the British press. England should not have stood by and seen a feeble people robbed, without raising a note of remonstrance.

I have done with the question of Texas—let me proceed to the general question. I will read you the laws of a part of the American states, regarding the relation of master and slave, the laws which created the row in the steamship Cambria, not because they are the worst I could select but because I desire to have them remain upon your memory. If more than seven slaves are found together without a white person, 20 lashes a piece; for letting loose a boat from where it is moored, 39 lashes, for the first, and for the second offence, the loss of an ear. For having an article for sale without a ticket from his master, 10 lashes. For travelling in the night without a pass, 40 lashes. Found in another person's quarters, 40 lashes. For being on horseback without a written permissions, 3 lashes; for riding without leave, a slave may be whipped, cropped or branded with the letter A, in the cheek. The laws may be found in Heywood's manual,[1] and several other works. These laws will be the laws of Texas. How sound these laws, Irishmen and Irish women, in your ears? These laws, as you are aware, are not the worst, for one law in North Carolina makes it a crime punishable with death for the second offence, to teach a slave to read.

My friends, I would wish to allude to another matter in relation to the religious denominations of Cork. My friends, all I have said respecting their brethren in America has been prompted by a regard for the bondman. I know what slavery is by experience. I know what my experience has been at the hands of religionists. The Baptist or Presbyterian that would desire me not to tell the truth, is a man who loves his sect more than he loves his God, [cheers.] To you who have a missionary spirit, I say, there is no better field than America. The slave is on his knees, asking for light; slaves who not only want the Bible, but some one to teach them to read its contents, [hear, hear.] Their cries come across the Atlantic this evening, appealing to you! Lift up your voices against this giant sin, [loud cheers.] Mr. President, I am glad to learn that the simple reading of my narrative by a minister in your town, was the cause of his preaching last Sabbath an able anti-slavery discourse, [hear, hear.] My friends, labor on in this good work, for hearts on the other side of the Atlantic have long been cheered by your efforts. When England with one effort wiped from her West Indies that stain of slavery, turning eight hundred thousand *things* into eight hundred thousand human beings, from that time the bondmen in our country looked with more ardent hope to the day when their chains would be broken, and they be permitted to enjoy that liberty in a Republic, which was now enjoyed under the mild rule of a Monarchical Government. This infused amongst us a spirit of hope, of faith, of liberty. Thus you have done much, but *don't feel your power ceases here.* Every one has an influence. ONLY SPEAK THE

---

1 Further information about this manual cannot be located.

TRUE WORD—BREATHE THE RIGHT PRAYER—TRUST IN THE TRUE GOD—and your influence will be powerful against all wrong! [loud and continued applause.]

Your land is now being travelled over by men from our country. Their whole code of justice is based on the changing basis of the color of a man's skin; for in Virginia, there are but three crimes for which a white man is hung, but in the same State, there are seventy-one crimes for which the black suffers death. I want the Americans to know that in the good city of Cork, I ridiculed their nation—I attempted to excite the utter contempt of the people here upon them. O that America were freed from slavery! Her brightness would then dazzle the Eastern world. The oppressed of all nations might flock to her as an asylum from monarchical or other despotic rulers, [applause.] I do believe that America has the elements for becoming a great and glorious nation. Those three millions of foes might be converted into three million of friends—but I am not going to say anything in her favor—I am an outlaw there—and it is time to bid you farewell!

Mr. Douglass sat down amidst the most enthusiastic applause, which was again and again repeated.

11. "The Folly of Our Opponents," *The Liberty Bell* (Boston, 1845), 166–72

[Douglass wrote this essay at the request of Maria Weston Chapman (see Appendix B5), editor of *The Liberty Bell*, a series of antislavery giftbooks that were published to raise money for the abolitionist campaign. In the Preface to her publication of Douglass's essay, Chapman inserted the following statement regarding his own admission concerning the seemingly impassable—yet in fact passable—chasm between slavery and freedom: "In a note enclosing this article, Mr. Douglass says:—'It was intended for a place in the Liberty Bell, but my literary advantages have been so limited, that I am ill prepared to decide what is, and what is not, appropriate for such a collection. I looked exceedingly strange in my own eyes, as I sat writing. The thought of writing for a book!—and only six years since a fugitive from a Southern cornfield—caused a singular jingle in my mind.'"]

Dr. DEWEY,[1] in his somewhat notorious defence of American Morals, published soon after his return to this country from Europe, where he had witnessed those morals subjected to a most rigid examination, treats of the conduct of the American people and Slavery; and,

---

1 Orville Dewey (1794–1882) was a white US minister, author, and philosopher who published his tract, *On American Morals and Manners*, in Boston in 1844.

in extenuation of their conduct, speaks of the existence of an "impassable barrier" between the white and colored people of this country, and proceeds to draw a most odious picture of the character of his colored fellow-countrymen. Mean and wicked as is this position, the Doctor assumes it; and in so doing, because the favorite representative of a large class of his divine order, as well as of his white fellow-citizens, who, like himself, being stung to very shame by the exposures abroad of their naked inhumanity at home, strive, with fig-leaf sophistry, to cover their guilt from the penetrating eye and scorching rebukes of the Christian world.

Fortunately for the cause of truth and human brotherhood, it has reached a period, when such mean-spirited efforts tend more to advance than retard its progress. Ingenious as are the arguments of its foes, they but defeat the object they are intended to promote. Their authors, in seeking thus to cover their sins, succeed only in lighting the lamp of investigation by which their guilt is more completely exposed. It is the decree of the Supreme Ruler of the universe, that he will confound the wisdom of the crafty, and bring to naught the counsels of the ungodly; and how faithfully is his decree executed upon those who bring their worldly wisdom to cover up the guilt of the American people! Their iniquity has grown too large for its robe. When one part is covered, another, equally odious and revolting, is made to appear. The efforts of priests and politicians to stretch the garment, to suit the dimensions of this giant sin, has resulted in tearing it asunder, and leaving the monster revealed as perhaps it never was before.

When they tell the world that the negro is ignorant, and naturally and intellectually incapacitated to appreciate and enjoy freedom, they also publish their own condemnation, by bringing to light those infamous Laws by which the Slave is compelled to live in the grossest ignorance. When they tell the world that the Slave is immoral, vicious and degraded, they invite attention to their own depravity: for the world sees the Slave stripped, by his accusers, of every safeguard to virtue, even of that purest and most sacred institution of marriage. When they represent the Slave as being destitute of religious principle—as in the preceding cases—they profit nothing by the plea. In addition to their moral condemnation they brand themselves with bold and daring impiety, in making it an offence punishable with fine and imprisonment, and even death, to teach a Slave to read the will of God. When they pretend that they hold the Slave out of actual regard to the Slave's welfare, and not because of any profit which accrues to themselves, as owners, they are covered with confusion by the single fact that Virginia alone has realized, in one short year, eighteen millions of dollars from the sale of human flesh. When they attempt to shield themselves by the grossly absurd and wicked pretence that the

Slave is contented and happy, and, therefore, "better off" in Slavery than he could be possessed of freedom, their shield is broken by that long and bloody list of advertisements for runaway Slaves who have left their happy homes, and sought for freedom, even at the hazard of losing their lives in the attempt to gain it. When it is most foolishly asserted by Henry Clay, and those he represents, that the freedom of the colored is incompatible with the liberty of the white people of this country, the wicked intent of its author, and the barefaced absurdity of the proposition, are equally manifest. And when John C. Calhoun and Senator Walker[1] attempt to prove that freedom is fraught with deafness, insanity and blindness to the people of color, their whole refuge of lies is swept away by the palpable inaccuracy of the last United States Census. And when, to cap the climax, Dr. Dewey tells the people of England that the white and colored people in this country are separated by an "impassable barrier," the hundreds of thousands of mulattoes, quadroons, &c. in this country, silently but unequivocally brand him with the guilt of having uttered a most egregious falsehood.

Bad, however, as are the apologies which the American people make in defence of themselves and their "peculiar institution," I am always glad to see them. I prize them very highly, as indications of a living sense of shame, which renders them susceptible of outward influences, and which shall one day bring them to repentance. Men seldom sink so deep in sin as to rid themselves of all disposition to apologise for their iniquity;—when they do, it is quite idle to labor for their reformation. Fortunately for our brethren under the accursed yoke, the American people have not yet reached that depth; and whilst there is a sense of shame left, there is strong ground for hope. The year eighteen hundred and forty-four has produced an abundant harvest of Anti-Slavery discussion. Slavery and prejudice cannot endure discussion, even though such discussion be had in its favor. The light necessary to reason by, is at once too painful to the eyes of these twin-monsters of darkness to be endured. Their motto is, "Put out the light!" Thanks to Heaven, "the morning light is breaking;" our cause is onward; the efforts of our enemies, not less than the efforts of our friends, are contributing to increase the strength of that sentiment at home, as well as abroad, which is very soon to dash down the bloody altar of Slavery, and "proclaim liberty through all the land, unto all the inhabitants thereof."

Lynn, Massachusetts, US

---

1 William Walker (1824–60) was born in Nashville, Tennessee, and was a white US lawyer, staunch supporter of slavery, and war-mongerer and colonizationist in Latin America.

12. "To My Old Master," *North Star*, 8 September 1848

To My Old Master.

THOMAS AULD—SIR:—The long and intimate, though by no means friendly, relation which unhappily subsisted between you and myself, leads me to hope that you will easily account for the great liberty which I now take in addressing you in this open and public manner. The same fact may possibly remove any disagreeable surprise which you may experience on again finding your name coupled with mine, in any other way than in an advertisement, accurately describing my person, and offering a large sum for my arrest. In thus dragging you again before the public, I am aware that I shall subject myself to no inconsiderable amount of censure. I shall probably be charged with an unwarrantable if not a wanton and reckless disregard of the rights and proprieties of private life. There are those North as well as South, who entertain a much higher respect for rights which are merely conventional, than they do for rights which are personal and essential. Not a few there are in our country who, while they have no scruples against robbing the laborer of the hard-earned results of his pertinent industry, will be shocked by the extremely indelicate manner of bringing your name before the public. Believing this to be the case, and wishing to meet every reasonable or plausible objection to my conduct, I will frankly state the ground upon which I justify myself in this instance, as well as on former occasions when I have thought proper to mention your name in public. All will agree that a man guilty of theft, robbery or murder, has forfeited the right to concealment and private life; that the community have a right to subject such persons to the most complete exposure. However much they may desire retirement, and aim to conceal themselves and their movements from the popular gaze, the public have a right to ferret them out, and bring their conduct before the proper tribunals of the country for investigation. Sir, you will undoubtedly make the proper application of these generally admitted principles, and will easily see the light in which you are regarded by me. I will not, therefore, manifest ill-temper, by calling you hard names. I know you to be a man of some intelligence, and can readily determine the precise estimate which I entertain of your character. I may therefore indulge in language which may seem to others indirect and ambiguous, and yet be quite well understood by yourself.

I have selected this day on which to address you, because it is the anniversary of my emancipation; and knowing of no better way, I am led to this as the best mode of celebrating, that truly important event. Just ten years ago this beautiful September morning, yon bright sun beheld me a slave—a poor degraded chattel—trembling at the sound of your voice, lamenting that I was a man, and wishing myself a brute. The hopes which I had treasured up for weeks of a safe and successful escape from your grasp, were powerfully confronted at this last hour by dark clouds of doubt and fear, making my person shake and my bosom to heave with the heavy contest between hope and fear. I have no words to describe to you the deep agony of soul which I experienced on that never-to-be-forgotten morning—(for I left by daylight)—I was taking a leap in the dark. The probabilities, so far as I could by reason determine them, were stoutly against the undertaking. The preliminaries and precautions I had adopted previously, all worked badly. I was like one going to war without weapons—ten chances of defeat to one of victory. One in whom I had confided, and one who had promised me assistance, appalled by fear at the trial-hour, deserted me, thus leaving the responsibility of success or failure solely with myself. As I look back to then I can scarcely realize that I have passed through a scene so trying. Trying however as they were, and gloomy as was the prospect, thanks be to the Most High, who is ever the God of the oppressed, at the moment which was to determine my whole earthly career, His grace was sufficient, my mind was made up. I embraced the golden opportunity, took the morning tide at the flood; and a free man, young, active, and strong, is the result.

I have often thought I should like to explain to you the grounds upon which I have justified myself in running away from you. I am almost ashamed to do so now, for by this time you may have discovered them yourself. I will, however, glance at them. When yet but a child about six years old, I imbibed the determination to run away. The very first mental effort that I now remember on my part, was an attempt to solve the mystery, Why am I a slave? and with this question my youthful mind was troubled for many days, pressing upon me more heavily at times than others. When I saw the slave-driver whip a slave-woman, cut the blood out of her neck, and heard her piteous cries, I went away into the corner of the fence, wept and pondered over this mystery. I had, through some medium, I know not what, got some idea of God, the Creator of all mankind, the black and the white, and that he had made the blacks to serve the whites as slaves. How he could do this and be *good*, I could not tell. I was not satisfied with this theory, which made God responsible for slavery, for it pained me greatly, and I have wept over it long and often. At one time, your first wife, Mrs. Lucretia, heard me singing and saw me shedding tears, and asked of me the matter, but I was afraid to tell her. I was puzzled with this question, till one night, while sitting in the kitchen, I heard some of the old slaves talking of their parents having been stolen from Africa by white men, and were sold here as slaves. The whole mystery was solved at once. Very soon after this, my aunt Jinny and uncle Noah ran away, and the great noise made about it by your father-in-law, made me for the first time acquainted with the fact, that there were free States as well as slave States. From that time, I resolved that I would some day run away. The morality of the act, I dispose of as follows: I am myself; you are yourself, we are two distinct person [sic], equal persons. What you are I am. You are a man, so am I.—God created both, and made us separate beings. I am not by nature bound to you, or you to me. Nature does not make your existence depend upon me, or mine to depend upon yours. I cannot walk upon your legs, or you upon mine. I cannot breathe for you, or you for me; I must breathe for myself, and you for yourself. We are distinct persons, and are each equally provided with faculties necessary to our individual existence. In leaving you, I took nothing but what belonged to me, and in no way lessened your means of obtaining an *honest* living. Your faculties remained yours, and mine became useful to their rightful owners. I therefore see no wrong in any part of the transaction. It is true, I went off secretly, but that was more your fault than mine. Had I let you into the secret, you would have defeated the enterprise entirely; but for this, I should have been really glad to have made you acquainted with my intention to leave.

You may perhaps want to know how I like my present condition. I am free to say, I greatly prefer it to that which I occupied in Maryland. I am, however, by no means prejudiced against that State as such. Its geography, climate, fertility and products, are such as to make it a very desirable abode for any man; and but for the existence of slavery there, it is not impossible that I might again take up my abode in that State. It is not that I love Maryland less, but freedom more. You will be surprised to learn that people at the North labor under the strange delusion that if the slaves were emancipated at the South, they would all flock to the North. So far from this being the case, in that event, you would see many old and familiar faces back again at the South. The fact is, there are few here who would not return to the South in the event of emancipation. We want to live in the land of our birth, and to lay our bones by the side of our fathers'; and nothing short of an intense love of personal freedom keeps us from the South. For the sake of this, most of us would live on a crust of bread and a cup of cold water.

Since I left you, I have had a rich experience. I have occupied stations which I never dreamed of when a slave. Three out of the ten years since I left you, I spent as a common laborer on the wharves of New Bedford, Massachusetts. It was there I earned my first free dollar. It was mine. I could spend it as I pleased. I could buy hams or herring with it, without asking any odds of anybody. That was a precious dollar to me. You remember when I used to make seven or eight, and even nine dollars a week in Baltimore, you would take every cent of it from me every Saturday night, saying that I belonged to you, and my earnings also. I never liked this conduct on your part—to say the best, I thought it a little mean. I would not have served you so. But let that pass. I was a little awkward about counting money in New Bedford. I like to have betrayed myself several times. I caught myself saying phip, for four pence; and one time a man actually charged me with being a runaway, whereupon I was silly enough to become one by running away from him, for I was greatly afraid he might adopt measures to get me again into slavery, a condition I then dreaded more than death.

I soon, however, learned to count money as well as to make it, and got on swimmingly. I married soon after leaving you: I fact, I was engaged to be married before I left you; and instead of finding my companion a burden, she was truly a helpmeet. She went to live—at service, and I to work on the wharf, and though we toiled hard the first winter, we never lived more happily. After remaining in New Bedford for three years, I met with Wm. Lloyd Garrison, a person of whom you have *possibly* heard, as he is pretty generally known among slaveholders. He put it into my head that I might make myself serviceable to the cause of the slave by devoting a portion of my time to telling my own sorrows, and those of other slaves which had come under my observation. This was the commencement of a higher state of existence than any to which I had ever aspired. I was thrown into society the most pure, enlightened and benevolent that the country affords. Among these, I have never forgotten you, but have invariably made you the topic of conversation—thus giving you all the notoriety I could do. I need not tell you that the opinion formed of you in these circles, is far from being favorable. They have little respect for your honesty, and less for your religion.

But I was going on to relate to you something of my interesting experience. I had not long enjoyed the excellent society to which I have referred, before the light of its excellence exerted a beneficial influence on my mind and heart. Much of my early dislike of white persons was removed, and their manners, habits and customs, so entirely unlike what I have been used to in the kitchen-quarters on the plantations of the South, fairly charmed me, and gave me a strong dis-relish for the coarse and degrading customs of my former condition. I therefore made an effort so to improve my mind and deportment, as to be somewhat fitted to the station to which I seemed almost Providentially called. The transition from degradation to respectability was indeed great, and to get from one to the other without carrying some marks of one's former condition, is truly a difficult matter.—I would not have you think that I am now entirely clear of all plantation peculiarities, but my friends here, while they entertain the strongest dislike to them, regard me with that charity to which my past life somewhat entitles me, so that my condition in this respect is exceedingly pleasant. So far as my domestic affairs are concerned, I can boast of as comfortable a dwelling as your own. I have an industrious and neat companion, and four dear children—the oldest a girl of nine years, and three fine boys, the oldest eight, the next six, and the youngest four years old. The three oldest are now going regularly to school— two can read and write, the other can spell with tolerable correctness words of two syllables. Dear fellows! they are all in comfortable beds, and are sound asleep, perfectly secured under my own roof. There are no slaveholders here to rend my heart by snatching them from my arms, or blast a proud mother's dearest hopes by tearing them from her bosom. These dear children are ours—not to work up into rice, sugar, and tobacco, but to watch over, regard, and protect, and to rear them up in the nurture and admonition of the gospel—to train them up in the paths of wisdom and virtue, and as far as we can, to make them useful to the world and to themselves. Oh! sir, a slaveholder never appears to me so completely an agent of hell, as when I think of and look upon my dear children. It is then that my feelings rise above my control. I meant to have said more with respect to my own prosperity and happiness, but thoughts and feelings which this recital has quickened, unfits me to proceed further in that direction. The grim horrors of slavery rise in all their ghastly terror before me, the wails of millions pierce my heart, and chill my blood. I remember the chain, the gag, the bloody whip, the deathlike gloom overshadowing the broke spirit of the fettered bondman, the appalling liability of his being torn away from wife and children and sold like a beast in the market. Say not this is a picture of fancy. You well know that I wear stripes on my back inflicted by your direction; and that you, while we were brothers in the same church, caused this right hand, with which I am now penning this letter, to be closely tied to my left, and my person dragged at the pistol's mouth, fifteen miles, from the Bay side to Easton, to be sold like a beast in the market, for the alleged crime of intending to escape from your possession. All this and more you remember, and know to be perfectly true, not only of yourself, but of nearly all the slaveholders around you.

At this moment, you are probably the guilty holder of at least three of my own dear sisters, and my only brother in bondage. These you regard as your property. They are recorded on your ledger, or perhaps have been sold to human flesh mongers, with a view to filling your own ever-hungry purse. Sir, I desire to know how and where these dear sisters are. Have you sold them? or are they still in your possession? What has become of them? are they living or dead? And my dear old grandmother, whom you turned out like an old horse, to die in the woods—

is she still alive? Write and let me know all about them. If my grand-mother be still alive, she is of no service to you, for by this time she must be nearly eighty years old—too old to be cared for by one to whom she has ceased to be of service, send her to me at Rochester, or bring her to Philadelphia, and it shall be the crowning happiness of my life to take care of her in her old age. Oh! she was to me a mother, and a father, so far as hard toil for my comfort could make her such. Send me my grandmother! that I may watch over and take care of her in her old age. And my sisters, let me know all about them. I would write to them, and learn all I want to know of them, without disturbing you in any way, but that, through your unrighteous conduct, they have been entirely deprived of the power to read and write. You have kept them in utter ignorance, and have therefore robbed them of the sweet enjoy-ments of writing or receiving letters from absent friends and relatives. Your wickedness and cruelty committed in this respect on your own fellow-creatures, are greater than all the stripes you have laid upon my back, or theirs. It is an outrage upon the soul—a war upon the immor-tal spirit, and one for which you must give account at the bar of our common Father and Creator.

The responsibility which you have assumed in this regard is truly awful—and how you could stagger under it these many years is mar-vellous. Your mind must have become darkened, your heart hardened, your conscience seared and petrified, or you would have long since thrown off the accursed load and sought relief at the hands of a sin for-giving God. How, let me ask, would you look upon me, were I some dark night in company with a band of hardened villains, to enter the precincts of your own elegant dwelling and seize the person of our own lovely daughter Amanda, and carry her off from your family, friends, and all the loved ones of her youth—make her my slave—compel her to work, and I take her wages—place her name of my ledger as prop-erty—disregard her personal rights—fetter the powers of her immortal soul by denying her the right and privilege of learning to read and write—feed her coarsely—clothe her scantily, and whip her on the naked back occasionally; more and still more horrible, leave her unpro-tected—a degraded victim to the brutal lust of fiendish overseers who would pollute, blight, and blast her fair soul—rob her of all dignity—destroy her virtue, and annihilate all in her person the graces that adorn the character of virtuous womanhood? I ask how would you regard me, if such were my conduct? Oh! the vocabulary of the damned would not afford a word sufficiently infernal, to express your idea of my God-provoking wickedness. Yet sir, your treatment of my beloved sisters is in all essential points, precisely like the case I have now supposed. Damning as would be such a deed on my part, it would be no more so than that which you have committed against me and my sisters.

I will now bring this letter to a close, you shall hear from me again unless you let me hear from you. I intend to make use of you as a weapon with which to assail the system of slavery—as a means of concentrating public attention on the system, and deepening the horror of trafficking in the souls and bodies of men. I shall make use of you as a means of exposing the character of the American church and clergy—and as a means of bringing this guilty nation with yourself to repentance. In doing this I entertain no malice towards you personally. There is no roof under which you would be more safe than mine, and there is nothing in my house which you might need for your comfort, which I would not readily grant. Indeed, I should esteem it a privilege, to set you an example as to how mankind ought to treat each other. I am your fellow man but not your slave,
FREDERICK DOUGLASS.
P.S.—I send a copy of the paper containing this letter, to save postage.—F.D.

13. Letter to Harriet Tubman, Rochester, 29 August 1868; in Sarah H. Bradford, *Scenes in the Life of Harriet Tubman* (Auburn: W.J. Moses, 1869)

[Frederick Douglass's letter was reproduced as an appendix in Sarah Bradford's first biography of Harriet Tubman. Tubman (1822–1913) was an Underground Railroad coordinator, Civil War nurse and intelligence officer, and lifelong civil rights campaigner.]

Letter from Frederick Douglass.
ROCHESTER, August 29, 1868.
DEAR HARRIET: I am glad to know that the story of your eventful life has been written by a kind lady, and that the same is soon to be published. You ask for what you do not need when you call upon me for a word of commendation. I need such words from you far more than you can need them from me, especially where your superior labors and devotion to the cause of the lately enslaved of our land are known as I know them. The difference between us is very marked. Most that I have done and suffered in the service of our cause has been in public, and I have received much encouragement at every step of the way. You, on the other hand, have labored in a private way. I have wrought in the day—you in the night. I have had the applause of the crowd and the satisfaction that comes of being approved by the multitude, while the most that you have done has been witnessed by a few trembling, scarred, and foot-sore bondmen and women, whom you have led out of the house of bondage, and whose heartfelt "God bless you" has been your only reward. The midnight sky and the silent stars

have been the witnesses of your devotion to freedom and of your heroism. Excepting John Brown[1]—of sacred memory—I know of no one who has willingly encountered more perils and hardships to serve our enslaved people than you have. Much that you have done would seem improbable to those who do not know you as I know you. It is to me a great pleasure and a great privilege to bear testimony to your character and your works, and to say to those to whom you may come, that I regard you in every way truthful and trustworthy.

Your friend, FREDERICK DOUGLASS.

---

1 John Brown (1800–59) was a white US farmer, surveyor, radical abolitionist, and military general. He launched an armed attack on the federal arsenal at Harpers Ferry in West Virginia, with the tragic result that he and his revolutionary supporters were executed in bloody reprisals, but his action can be considered a harbinger of the Civil War.

Appendix D: Family

1. Portraits

a. Anna Murray Douglass (National Park Service, Cedar Hill, Washington, DC, n.d.)

[Born free in Denton, Maryland, in 1813, Anna Murray Douglass died in Washington, DC, on 4 August 1882. She became romantically involved with Frederick Douglass when he was still enslaved and living as Frederick Bailey. She not only assisted him in gaining access to Baltimore's free Black community but also provided him with financial assistance to enable his escape, after which they were married in New York in 1838. Anna Murray was a chef, laundrist, domestic manager, foster mother, antislavery campaigner, Underground Railroad operator, and political commentator.]

Figure 18: Anna Murray Douglass Portrait, n.d. (National Park Service: Frederick Douglass National Historic Site, Cedar Hill, Washington, DC).

b. Rosetta Douglass Sprague (National Park Service, Cedar Hill, Washington, DC, n.d.)

[Born Rosetta Douglass, Rosetta Douglass Sprague was born on 24 June 1839 in New Bedford, Massachusetts, and died on 25 November 1906 in Washington, DC. The eldest of the Douglass children, she married Nathan Sprague (1841–1907), a man who had been born into slavery and who had gained his own freedom, with whom she had seven children. She was a women's rights campaigner, political activist, orator, writer, office worker, business manager, housewife, proofreader, and amanuensis for her father.]

Figure 19: Rosetta Douglass Sprague Portrait, n.d. (National Park Service: Frederick Douglass National Historic Site, Cedar Hill, Washington, DC).

c. Lewis Henry Douglass (National Park Service, Cedar Hill, Washington, DC, n.d.)

[Lewis Henry Douglass was born on 9 October 1840 in New Bedford, Massachusetts, and died in Washington, DC, in 1908. The eldest son in the Douglass family, he served as sergeant major in the Fifty-Fourth Massachusetts Regiment during the Civil War. Following his discharge, he married Helen Amelia Loguen, daughter of a formerly enslaved man turned Underground Railroad operator, Reverend Jermain Wesley Loguen, and his wife, Catherine Loguen. During his lifetime, Lewis Henry was a government employee, journalist, printer, civil rights campaigner, political commentator, orator, essay-writer, real-estate broker, newspaper editor, and archivist of his father's papers.]

Figure 20: Lewis Henry Douglass Portrait, n.d. (National Park Service: Frederick Douglass National Historic Site, Cedar Hill, Washington, DC).

d. Frederick Douglass Jr. (National Park Service, Cedar Hill, Washington, DC, n.d.)

[Frederick Douglass Jr. was the second-eldest son in the Douglass family. He was born in New Bedford, Massachusetts on 3 March 1842 and died on 26 July 1892 in Washington, DC, a few years before his father's death. A recruiter during the Civil War, in 1871 he married Virginia Hewlett, a teacher and daughter of A. Moylneaux Hewlett, professor of physical training at Harvard University; they had seven children, many of whom tragically never reached adulthood. Despite undertaking many professions, including printer, essayist, grocer, journalist, court bailiff, and newspaper manager, Frederick Jr. suffered many hardships in the pursuit of financial independence. A radical thinker and political philosopher, he remained a committed campaigner for equal civil rights until the day he died.]

Figure 21: Frederick Douglass Jr. Portrait, n.d. (National Park Service: Frederick Douglass National Historic Site, Cedar Hill, Washington, DC).

e. Charles Remond Douglass (National Park Service, Cedar Hill, Washington, DC, n.d.)

[Charles Remond Douglass was named after Frederick Douglass's close friend and fellow campaigner on the antislavery circuit Charles Remond (1810–73), who had been born a free man in Salem, Massachusetts. Douglass's son Charles Remond was born in Lynn, Massachusetts, on 21 October 1844 and was the last surviving family member, dying on 23 November 1920 in Washington, DC. During the Civil War, he initially registered in the Fifty-Fourth Massachusetts Regiment, only to later join the Fifth Massachusetts Calvary when he became a first sergeant. In 1866 he married Mary Elizabeth Murphy, with whom he had six children. Following her death in 1878, he married his second wife, Antoinette Haley, with whom he had one child. One of the sons born during his first marriage, Joseph Henry Douglass (1871–1935), became a world-famous violinist and composer. In a post-emancipation era, Charles Remond Douglass not only played key roles in the Grand Army of the Republican Veterans' Association but also served as a government employee in various roles, as well as a real-estate broker, orator, printer, and newspaper editor.]

Figure 22: Charles Remond Douglass Portrait, n.d. (National Park Service: Frederick Douglass National Historic Site, Cedar Hill, Washington, DC).

2. Letters from Rosetta Douglass to Frederick Douglass (1845–46)

a. Rosetta Douglass to Frederick Douglass, Albany, 20 October 1846

[This letter and the next were reprinted in an article titled "NEW LIGHT ON DOUGLASS: Infant Daughter of the Great Agitator a Genius at Letter Writing," published in the *Afro-American,* a Baltimore-based newspaper, a few years after Rosetta died, on 16 October 1909. The unidentified reporter published these letters alongside this comment: "The following letters were written to Frederick Douglass by his little seven-year-old daughter Rosetta while he was in England in 1846. This is the first time they have ever been made public."]

Albany, Oct. 20, 1845.
My Dear Father—I wish to write to you now to tell you that my eyes are almost well. Miss Mott says that you will feel uneasy and anxious to know. I was very blind when Miss Mott wrote her letter. I have just begun to read and write again. Oh, how happy you will be to hear that I can see again! I thought how you would pity me if only you knew how blind I was. Miss Mott held me in her arms all this time I was not asleep.

Miss Mott told me that you visited a great many blind children and they felt of you because they could not see you and they had heard of you before you came to see them. Oh, how sorry I felt for them that they could not see you!

I wonder if it snows where you are. It snows here today, and I love to see it snow. The flakes are almost as large as the palm of my hand. They look so beautiful falling upon the green leaves of the chestnut tree in front of the parlor windows. The leaves are bright green. They have now a beautiful green edge.

My dear father, if you were here now, oh, happy, how happy, I should be!

b. Rosetta Douglass to Frederick Douglass, Albany, 23 October 1846

Oct. 23
Oh, my dear friend, how glad I was this morning when Miss Mott handed me your letter! I kissed it over and over again, and when I read it, oh, happy, oh, how happy it made me! It was such a dear, sweet letter. Why, my dear father, how can I forget you when we talk about you every hour in the day? Oh, no, my dear father, your little Rosa can

never forget you. Then I have so many of your dear letters, and you tell me how you love me.

Miss Abigail and Miss Lydia are very much delighted with your last letter. They thought Mr. Sanderson wrote me a beautiful letter, but it did not come from my dear father, although he calls himself my oldest brother. Do you know that, father?

Miss Nash says that she is very much obliged to you for your love to her, but she says she wonders how you have any love left for her when you send a whole heart full to me.

My dear father, you say that you show my letters to little girls. Why, father, I did not think that you would show them. There is something private in them.

Father, you say that you dreamed that I did not know you when you met me; I did not smile or look pleased. That was very strange for you to dream that I did not know you, for I shall know you if I only hear you say "Rosa," even though you would speak to me in the dark. I do not dream. I sleep so sweetly. I do not remember what I think when I am asleep, but Miss Abigail says she can give me her dream as an offset to my father's dream. She dreamt that she met you in some company and you would not shake hands with her for some time. After awhile you put out your hand very indifferently and spoke coldly to her. But Miss Mott says she doesn't believave [sic] in dreams. Do you, father?

Miss Lydia desires me to give a great deal of love to you. This is from your loving little daughter.

ROSETTA DOUGLASS.

3. Letter from Annie Douglass to Frederick Douglass, Rochester, 7 December 1859 (Frederick Douglass Papers, Library of Congress)

[As Anna Murray and Frederick Douglass's last born child, Annie Douglass was born in 1849 and died tragically young in 1860 while her father was on the run from the US government. He had escaped to the British Isles to avoid arrest by Governor Henry Wise in the wake of John Brown's revolutionary activism in Harpers Ferry, Virginia, in October 1859.]

Rochester Dec 7th 1859

My Dear Father

I am proceeding in my German very well for my teacher says so. I am in the first reader and I can read. I expect that you will have a German letter from me in a very short time. I have learned another piece and it is Anti-Slavery I am going to speak it in school, my piece is this.

> O he is not the man for me
> Who buys or sells a slave
> Nor he who will not set him free
> But send him to his grave
> But he whose noble hearts beats warm
> For all men's life and liberty
> Who loves alike each human form
> O that's the man for me

It is in the Garland of Freedom and for four verses of it.[1] My letter will not be very long. Poor Mr. Brown[2] is dead. That hard hearted man said he must die and they took him in and open field and about half a mil[e] from the jail and hung him. The German children like me very much but I have gone a head of them and they have been there longer than me too.

They all send their love.

From your affectionate
Daughter
Annie Douglass
Two a life of labor I am

4. Letters from Frederick Douglass to Harriet Bailey / Ruth Cox[3] (1846–47)

a. Frederick Douglass to Harriet Bailey / Ruth Cox, 16 May 1846 (Frederick Douglass Papers, Library of Congress)

A few loving words to my own dear sister Harriet. You will observe that I commence to write very plain. I don't know how I shall hold out— at any rate I think you will be able to read it. I'll try to make it so that you can with out much trouble. I write not because I have much to say but because I guess you will be pleased to get a word directly from

---

1 From *Garland of Freedom: A Collection of Poems, Chiefly Anti-Slavery*, edited by white British Quaker and abolitionist Wilson Armistead (1819–68) and published in London by printer William Tweedie in 1853. Annie chose to quote from an anonymous poem titled "The Man For Me" (23).

2 See p. 242, n. 1.

3 For further informaiton regarding Douglass's relationship to this addressee, who was known as both Harriet Bailey and Ruth Cox, see the discussion in the Introduction (p. 51).

your Brother's pen. Do I guess right? Now having introduced my letter let me say a word about my health. It is only tolerable. I never feel very well in the Spring. I however think I feel as well this Spring as I remember to have felt at any time in the Spring during the last five years. Harriet ... [text obscured] a few days ago—quite down at the mouth. I felt worse than "get out!" My under lip hung like that of a motherless Colt I looked so ugly that I hated to see myself in a glass. There was no living for me. I was so snappish I would have kicked my grand "dadda"! I was in a terrible mood—dats a fac! Ole missus is you got any ting for poor nigger to eat!!! Oh, Harriet could I have seen you then. How soon I would have been relieved from that Horrible feeling. You would have been so kind to me. You would not have looked cross at me. I know you would not. Instead of looking cross at me, you would have with your own Dear sisterly hand smoothed and stroked down my feverish forehead and spoken so kindly as to make me forget my sadness.

Harriet you were always dear to me but never so dear as now—your devotion to my little boys[.] Your attention to Dear Anna. Your smartness in learning to read and write and your loving letters to me had made you doubly dear to me. I will not forget you. What you do for my anna and my children I shall consider as done to myself and will reward you with a brother's love and a father's care. I am going on bravely with my antislavery work. My book is selling slowly but I have fourteen hundred copies to dispose of before I come home[.] I wish I could see my way clear to come home in July with my old friend and brother James with whom you may confidently expect to shake hands on the 18th of july. If I could sell what books I have on hand by that time I would come but this I do not expect so I submit to my fate and will try to make myself contented. The right way when we can do no better and I advise every body to keep clear of it who can and whose who cant to buy a fiddle. They say music is good for insane people and I believe every body is more or less insane at times. I feel very foolish when I come out of my fits of insanity. I mean my fits of melancholy— all the same—you know. Do you ever have them Dear Harriet? If you do just take down my old fiddle I am sure it will do you good. Read the enclosed letter which I send to my dear Anna over and over again till she can fully understand its contents. Remember me very affectionately to all who make friendly enquiries after me. Speak kindly of me to our mutually Dear Friend Mrs Fletcher. Take care of all the papers which I send look after my little Ones kiss all my dear boys for me—and believe me always your Brother Frederick Douglass.

b. Frederick Douglass to Harriet Bailey / Ruth Cox, 17 July 1846
    (Frederick Douglass Papers, Addition II, Library of Congress)

[Belfast Ire. 17 July 1846]

MY OWN DEAR SISTER HARRIET,

I am not unmindful of you although I did not write to you by the last
steamer. I always think of you among the beloved one's of my family.
The enclosed letter is to my Dear Anna. I have written one which will
be read by Jerrimiah [sic].[1] You will see both—and both of them I want
you to read over and over again until Dear Anna shall fully understand
their contents. I did shall not send any caps for our Boys or a shawl for
Dear Anna—as James has too many things to bring home for himself
to be troubled with mine. I shall send a beautiful work box to you
which I bought in London and gave six dollars for it. You will be
pleased with it I know. The Boys must wait for presents till I come
home, or until they come to this country. You will get this letter about
two weeks before you see friend [James] Buffum. Write me by the next
steamer. What you think of coming to this country and __? [sentence
obscured in the original letter because it has been torn and taped
together] Speak Dear Harriet just what you think—even though differ
from me—I will love you all the more for speaking out.
Your Brother
    F. DOUGLASS

c. Frederick Douglass to Harriet Bailey / Ruth Cox, 18 August 1846
    (Frederick Douglass Papers, Addition II, Library of Congress)

London Eng. 18 Aug 1846

MY DEAR HARRIET,
Your Dear Letter has just reached me and as you may well suppose its
contents shocked and surprised me. Is it possible that you are engaged
to be married? From what you say I suppose the whole thing is determined upon. Even the time is fix—and I am invited to attend and all
this without my knowing who your lover is, what his name—or where
he lives—how long he has visited you or any thing about it. Whether he
is good—bad or indifferent. This is strange—passing strange something
I cannot understand or account for. I am not however disposed to

---

1   This letter has not survived. Here Douglass is referring to a close family
    friend, Jeremiah B. Sanderson, an African American radical abolitionist and
    activist. See p. 217, n. 3.

censure you for not mentioning to me the name of your intended husband—as I suppose you withheld it from mere modesty or bashfulness. I should cirtainly [sic] like to know something about your lover previous to your getting married. I think this much due to me. But harken Dear Harriet I will not throw a single straw in the way of your Marriage. If I was absolutely cirtain [sic] that you were on the brink of distruction [sic] I might warn you—if you asked my advice. But you don't honor me so much as to ask my advice. No—no. My Dear you do not even say brother do you think it is best. All you wish from me is a dress a light silk dress—a wedding Dress. A dress to marry some body in—but who I don't know nor you don't tell me who it is. Now My Dear Harriet—this is not treating me well—it is not treating me as a sister ought to treat a brother. Now let me tell you—so far as this dress is concirned [sic], I am perfectly willing to give one—or any thing else within my power but before you ought expect this, you ought to let me know who you are about to Marry—giving you a dress to marry some one I do not know—and have no means of knowing is asking me to take a leap in the dark such as I am not prepared for. I can not do any thing that looks like favoring a thing which I know nothing about—especially a thing envolving [sic] so grave a matter as that of marriage. It is a solemn Matter. I wish I had time to write you such a letter as the solemn importance of the subject demands. Marriage—is one act of our lives—once performed It cannot be undone. It is not a thing which may be entered into to day and given up to morrow—but must last so long as life continues. I therefore counsel that you sereously [sic] consider before you take the step—it may lead to a life of misery and wretchedness—for which you alone must be responsible. Think of it. But my Dear Harriet—and you are Dear to me and never Dearer than at this moment—Do not understand me to be opposed to you getting married—not at all. Although I love to have you in my family and it will be a soar [sic] trial for me to part with you—yet I should rejoice to see you married to morrow if I felt you were marrying some-one worthy of you. It would indeed spread a dark cloud over my soul to see you marry some ignorant—idle worthless person unable to take care of you or himself ether. I would rather follow you to your grave than to do that. You ought not to marry any ignorant and unlearned person. You might as well tie yourself to a log of wood as to do so. You are altogether too refined and intelegent [sic] for any such marriage. But I have no time to continue this subject further. What I have said I have said as a brother—as one having no object in view but your own good—and that I will always seek whether you be married or single. The man who marries you should remember he takes you from a brothers house and a brothers home—and he should at least see that you have as good a home after marriage as before marriage. God bless you Dear Harriet—

and remember that whether married or single, you are still my sister. Remember you need never be out of Doors while I have a house to shelter my self and family. I shall come home before you are married—if you are not in too great haste. But don't wait for me unless you wish to do so. You are of age and much be your own judge as to what is best. Upon your own shoulders rests the responsibility. May God bless—My Dear Harriet—and guide you in the path of happiness—a path you may not be sorry for in time come—is the sincerest wish my heart. Your affectionate Brother,
FREDERICK DOUGLASS

d. Frederick Douglass to Harriet Bailey / Ruth Cox, Leamington, 31 January 1847 (Frederick Douglass Papers, Addition II, Library of Congress)

Leamington, 31 Jan 1847
MY DEAR HARRIET—
I am now almost persuaded that I have done you serious injustice if so—I am very sorry for it—and hope to be forgiven for it—and that at once—you know me too well and too long to imagine that I could take pleasure in harshly hurting you—in whom I have so long trusted, and have loved as a true friend, and even as a sister. It was with no little pain that I spoke as I did to you—in the letter asking you to leave my house, I suffered as much in sending that letter as you could possibly do in receiving it. If you have not absolutely resolved to leave, I now wish you to stay in my family—But do not stay on my account—if you think you can be happier out of my family than in it—why consult your own happiness—I would be glad to have you stay—but not my will—pursue your own course. You are your own woman—seek your own happiness—I shall always wish you well—and stand ready to render you any assistance I possess the power to do—and this shall be the case no matter what course you take. My regard for you has never been a selfish regard—but always—a regard for your own welfare—and such it shall ever be.

There are many things I should like to write about—but I am not in a state of mind to write—I am miserable—unhappy—and it seems I must so live and Die. I wish to mercy I could see you and talk with—I could soon relieve my mind—but I am too far a way—and writing seems only to make matters worse. It is absolutely too bad that I should be so harassed in my feelings.

Fare well Harriet—and receive my heartfelt good wishes—Write to me soon
    Yours sincerely
        FREDERICK DOUGLASS

5. Jane Marsh Parker, "Reminiscences of Frederick Douglass," *The Outlook* 51.14 (6 April 1895)

[Jane Marsh Parker (1836–1913) was a white US author and journalist. She was born into a religious antislavery family and lived in Rochester, New York, when she became a close friend of the Douglass family. Only months following Douglass's death, she published "Reminiscences of Frederick Douglass" in *The Outlook*, a weekly magazine published in New York City.]

How well I remember the flutter our suburban and aspiring neighborhood was thrown into when, some time in 1847, soon after Frederick Douglass came to Rochester to live, it was known that he had bought a house on our street—and a very good house, too—and was about to move his family into the same! He had bought of an Abolitionist, and the property-owners on either side of him were Abolitionists, one of whom was my father. Naturally, there was open protest from the rest; but soon after the arrival of the new neighbors, all opposition to their presence disappeared. Frederick Douglass was a gentleman, and a good neighbor. Mrs. Douglass chose seclusion, and the children were models of behavior.

That house on Alexander Street, a two-story brick, of about nine rooms, on a large lot about one hundred feet in width, was a handsome property for an ex-slave to buy, a runaway of only ten years before, whose manumission papers bore date December 5, 1846. It must have been the first house he ever owned. One of the first things he did after settling in it, and making a private study of a hall bedroom on the upper floor, was to write a letter to his old master, Thomas Auld, in which he said: "So far as my domestic affairs are concerned, I can boast of as comfortable a dwelling as your own."[1] It may be doubted if many slave-kept homes were as comfortable and well ordered, for Mrs. Douglass was a model housekeeper, her thrifty care of her family and her watchful supervision of expenditure making the financial venture of her husband in undertaking the "North Star" far less hazardous than many believed. She was laying the foundations of his prosperity, insuring his future independence. Anna Murray Douglass was a free woman when she helped her lover to escape from Maryland, following him at no small peril to New York, where they were married, she going out to service until he found steady employment on the docks of New Bedford. She was a pure-blooded negro, of the best type, with severe notions of the proprieties and duties of life.

---

1 See Appendix C12.

Her training had evidently been in Southern families of high standing; for, like her husband, she had what her new neighbors called "very aristocratic ideas." She read character with marvelous accuracy, and was a wholesome check on her husband's proneness to being imposed upon. Her greatest discontent was when his admirers persisted in dragging her into notice—when she had to receive visitors merely to gratify curiosity. Little if any service was hired in that admirably kept home. A sister of Mrs. Douglass assisted her in the housekeeping; the children were trained to self-helpfulness and systematic industry. Did not Rosetta make a shirt for her father, every stitch, before she was ten years old? Mrs. Douglass disapproved, decidedly, of the idle, pleasure-taking ways of the other little girls in the neighborhood, and she did not hesitate to correct their lapses in good manners. This is to show the footing the family soon had in the neighborhood.

Every one of note who came to the city was pretty sure to call upon Frederick Douglass; we had only to watch his front door to see many famous men and women; which, with his connection with the Underground Railroad (known only to his anti-slavery neighbors), added much to a locality which before had been rather dull. Frederika Bremer[1] was one of his most famous visitors in those days; and what a thrill it gave me to turn over the pages of the full set of her writings which she had left upon the Douglass parlor table, her autograph on the fly-leaf of each volume!

"For Frederick's sake," Mrs. Douglass, that first summer of their living on Alexander Street, consented, rather reluctantly, to have a teacher in the house for herself as well as the children—an English woman, of whom she faithfully tried for a while to learn to read and write; but when it came to neglecting housewifely duties for copy-book and speller, the experiment ended; and Mrs. Douglass was glad to be released, referring to the episode afterwards as an amusing experience to Frederick as well as herself, and one that had settled the matter of her ever becoming an educated woman. Small circles of young ladies used to meet at the house in those times to make fancy articles for the anti-slavery fairs, and once, when one of them had finished a book-mark with *Fredrick* Douglass upon it in cross-stitch, Mrs. Douglass was the first to see the mistake, showing that there was one name in the world that she could read and spell, even if she did make her signature with her X.

But the excitement caused in the neighborhood by the settlement of the Douglass family among us was as nothing to what came to pass

---

1 Swedish-born Frederika Bremer (1801–65) was a radical feminist and celebrated novelist who enjoyed fame in Britain and the US.

when two English sisters arrived,[1] spinsters of means and culture, and it was announced that they were to be members of the Douglass household for some time, and co-workers with Frederick Douglass in the anti-slavery cause, assisting in the office of the "North Star." Enthusiasts for the abolition of American slavery, these two English ladies had consecrated their means and service to the cause. The appearance upon the main street of Frederick Douglass with one of these ladies on either arm seriously threatened the order of the town for a while, and threats were openly made of what would be done if such aggressive demonstration of race-mixture were persisted in. Frederick Douglass kept his head high as ever, the ladies filling the role of possible martyrs unflinchingly. After a while the threatenings of storm died away; one of the ladies married a leading Abolitionist, and the elder remained for several years the associate editor of the "North Star," giving to Frederick Douglass that assistance in his work which he could ill have done without. "Think what editing a paper was to me before Miss [Julia] Griffiths came! I had not learned how to spell; my knowledge of the simplest rules of grammar was most defective. I wrote slowly and under embarrassment—lamentably ignorant of much that every school-boy is supposed to know." He rewrote his autobiography under her supervision, and she did much for his education in many ways, returning to England after a few years, when she was married to a clergyman[2] of the Established Church.

That little den-like upstairs study of Frederick Douglass, with its small table and a few books—how well I remember it! and how he used to keep there a list of the words he found it hard to spell. He did learn to spell, however, and in a very short time. Had he drawn up the Constitution of John Brown's Asylum Republic (the original copy as written by John Brown was one of the treasures of Cedar Hill), there would not have been those slips in orthography.[3]

Frederick Douglass was highly esteemed by his neighbors, and most popular with the children. When the boys stole his apples he made them ashamed, and they became his loyal admirers forever after.

---

1 Julia Griffiths Crofts (c. 1821–1895) not only worked alongside Douglass by editing *The North Star* but was also his business manager and a founding member of the Rochester Ladies Antislavery Society. Her sister, Eliza Griffiths, married the printer at *The North Star*, John Dick, in 1850.

2 Julia Griffiths married Henry O. Crofts, a Methodist minister, in 1859.

3 While he was planning his attack and in the run-up to his revolutionary action in Harpers Ferry, John Brown stayed with the Douglass family. As Douglass later recalled in his final autobiography, *Life and Times*, "sundry letters and a constitution written by John Brown were locked up in my desk in Rochester" (377).

If he knew that a group of children were gathered before his window on a warm summer night when he was singing to his violin, he was sure to give them what he knew they were waiting for—"Nelly was a Lady" or "Old Kentucky Home"—coming to the door and bowing his acknowledgement of their hearty applause. Nobody could sing "Oh, carry me back to ole Virginny" as he could. He had a rich baritone voice and a correct ear, and it was something to hear him sing in the latter years of his life from "The Seraph," the very same old singing-book which he had slipped into his bundle when he skipped out of Maryland for freedom. There was another book in his library that had much to do with his destiny—"The Columbian Orator," the identical book he had bought with his carefully hoarded pennies when a slave boy, that he might learn something to speak at the Sabbath-school exhibitions of the free negroes, which he attended by stealth, and where he was beginning to shine as an orator. That "Columbian Orator" contained a dialogue between a master and a slave (a Turkish master), and he, as a boy, delighted to repeat the long, big-worded soliloquy of the slave—"… all nature's smiles are frowns to him who wears the chains of slavery."

Later on Mr. Douglass bought a house with much larger grounds on the woody hillside south of the city—a neighborless place, its only roadway at the time the private road leading to his door. It was there that John Brown visited him, full of his project of raiding the border slave States and of establishing a refuge for fugitives in the mountains, and there that he laid his plans, often demonstrating, to the delight of the Douglass children, each detail with a set of blocks, making long tramps along over the hills when he had a hard problem to solve. Mr. Douglass was absent from home much in those days, a great part of his time being spent in Washington and in lecturing and attendance upon conventions.

Frederick Douglass had his education in four great schools, graduating from one to the other in natural sequence and with honors—Methodism, Garrisonianism, Journalism, Political Campaignism. Had not the great mass of the slaves been religious, had they not been held in check by their strong emotional religious feeling, surely slavery would have been terribly different from what it was. And so, had not Frederick Douglass been a Methodist, had the deepest springs of his nature been unlocked by some other force, might they not have found an outlet sweeping him to disaster rather than salvation? It was in the Methodist prayer-meetings that he found that he could speak so that every one would listen to him, and that few, if any, could speak as he could. He was innately religious—it was his temperament; his underlying characteristic was a reverent faith in the Unseen. Irreverence always shocked him. Religious cant—or, as he would call it, *ir*religious cant,—was his aversion. He subscribed to no creed, having tolerance for all. He knew the Bible better than most men; he read it more; his readiness in quoting texts never failed him; that was one secret of his old-time telling assaults upon a slave-defending Christianity. He has been heard to say in his later years, "I have no uneasiness about the hereafter. I am in the trade-winds of God. My bark was launched by him, and he is taking it into port." Again, "Perhaps I should have made a good Roman Catholic. I have a kinship with that Church, I think sometime; but one must be born with it, nurtured in it, or always an alien." Once, when urged by an overzealous Churchman to join the Episcopal Mission at the foot of Cedar Hill, he mused some time in silence. "I can't forget," he said, softly, "that your Church would not baptize slave babies. The Episcopal Church was consistent there, as it is in everything, but it left me out." He was the warm friend of Robert G. Ingersoll,[1] their acquaintance beginning, if my memory is right, long before Ingersoll was known to the world, and when he opened his door one night to Frederick Douglass, who otherwise would have walked the street, the hotels refusing him admission. "I was a stranger—more than that, a negro—and he took me in."

"One of the hardest things I had to learn when I was fairly under way as a public speaker was to stop telling so many funny stories. I could keep my audience in a roar of laughter—and they liked to laugh, and showed disappointment when I was not amusing—but I was convinced that I was in danger of becoming something of a clown, and that I must guard against it." His keen sense of the ludicrous saved him from many a mistake; his quick wit in repartee could effectually silence his antagonists. Under it all was the deep minor key of his prevailing melancholy—that depth of feeling he seldom suffered to master his outward cheerfulness.

As "a graduate from slavery, with his diploma written on his back," the Garrisonian platform gained much in enrolling him under its banner; and he found upon it, perhaps, the single door for advancement beyond the menial calling but which he had barely earned his bread. As a Methodist exhorter he had learned to speak so fluently and well that it was no wonder that many who heard him in the anti-slavery meetings had doubts if he had even [been] a slave, and said so openly.

Public speaking and the drill of conventions fitted him for journalism as nothing else could have done. Again his horizon was widened, and he was brought into fuller touch with men of the world and public affairs. Only ten years out of slavery, and seated in an editorial chair!

---

1 Robert G. Ingersoll (1833–99) was a white US lawyer and Civil War veteran.

Who, then, was so qualified in his peculiar way for "stumping the North" in Presidential campaigns? From Fremont to Harrison,[1] great was his service to the Republican party.

It has been said that the career of Douglass would have had its fitting and glorious ending on the scaffold with John Brown. He never thought so. His heart was never fully given to John Brown's scheme; he had discouraged it; had thought it visionary and impracticable; and yet his complication with it nearly cost him his life. He was always open in saying that he did not boast of having much martyr-stuff in him—that is, when he could just as well live for the cause as die for it. The intensity of his emotional nature, when aroused, had given him a habit, in denunciation, of shutting his jaws tightly together at the close of his sentences. Once, when speaking before a large audience, he actually crushed his upper front teeth, but so perfect was his self-control that he betrayed nothing in his delivery or facial expression, but finished his address before leaving the platform.

He never became a student, even when the victory of his cause had been won, and he had the leisure for study. Composition was never easy for him, unless his soul was stirred in its depths; nor was public speaking, unless his tongue was on fire. His literary lectures upon subjects foreign to his personal experience was largely disappointing. "The Honorable Frederick Douglass" was never the orator that "Fred Douglass" had been in the old pre-emancipation days. He sometimes said in his old age that he had outlived his cause. "Never did I dream, in my most hopeful moods, when I was pleading for my brothers in bonds, that I would ever see the end of American slavery." He liked a good novel—of the stirring kind. Dumas was one of his favorites, and of "The Three Musketeers"[2] he never tired. Nothing pleased him more, upon his arrival in Port-au-Prince, than to be told by the Parisian Haytians [sic] that he bore a strong resemblance to Victor Hugo.[3]

---

1 Savannah-born white US politician John Charles Frémont (1813–90) was a presidential candidate for the Republican Party in 1856. Ohio-born white US lawyer and politician Benjamin Harrison (1833–1901) served as 23rd president from 1889 to 1893.

2 Alexandra Dumas (1802–70) was a French author who was born to a white French woman and the son of a nobleman and an enslaved woman of African Caribbean heritage. A worldwide bestselling author, he published *The Three Musketeers* in 1844. Despite his personal protest regarding Dumas's lack of political activism in favor of human rights, his novel *The Count of Monte Cristo* (1844–45) remained one of Douglass's favorite works of literature.

3 Victor Hugo (1802–85) was a world-renowned French author who published his bestselling novel, another of Frederick Douglass's favorite books, *Les Misérables*, in 1862.

6. Rosetta Douglass Sprague, *My Mother as I Recall Her*, 10 May 1900 (Frederick Douglass Papers, Library of Congress)

[Rosetta Douglass Sprague originally delivered this speech on her mother's life before the Anna Murray Douglass Union on 10 May 1900. Over two decades later, following her death, her speech was reprinted on 14 February 1923 by her daughter, Fredericka Douglass Sprague Perry (1872–1943) and "Dedicated to the Noble Women" of the National Association of Colored Women. In the same year, Douglass Sprague's pamphlet was also published without Sprague Perry's Foreword in *The Journal of Negro History* 8.1 (January 1923): 93–101.]

FOREWORD

In a little autograph album that I gave my mother on the occasion of her birthday, my grandfather wrote:

"Few things can bring more happiness to the heart of a parent than the confidence and love of a child."

This tribute to her MOTHER by my MOTHER brings to mind that statement from a father who knew by experience just such joys and who rejoiced to see his daughter enjoying the same.

My mother's devotion to her parents was complete and I am publishing this little booklet that the world may learn some thing of the noble woman who was the wife of a great man, well known—and the mother of his children.

Too often are the facts of the great sacrifices and heroic efforts of the wives of renowned men overshadowed by the achievements of the men and the wonderful and beautiful part she has played so well is overlooked.

From afar Anna Murray Douglass has watched these many years the gradual decay of the house she loved and wherein she made it cheerfully homelike.

But to-day she stretches out her motherly arms and gathers to her grateful bosom the daughters of her race, joyous over their wonderful accomplishment—the restoration of the home of Anna Murray Douglass the

"MOTHER OF CEDAR HILL."
"God thought to give the sweetest thing
In His Almighty power
To earth; and deeply pondering
What is should be, one hour,
In fondest joy and love of heart
Our weighing every other,
He moved the gates of heaven apart
And gave to earth—YOU—mother!" F.D.S.P.[1]

PREFACE

The traveler standing at the base of a high mountain viewing for the first time its lofty peak as it towers above him feels his insignificance. He scans its rugged sides with an irresistible desire to know what is hiding at its summit. Not content to stand looking upward, feeding his imagination by silently gazing, he must mount and explore and with no realization of the obstacles to be encountered, but with a determined purpose, he prepares to ascend.

This but epitomizes life. Real life is a struggle, an activity, a will to execute. Desire precedes effort. Life with no desire, no effort is merely an existence, and is void of the elements that make life worth the living.

There have been many who have iterated and re-iterated this idea in as many forms of expression as the individuality of the writers themselves. Life is as the mountain, it may be said to have its base, its rugged sides and its summit.

Looking backward over a space of fifty years or more, I have in remembrance two travelers whose lives were real in their activity; two lives that have indelibly impressed themselves upon my memory; two lives whose energy and best ability were exerted to make my life what it should be, and who gave me a home, where wisdom and industry went hand in hand; where instruction was given that a cultivated brain and an industrious hand were the twin conditions that lead to a well balanced and useful life.

These two lives were embodied in the personalities of Frederick Douglass and Anna Murray Douglass, his wife.

They met at the base of a mountain of wrong and oppression, victims of the slave power as it existed over sixty years ago. One, smarting under the manifold hardships as a slave, the other in many ways suffering from the effects of such a system.

---

1 Fredericka Douglass Sprague Perry (1872–1943), granddaughter of Frederick Douglass and daughter of Rosetta Douglass Sprague and Nathan Sprague.

The story of Frederick Douglass' hopes and aspirations and longing desire for freedom has been told—you all know it. It was a story made possible through the unswerving loyalty of Anna Murray, to whose memory this paper is written.

ANNA MURRAY was born in Denton, Caroline Co., Maryland, an adjoining county to that in which my father was born. The exact date of her birth is not known. Her parents Bambarra Murray and Mary his wife were slaves, their family consisted of twelve children seven of whom were born in slavery and five born in freedom. My mother the eighth child escaped by the short period of one month the fate of her older brothers and sisters, and was the first free child. Remaining with her parents until she was seventeen, she felt it time that she should be entirely self-supporting and with that idea she left her country home and went to Baltimore, sought employment in a French family by the name of Montell whom she served two years. Doubtless it was while with them she gained her first idea as to household management which served her so well in her after years and which gained for her the reputation of a thorough and competent housekeeper. On leaving the Montells', she served in a family by the name of Wells living on S. Caroline Street, Mr. Wells was Post-master at the time of my father's escape from slavery. It interested me very much in one of my recent visits to Baltimore, to go to that house accompanied by an old friend of my parents of those early days, who as a free woman was enabled with others to make my father's life easier while he was a slave in that city. This house is owned now by a colored man. In going through the house I endeavored to remember its appointments, so frequently spoken of by my mother, for she had lived with this family seven years and an attachment sprang up between her and the members of that household, the memory of which gave her pleasure to recall.

The free people of Baltimore had their own circles from which the slaves were excluded, the ruling of them out of their society resulted more from the desire of the slaveholder than from any great wish of the free people themselves. If a slave would dare to hazard all danger and enter among the free people he would be received. To such a little circle of free people—a circle a little more exclusive than some others, Frederick Bailey was welcome. Anna Murray, to whom he had give his heart, sympathized with him and she devoted all her energies to assist him.[1]

The three weeks prior to the escape were busy and anxious weeks for Anna Murray. She had lived with the Wells family so long and

1 [Original note:] Attaining freedom, Frederick Bailey changed his name to Douglass.

having been able to save the greater part of her earnings was willing to share with the man she loved that he might gain the freedom he yearned to possess. Her courage, her sympathy at the start was the main-spring that supported the career of Frederick Douglass. As is the condition of most wives her identity became merged into that of the husband. Thus only the few of their friends in the North really knew and appreciated the full value of the woman who presided over the Douglass home for forty-four years. When the escaped slave and future husband of Anna Murray had reached New York in safety, his first act was to write to her of his arrival and as they had previously arranged she was to come on immediately—reaching New York a week later, they married and at once took their wedding trip to New Bedford.

In "My Bondage and Freedom," by Frederick Douglass, a graphic account of that trip is given. The little that they possessed was the outcome of the industrial and economical habits that were characteristic of my mother. She had brought with her sufficient goods and chattels to fit up comfortably two rooms in her New Bedford home— a feather bed with pillows, bed linen, dishes, knives, forks and spoons, besides a well filled trunk of wearing apparel for herself. A new plum colored silk dress was her wedding gown. To my child eyes that dress was very fine. She had previously sold one of her feather beds to assist in defraying the expenses of the flight from bondage. The early days in New Bedford were spent in daily toil, the wife at the wash board, the husband with saw, buck and axe. I have frequently listened to the rehearsal of those early days of endeavor. Looking around me at the well appointed home built up from the labors of the father and mother under so much difficulty, I found it hard to realize that it was a fact. After the day of toil they would seek their little home of two rooms and the meal of the day that was most enjoyable was the supper, nicely prepared by mother. Father frequently spoke of the neatly set table with its snowy white cloth—coarse tho' it was. In 1890 I was taken by my father to these rooms on Elm Street, New Bedford, Mass., overlooking Buzzards Bay. This was my birth place. Every detail as to the early housekeeping was gone over, it was indelibly impressed upon his mind, even to the hanging of a towel on a particular nail. Many of the dishes used by my mother at that time were in our Rochester home and kept as souvenirs of those first days of housekeeping. The fire that destroyed that home in 1872, also destroyed them.

Three of the family had their birthplace in New Bedford. When after having written his first narrative, father built himself a nice little cottage in Lynn, Mass., and moved his family there, before making his first trip to Europe.[1]

He was absent during the years '45 and '46. It was then that my mother with four children, the eldest in her sixth year struggled to maintain the family amid much that would dampen the courage of many a young woman of to-day. I had previously been taken to Albany by my father as a means of lightening the burden for mother. Abigail and Lydia Mott cousins of Lucretia Mott desire to have the care of me. During the absence of father, mother sustained her little family by binding shoes. Mother had many friends in the Anti-slavery circle of Lynn and Boston who recognized her sterling qualities, and who encouraged her during the long absence of her husband. Those were days of anxious worry. The narrative of Frederick Douglass with its bold utterances of truth, with the name of the parties with whom he had been associated in slave life, so incensed the slaveholders that it was doubtful if ever he would return to this country. There was also the danger that mother and those who had aided in his escape might be pursued. It was with reluctance father consented to leave the country, and not until he was assured by the many friends that mother and the children would be carefully guarded, would he go.

There was among the Anti-Slavery people of Massachusetts a fraternal spirit born of the noble purpose near their heart that served as an uplifter and encouraged the best energies in each individual, and mother from contact with the great and noble workers grew and improved even more than ever before. She was a recognized co-worker in the Anti-Slavery Societies of Lynn and Boston, and no circle was felt to be complete without her presence. There was a weekly gathering of the women to prepare articles for the Annual Anti-Slavery Fair held in Faneuil Hall, Boston. At that time mother would spend the week in attendance having charge, in company with a committee of ladies of which she was one, of the refreshments. The New England women were all workers and there was no shirking of responsibility— all worked. It became the custom of the ladies of the Lynn society each to take her turn in assisting mother in her household duties on the morning of the day that the sewing circle met so as to be sure of her meeting with them. It was mother's custom to put aside the earnings from a certain number of shoes that she had bound as her donation to the Anti-Slavery cause. Being frugal and economical she was also able to put by a portion of her earnings for a rainy day. I have often heard

---

1   [Original note:] The Douglass children were Rosetta (first born), Lewis Henry, Frederic, Charles Remond, Anna (d. at 6).

my father speak in admiration of mother's executive ability. During his absence abroad, he sent, as he could, support for his family, and on his coming home he supposed there would be some bills to settle. One day while talking over their affairs, mother arose and quietly going to a bureau drawer produced a bank book with the sums deposited just in the proportion father had sent, the book also contained deposits of her own earnings—and not a debt had been contracted during his absence.

The greatest trial, perhaps, that mother was called upon to endure, after parting from her Baltimore friends several years before, was the leaving her Massachusetts home for the Rochester home where father established the "North Star." She never forgot her old friends and delighted to speak of them up to her last illness. Wendell Phillips, Wm. Lloyd Garrison, Sydney Howard Gay[1] and many more with their wives were particularly kind to her. At one of the Anti-Slavery conventions held in Syracuse, father and mother were the guests of Rev. Samuel J. May,[2] a Unitarian minister and an ardent Anti-Slavery friend. The spacious parlors of the May mansion were thrown open for a reception in their honor and where she could meet her old Boston friends. The refreshments were served on trays, one of which placed upon an improvised table made by the sitting close together of Wendell Phillips, Wm. Lloyd Garrison and Sydney Howard Gay, mother was invited to sit, the four making an interesting tableaux [sic]. Mother occasionally traveled with father on his short trips, but not as often as he would liked as she was a housekeeper who felt that her presence was necessary in the home, as she was wont to say "to keep things straight." Her life in Rochester was not less active in the cause of the slave, if anything she was more self-sacrificing, and it was a long time after her residence there before she was understood. The atmosphere in which she was placed lacked the genial cordiality that greeted her in her Massachusetts home. There were only the few that learned to know her, for she drew around herself a certain reserve, after meeting her new acquaintances that forbade any very near approach to her. Prejudice in the early 40's in Rochester ran rampant and mother became more distrustful. There were a few loyal co-workers and she set herself assiduously to work. In the home, with the aid of a laundress only, she managed her household. She watched with a great deal of interest and no little pride the growth in the public life of my father, and in every possible way that she was capable of aided him by

1 Sydney Howard Gay (1814–88) was a white US abolitionist, Underground Railroad operator, and editor of the *National Anti-Slavery Standard*.
2 Samuel Joseph May (1797–1871) was a white US radical reformer and abolitionist campaigner.

relieving him of all the management of the home as it increased in size and its appointments. It was her pleasure to know when he stood up before an audience that his linen was immaculate and that she had made it so, for no matter how well the laundry was done for the family, she must with her own hands smooth the tucks in father's linen and when he was on a long journey she would forward ·at a given point a fresh supply. Being herself one of the first agents of the Underground Railroad she was an untiring worker along that line. To be able to accommodate in a comfortable manner the fugitives that passed our way, father enlarged his home where a suite of rooms could be made ready for those fleeing to Canada. It was no unusual occurrence for mother to be called up at all hours of the night, cold or hot, as the case might be, to prepare supper for a hungry lot of fleeing humanity.

She was greatly interested in the publication of the "North Star" or Frederick Douglass' paper as it was called later on, and publication day was always a day for extra rejoicing as each weekly paper was felt to be another arrow sent on its way to do the work of puncturing the veil that shrouded a whole race in gloom. Mother felt it her duty to have her table well supplied with extra provisions that day, a custom that we, child-like, fully appreciated. Our home was two miles from the center of the city, where our office was situated, and many times did we trudge through snow knee-deep, as street cars were unknown. During one of the Summer vacations the question arose in father's mind as to how his sons should be employed, for them to run wild through the streets was out of the question. There was much hostile feeling against the colored boys and as he would be from home the most of the time, he felt anxious about them. Mother came to the rescue with the suggestion that they be taken into the office and taught the case.[1] They were little fellows and the thought had not occurred to father. He acted upon the suggestion and at the ages of eleven and nine they were perched upon blocks and given their first lesson in printer's ink, besides carrying papers and mailing them.

DEVOTION

Father was mother's honored guest. He was from home so often that his home-comings were events that she thought worthy of extra notice, and caused renewed activity. Everything was done that could be to add to his comfort. She also found time to care for four other boys at different times. As they became members of our home circle, the care of

---

1   The reference to Douglass's sons being "taught the case" refers to their being apprenticed to the trade of learning how to prepare a printer's case of type.

their clothing was as carefully seen to as her own children's and they delighted in calling her MOTHER.

In her early life she was a member of the Methodist church as was father, but in our home there was no family altar. Our custom was to read a chapter in the Bible around the table, each reading a verse in turn until the chapter was completed. She was a person who strived to live a Christian life instead of talking it. She was a woman strong in her likes and dislikes and had large discernment as to the character of those who came around her. Her gift in that direction being very fortunate in the protection of father's interests, especially in the early days of his public life, when there was a great apprehension for his safety. She was a woman firm in her opposition to alcoholic drinks, a strict disciplinarian—her no meant no and yes, yes, but more frequently the no's had it, especially when I was the petitioner. So far as I was concerned, I found my father more yielding than my mother, altho' both were rigid as to the matter of obedience.

There was a certain amount of grim humor about mother and perhaps such exhibitions as they occurred were a little starting to those who were unacquainted with her. The reserve in which she held herself made whatever she might attempt of a jocose nature somewhat acrid. She could not be known all at once, she had to be studied. She abhorred shams. In the early 70's she came to Washington and found a large number of people from whom the shackles had recently fallen. She fully realized their condition and considered the gaieties that were indulged in as frivolous in the extreme.

On one occasion several young women called upon her and commenting on her spacious parlors and the approaching holiday season, thought it a favorable opportunity to suggest the keeping of an open house. Mother replied: "I have been keeping open house for several weeks. I have it closed now and I expect to keep it closed." The young women thinking mother's understanding was at fault, endeavored to explain. They were assured, however, that they were fully understood. Father, who was present, laughingly pointed to the new bay window, which had been completed only a few days previous to their call. Perhaps no other home received under its roof a more varied class of people than did our home. From the highest dignitaries to the lowliest person, bond or free, white or black, were welcomed, and mother was equally gracious to all. There were a few who presumed on the hospitality of the home and officiously insinuated themselves and their advice in a manner that was particularly disagreeable to her. This unwelcome attention on the part of the visitor would be vigorously repelled, in a manner more forceful than the said party would deem her capable of. From such a person an erroneous impression of her temper and qualifications would be given, and criticisms sharp and unjust would be made; so that altho' she had her triumphs, there were trials, and only those who knew her intimately could fully understand and appreciate the enduring patience of the wife and mother.

During her wedded life of forty-four years, whether in adversity or prosperity, she was the same faithful ally, guarding as best she could every interest connected with my father, his life-work and the home. Unfortunately an opportunity for a knowledge of books had been denied to her, the lack of which she greaty [sic] deplored. Her increasing family and household duties prevented any great advancement, altho' she was able to read a little. By contact with people of culture and education, and they were her real friends, her improvement was marked. She took a lively interest in every phase of the Anti-Slavery movement, an interest that father took full pains to foster and to keep her intelligently informed. I was instructed to read to her. She was a good listener, making comments on passing events, which were well worth consideration, altho' the manner of the presentation of them might provoke a smile. Her value was fully appreciated by my father, and in one of his letters to Thomas Auld (his former master), he says: "Instead of finding my companion a burden she is truly a helpmeet."[1]

In 1882, this remarkable woman, for in many ways she was remarkable, was stricken with paralysis, and for four weeks was a great sufferer. Altho' perfectly helpless, she insisted from her sick bed to direct her home affairs. The orders were given with precision and they were obeyed with alacrity. Her fortitude and patience up to within ten days of her death were very great. She helped us to bear her burden. Many letters on condolence from those who had met her and upon whom pleasant impressions had been made, were received. Hon. J.M. Dalzell[2] of Ohio, wrote thus:

"You know I never met your good wife but once and then her welcome was so warm and sincere and unaffected, her manner altogether so motherly, and her good-bye so full of genuine kindness and hospitality, as to impress me tenderly and fill my eyes with tears as I now recall it."

Prof. Peter H. Clark of Cincinnati, Ohio, wrote: "The kind treatment given to us and our little one so many years ago won for her a place in our hearts from which no lapse of time could move her. To us she was ever kind and good and our mourning because of her death, is heartfelt."

There is much room for reflection in the review of the life of such a woman as Anna Murray Douglass. Unlettered tho' she was, there was a strength of character and of purpose that won for her the respect

---

1 See Appendix C12, p. 238.
2 James M. Dalzell (1841–94) was a white US lawyer and educator.

of the noblest and best. She was a woman who strove to inculcate in the minds of her children the highest principles of morality and virtue both by precept and example. She was not well versed in the polite etiquette of the drawing room, the rules for the same being found in the many treatises devoted to that branch of literature. She was possessed of a much broader culture, and with decernment [sic] born of intelligent observation, and wise discrimination she welcomed all with the hearty manner of a noble soul.

I have thus striven to give you a glimpse of my mother, in so doing I am conscious of having made frequent mention of my father. It is difficult to say anything of mother without the mention of father, her life was so enveloped in his. Together they rest side by side, and most befittingly, within sight of the dear old home of hallowed memories and from which the panting fugitive, the weary traveler, the lonely emigrant of every clime, received food and shelter.

7. Lewis Henry Douglass, undated and untitled handwritten statement [c. 1905] (Frederick Douglass Papers, Library of Congress)

[Lewis Henry Douglass wrote this undated and untitled handwritten statement in response to Archibald H. Grimké's article "Cedar Hill or the Famous Home of Frederick Douglass," published in *Voice of the Negro* on 1 November 1901. Douglass took issue with Grimké's focus on the personal suffering of his father's second wife, Helen Pitts Douglass, who, Grimké (1849–1930) writes, "denied herself food and proper clothing" (764) in a lifelong quest to preserve Cedar Hill to his memory. Lewis Henry Douglass was anxious to set the record straight by doing justice to the lifelong struggles of Douglass's first wife, Anna Murray, and of his own brothers and sisters in his father's campaigns for justice.]

Archibald Grimke [sic], in his eloquent article on the character of Frederick Douglass published in the Voice of the Negro for the month of ~~February~~ November gives us a glowing recital of the impression made by that truly great and remarkable man in his work of uplifting the people of his race. We can but sincerely wish that he would have been able to have gone all along the line of his work from the beginning of the first days of his labors and shown what were the distresses, the anxieties, and the hardships that he and his family had to undergo in the struggle for the cause of liberty. How the wife—the first Mrs. Douglass—worked early and late by the sunlight of day and the burning of the midnight oil at her duties of the household—at work binding shoes for the manufacturers of shoes in Lynn, Mass, and giving her attention and what she could share in money to aid in the cause of Abolition, and at the same time having four children while her husband was away in the labors that engaged the men of whom Garrison, Phillips, Remond and a score of others were a part—were fighting for the Emancipation of the people of her race. This was at a time when all was dark for the race with which Frederick Douglass was identified. No sunshine lit up the path the black man trod all was enmity, hatred and proscription. The children ~~had to partake~~ partook of the ill feelings manifested on the part of the so-called superior race and were bound down to the oppression that ruled in the dark days when pro-slavery was on deck and in command.

It was at this time when Frederick Douglass conceived the idea of publishing a weekly paper devoted to the advocacy of the principles of the Anti-slavery cause. How he performed that work, with what tremendous odds he had to encounter, both from the enemies of the Abolition cause, and the white friends of the Garrisonian party who could not ~~contemplate~~ tolerate a Negro ~~with~~ going into a work in which they ~~could~~ considered ~~that~~ only white people should participate ~~in and~~ thus he had to face what may be called the prejudices of the men who otherwise were in sympathy with the cause of Freedom. But he struggled on. With what labor was it? Few ~~who~~ know how the work was done; how many sleepless nights and how many days were given up by his family his wife two sons and one daughter to succeed in the way of getting the paper to press ~~and~~ in mailing it and engaging in setting in type. ~~And~~ For years the family worked on ~~and~~ only encouraged by the thought that they were working for the cause in which their father and mother were interested—namely the emancipation of the slave. This was a work done for a purpose, with no thought of any ___[?] but ~~for~~ the grandeur of doing good. The mother labored and saved. She it was ~~that~~ who went without the luxuries that came and went into the hands of another Mrs. Douglass of whom it is a mockery to speak of doing any thing for the good of the cause for which we had ~~all~~ labored and worked unceasingly.

To the subsequent wife of Frederick Douglass, poor though she had been, came ~~all~~ the results of the savings of the former Mrs. Douglass. ~~And~~ To the family who ~~knew~~ understands everything ~~that is in every way~~ connected with the history of Frederick Douglass, the money that was paid to his second wife and the amount ~~that was~~ lavished on her in ~~horses and carriages~~ equipages, furniture and travel in Europia [sic], ~~Asia~~ and Africa it appears to me that Archibald Grimke must have allowed himself a great deal ~~of~~ more than the usual allowance of acumen to have written that Mrs. Helen Douglass "denied ~~to~~ herself sufficient food and proper clothing, ah! in many ways, she denied herself, especially during the last years of her life, that Cedar Hill might become to her husband's memory what Mt. Vernon is to the memory of Washington." Mr. Grimke has been led into an error and to convince himself he may apply ~~himself~~ to the records of my Administration of the estate of Frederick Douglass ~~and to~~ ones all of which he is welcome to read and ponder. We think that, though unintentional, a reflection is cast upon our father and his children by representing any thing that can be construed into a want of money or food or clothing by Mrs. Douglass when there is abundance of evidence ~~that is quite~~ overwhelmingly true to the contrary.

However much we may be chagrined by the soliciting of alms for the purpose of establishing a place for ~~to be~~ a memorial to our father is it more than shameful to have it published ~~to the world~~ that my father left his wife penniless and suffering for the necessaries of life. Ah! that is an evidence of too much zeal on the part of those who would make the impression that my father left his wife in ~~any~~ a way that she would be subjected to begging for food and clothing. No, there was no necessity for ~~any~~ anything like it. The way my father left his widow was not penniless, was not in want of proper food and clothing. He left her well off. That is easily proven by the examination of the legacy left by my father's will and the amount of fees for the performance of a duty that I alone carried out, and the loan that was obtained on her property and the dower ~~dowry~~ all of which amounted to many thousands of dollars.

In this scheme of the Memorial no member of our family has been allowed to partake. ~~However much we were feel willing to go into it, but not by falsely alleging poverty, no offer on our part has been listened to.~~ We have also been true to our father's ideals. ~~None more so.~~ In the days ~~that have gone~~ gone by we labored with our father ~~in~~ when we have had fear for his safety as a constant companion and anxiety for his ~~safety~~ return to us from his work. We have been compelled to undergo all this but now we have to put up with what we have to look up as scandalously untrue by those who had undoubtedly been mislead into perversions of facts. It is shameful.

~~There is a history to be related in connection with this Memorial. It was contrived some of by those who are now at work upon the scheme. Not the least is the endeavor to close the door of any connection with the memorial, of any member of my father's family. At a future time not long in the distance I shall have reason to go into the matter more in detail~~

~~Lewis H. Douglass~~

What is to be gained by representing or rather misrepresenting the condition of Mrs. Douglass with regard to her being in want? She had plenty. This was well known to myself as I was the one who paid the money that came from my father's estate and I hold the vouchers for the payment.

Lewis H. Douglass

Works Cited and Select Bibliography

Andrews, William L., ed. *Critical Essays on Frederick Douglass.* Boston: G.K. Hall, 1991.

———. *To Tell a Free Story: The First Century of Afro-American Autobiography, 1760–1865.* Urbana: U of Illinois P, 1986.

Antislavery Collection, Boston Public Library. https://archive.org/details/bplscas.

Armistead, Wilson. *A Tribute for the Negro.* Manchester: W. Irwin, 1848.

Assing, Otillie. Untitled article. n.d. "Speech Article and Book File," Frederick Douglass Papers, Library of Congress.

Bernier, Celeste-Marie. *Characters of Blood: Black Heroism in the Transatlantic Imagination.* Charlottesville: U of Virginia P, 2012.

———. *Living Parchments: Artistry and Authorship in the Life and Works of Frederick Douglass.* New Haven, CT: Yale UP, forthcoming.

———. *My Bondage and My Freedom.* 1855. Oxford: Oxford UP, forthcoming.

———. *Struggle for Liberty: Frederick Douglass's Family Letters, Speeches, Essays and Photographs.* Philadelphia: Temple UP, forthcoming.

———, and Bill E. Lawson, eds. *Pictures and Power: Imaging and Imagining Frederick Douglass (1818–2018).* Liverpool: Liverpool UP, forthcoming.

———, and Andrew Taylor. *If I Survive: Frederick Douglass's Family Letters, Speeches, Essays and Photographs in the Walter O. Evans Collection.* Edinburgh: Edinburgh UP, 2018.

Bingham, Caleb. *The Columbian Orator.* Ed. David Blight. New York: New York UP, 1998.

Blassingame, John W., ed. *The Frederick Douglass Papers: Series One, Speeches, Debates, and Interviews.* Vol. 1, 1841–46. New Haven, CT: Yale UP, 1979.

Blassingame, John W., and John R. McKivigan, eds. *The Frederick Douglass Papers: Series One, Speeches, Debates, and Interviews.* 5 vols. New Haven, CT: Yale UP, 1979–92.

Blassingame, John W., John R McKivigan, Peter P. Hinks. Joseph R. McElrath, and Jesse S. Crisler, eds. *Narrative of the Life of Frederick Douglass, an American Slave.* New Haven, CT: Yale UP, 1999.

Blight, David W. *Beyond the Battlefield: Race, Memory and the American Civil War.* Amherst: U of Massachusetts P, 2002.

Chaffin, Tom. *Giant's Causeway: Frederick Douglass's Irish Odyssey and the Making of an American Visionary.* Charlottesville: U of Virginia P, 2014.

Chapman, Maria Weston. "Narrative." *National Anti-Slavery Standard* 12 June 1845.

Davis, Charles T., and Henry Louis Gates Jr. *The Slave's Narrative.* New York: Oxford UP, 1985.

Douglass, Frederick. *Frederick Douglass.* Annapolis: Archives of Maryland. http://msa.maryland.gov/msa/speccol/sc3500/sc3520 /013800/013800/html/msa13800.html.

———. *Frederick Douglass National Historic Site.* https://www.nps.gov/frdo/index.htm.

———. *Frederick Douglass Papers.* Savannah, GA: Walter O. Evans Collection.

———. *Frederick Douglass Papers.* Washington, DC: Moorland-Spingarn Research Center, Howard U.

———. *Frederick Douglass Papers 1841–1964.* Washington, DC: Library of Congress. https://www.loc.gov/collection/frederick-douglass-papers/about-this-collection/.

———. *Frederick Douglass Project: University of Rochester.* http://rbscp.lib.rochester.edu/2494.

———. *The Heroic Slave. Autographs for Freedom.* Ed. Julia Griffiths. Boston: John P. Jewett, 1853.

———. *Life and Times of Frederick Douglass.* Boston: De Wolfe & Fiske Co., 1892.

———. *My Bondage and My Freedom.* New York: Miller, 1855.

———. *Narrative of the Life of Frederick Douglass, an American Slave.* Boston: Anti-Slavery Office, 1845.

———. *Narrative of the Life of Frederick Douglass, an American Slave.* Dublin: Webb and Chapman, 1845.

———. *Narrative of the Life of Frederick Douglass, an American Slave.* 2nd [Irish] ed. Dublin: Webb and Chapman, 1846.

Douglass, Joseph L. *Frederick Douglass: A Family Biography 1733–1936.* Shelbyville: Winterlight Books, 2011.

———. "Harriet Bailey: Presumed Sister of Frederick Douglass." *Journal of the Afro-American Historical and Genealogical Society* 21 (2002): 6–11.

Ernest, John, ed. *Douglass in His Own Time.* Iowa City: Iowa UP, 2014.

———, ed. *The Oxford Handbook of the African American Slave Narrative.* Oxford: Oxford UP, 2017.

Fisch, Audrey A., ed. *The Cambridge Companion to the African American Slave Narrative.* Cambridge: Cambridge UP, 2007.

Foner, Philip S., ed. *Frederick Douglass on Women's Rights*. Westport, CT: Greenwood P, 1976.

——, ed. *Frederick Douglasss: Selected Speeches and Writings*. Chicago: Chicago Review Press, 2000.

——, ed. *The Life and Writings of Frederick Douglass*. 5 vols. New York: International Publishers, 1950–75.

Foster, Helen B. *"New Raiments of Self:" African American Clothing in the Antebellum South*. New York: Berg, 1997.

Fought, Leigh. *Women in the World of Frederick Douglass*. Oxford: Oxford UP, 2017.

Fredrickson, George. *The Black Image in the White Mind: The Debate on Afro-American Character and Destiny, 1817–1914*. New York: ACLS Humanities, 2008.

Fulkerson, R. Gerald, "Frederick Douglass and the Antislavery Crusade: His Career and Speeches, 1817–1861." Doctoral dissertation, U of Illinois, 1971.

Gregory, James M. *Frederick Douglass, the Orator*. Springfield, MA: Wiley Co., 1907.

Grimké, Archibald H. "Cedar Hill or the Famous Home of Frederick Douglass." *Voice of the Negro* 1 Nov. 1901.

Hairston, Eric Ashley. *The Ebony Column: Classics, Civilization, and the African American Reclamation of the West*. Knoxville: U of Tennessee P, 2013.

Holland, Frederic May. *Frederick Douglass: The Colored Orator*. New York: Funk & Wagnalls, 1895.

Huggins, Nathan Irving. *Slave and Citizen: The Life of Frederick Douglass*. Boston: Little, Brown, 1980.

Impey, Catherine. "Extracts from the Editor's Diary of a Visit to Cedar Hill." *Anti-Caste* 7 (1895): 14–16.

James, Thomas. *Life of Rev. Thomas James*. Rochester: Post Express Printing, 1886. http://docsouth.unc.edu/neh/jamesth/jamesth.html.

Johnson, Tekla Ali, John R. Wunder, and Abigail B. Anderson. "Always on My Mind: Frederick Douglass's Nebraska Sister." *Nebraska History* 91 (2010): 122–35.

Lampe, Gregory P. *Frederick Douglass: Freedom's Voice, 1818–45*. East Lansing: Michigan State UP, 1998.

Lawson, Bill E., and Frank Kirkland, eds. *Frederick Douglass: A Critical Reader*. Malden, MA: Blackwell, 1999.

Lee, Julia Sun-Joo. *The American Slave Narrative and the Victorian Novel*. New York: Oxford UP, 2012.

Lee, Maurice S., ed. *Cambridge Companion to Frederick Douglass*. Cambridge: Cambridge UP, 2009.

Leone, Mark P., and Lee Jenkins, eds. *Atlantic Crossings in the Wake of*

Frederick Douglass: Archaeology, Literature and Spatial Culture. Boston: Brill, 2017.

Levine, Robert S. *The Lives of Frederick Douglass.* Cambridge, MA: Harvard UP, 2016.

Levine, Robert S., John Stauffer, and John R. McKivigan, eds. *The Heroic Slave: A Cultural and Critical Edition.* New Haven, CT: Yale UP, 2015.

Martin, Waldo E. *The Mind of Frederick Douglass.* Chapel Hill: U of North Carolina P, 1984.

McFeely, William S. *Frederick Douglass.* New York: Norton, 1991.

McKivigan, John R., ed. *The Frederick Douglass Papers: Series Three: Correspondence, Volume 1: 1842–1852.* New Haven, CT: Yale UP, 2009.

Merrill, Walter, ed. *The Letters of William Lloyd Garrison: Volume III.* Boston: Belknap P, 1974.

Murray, Hannah-Rose. *Frederick Douglass in Britain.* http://www.frederickdouglassinbritain.com.

——. *"It Is Time for the Slaves to Speak": Transatlantic Abolitionism and African American Activism in Britain 1830–1895.* Nottingham: U of Nottingham, 2017.

——. "A Negro Hercules: The Legacy of Frederick Douglass' Celebrity in Britain." *Journal of Celebrity Studies* 7.2 (2016): 264–79.

Pettinger, Alasdair. "Frederick Douglass in Scotland." http://www.bulldozia.com/projects/index.php?id=258.

Preston, Dickson J. *Young Frederick Douglass: The Maryland Years.* Baltimore: Johns Hopkins UP, 1980.

Quarles, Benjamin. *Frederick Douglass.* Englewood Cliffs, NJ: Prentice-Hall, 1968.

Rice, Alan J., and Martin Crawford, eds. *Liberating Sojourn: Frederick Douglass and Transatlantic Reform.* Athens: U of Georgia P, 1999.

Ripley, C. Peter, ed. *The Black Abolitionist Papers: Vol. III: The United States, 1847–1858.* Chapel Hill: U of North Carolina P, 1991.

Sekora, John. "Black Message/White Envelope: Genre, Authenticity, and Authority in the Antebellum Slave Narrative." *Callaloo* 32 (1987): 482–515.

Stauffer, John. *The Black Hearts of Men: Radical Abolitionists and the Transformation of Race.* Cambridge, MA: Harvard UP, 2004.

Stauffer, John, and Henry Louis Gates Jr., eds., *The Portable Frederick Douglass.* New York: Penguin Classics, 2016.

Stauffer, John, Zoe Trodd, and Celeste-Marie Bernier, eds. *Picturing Frederick Douglass.* New York: Norton, 2015.

Storey, Graham, and Kenneth Fielding, eds. *The Pilgrim Edition of the Letters of Charles Dickens.* Vol. 5: 1847–48. Oxford: Clarendon P, 1981.

Sundquist, Eric J., ed. *Frederick Douglass: New Literary and Historical Essays.* New York: Cambridge UP, 1990.

Sweeney, Fionnghuala. *Frederick Douglass and the Atlantic World.* Liverpool: Liverpool UP, 2007.

Wallace, Maurice O., and Shawn Michelle Smith, eds. *Pictures and Progress: Early Photography and the Making of African American Identity.* Durham: Duke UP, 2012.

Weld, Theodore. *American Slavery as It Is: Testimony of a Thousand Witnesses.* New York: American Anti-Slavery Society, 1839.